KEN HOM'S
CHINESE COOKERY

KEN HOM'S
CHINESE
COOKERY

譚榮輝
中國烹飪

HARPER & ROW, PUBLISHERS, NEW YORK

Cambridge, Philadelphia, San Francisco,
London, Mexico City, São Paulo, Singapore, Sydney

For Craig Claiborne,
mentor and friend

First published in Great Britain by the
British Broadcasting Corporation,
London, England.

KEN HOM'S CHINESE COOKERY.
Text copyright © 1984 by Ken Hom.
Photographs copyright © 1986
by Victor Budnik.

FIRST U.S. EDITION 1986

Designed by Thomas Ingalls + Associates
    and David Barich
 Photography by Victor Budnik

Harper & Row, Publishers, Inc.,
New York, would like to thank the
following for the loan of equipment and
accessories for the photographs:
Almanac Antiques, Palo Alto, California;
Courtyard Antiques, Palo Alto, California;
Dr. Susanne Forrest; Clay Feet, Palo Alto,
California; and Dianne McKenzie.

LIBRARY OF CONGRESS
CATALOGING IN PUBLICATION DATA

Hom, Ken.
   Ken Hom's Chinese cookery.
   Includes index.
   1. Cookery, Chinese. I. Title. II. Title:
Chinese cookery.
TX724.5.C5H65 1985   641.5951   85-45203
ISBN 0-06-181386-9
ISBN 0-06-097016•2 (pbk.)

88 89 90 WAK 9 8 7 6 5

ACKNOWLEDGMENTS

Many people were involved in the production of the BBC television series and the different editions of this cookbook which act as a companion to the series. The first was Madhur Jaffrey, the brilliant Indian actress, cook, and author. It was at her suggestion that the BBC decided to audition me for the television series, and it is proper that she should head this list of acknowledgments.

The huge success of the series and the book testifies to the creative talents and professionalism of Jenny Stevens, the producer and book editor. Her determination forged a clear path for the success of the project. I am most grateful to her, and to our production team at the BBC: Damaris Pitcher, Anne O'Dwyer, Mary Cadogan, Jenny Lo, and Daniel Taurines. Special thanks to Gerry Cavanaugh for his assistance. Applause also goes to the film crew in Hong Kong—Nigel Meakin, Tony Bragg, Ron Brown, and John Collins—and of course to the numerous crews at the BBC studios. The people at BBC Publications were wonderful, especially John Holmes, Roger Chown, Graham Crossley, and Nigel Bradley.

More thanks go to David Barich and the talented Tom Ingalls, who took the British edition of the book and totally redesigned it. I love the way it looks, and the beautiful photography by Victor Budnik, who was assisted by Joy Deaderick and by the stylist Karen Hazarian. I was fortunate to have as cook-in-arms Gordon Wing. His wit, good taste, and sensible approach to cooking were of immense help. Thanks, too, to Todd Koons, who kept us on our toes with his energy and good humor, and to Kathie Ness, who in the midst of chaos and under severe time pressure, restored the manuscript to its original "American English."

Good food with beautiful ingredients would never have been possible without the cooperation of Monterey Produce and Monterey Fish of Berkeley. And a good book cannot exist without a wonderful editor who cares—and that is exactly what Ann Bramson is.

A toast to Susie Maurer, who opened up the window in Hong Kong which made all this possible.

Finally, special thanks must go to Martha Sternberg, my American literary agent, for her friendship and hard work, and to Ted Lyman, my attorney and international agent extraordinaire. I have benefited immensely from their guidance.

AUTHOR'S NOTE

The recipes in this book were chosen after careful deliberation, the criteria being that they be simple and accessible without compromising authenticity, that they offer a mix of the familiar and the unfamiliar, and that the resulting tastes be very appealing, often surprising, and always satisfying.

There is nothing daunting about the food in this book; all the recipes are straightforward and do-able. I do ask, though, that you read the introductory chapters, particularly the one on ingredients, before you begin to cook. In that chapter and again here, I want to emphasize that good ingredients make for good flavor, and good flavor makes great food.

The spellings of Chinese words and place names in the book follow the pinyin system of converting Chinese characters to the Roman alphabet. This system has been officially adopted by the People's Republic of China since 1979 and it closely resembles actual Mandarin pronunciation. Since this is a relatively new system you may find that it takes you a while to get used to seeing Beijing for Peking and Sichuan instead of Szechuan. I have used the new system throughout except for the spellings of very well-known dishes, such as Peking Duck and dim sum, and for a few ingredients which are Cantonese. In the case of the better-known places in China the pinyin spelling is followed by the other spelling, as, for example, Guangzhou (Canton).

CONTENTS

Good food has been an important part of my life since my earliest childhood. I well remember my family gathered around the dinner table, endlessly discussing what we were to eat, how it would be prepared, what our favorite dishes were, the best methods for cooking various delicacies, and so forth. In fact this is a common experience for most Chinese—food is our favorite topic of conversation. For us food is more than a passion, it is an obsession, and good eating is believed to be essential to good living. We Chinese have an expression: *"Chi fan le mei you?,"* which literally means: "Have you eaten yet?" It is used universally as a greeting, just as one would ask in English, "How are you?" It is also a wish for one's health and happiness. It is an entirely appropriate phrase, since food to the Chinese has always meant much more than mere sustenance, and the processes of cultivating, selecting, cooking and consuming it are completely embedded into Chinese culture.

Like all Chinese children I absorbed a great deal of knowledge about Chinese cuisine simply by listening to the dinner-table conversations of my relations. My real culinary training, however, took place in my uncle's restaurant in Chicago, where I started to work part-time at the age of 11. In those early days I had all the routine, unpleasant jobs. I remember peeling hundreds of pounds of shrimp, a tedious and painful chore. I also have memories of cleaning what seemed like mountains of huge sea snails, which were delivered to the kitchen in enormous burlap bags. All the time I was thus employed I was surrounded by the wonderful aromas of the mouth-watering dishes being prepared by the expert chefs. Slowly they taught me why a particular spice went with a certain meat, why this sauce suited that vegetable—in short, the essence of Chinese cooking technique.

Although my family were originally from Guangdong (Kwantung Province), my uncle employed chefs from many different parts of China. Many people think that all Chinese cooking is similar, which is understandable since all Chinese cooks share a common technique, and since so many restaurants in the West blur the distinctions between the various regional styles. But China is a vast country with great variations in climate, agricultural tradition and available foodstuffs. It is no wonder, then, that there are actually many variations in culinary style within China. They can be separated into four key regional categories:

THE SOUTHERN SCHOOL

This is the region of Guangdong (Cantonese) cuisine, which is probably the best known in the West because in the nineteenth century many Chinese families emigrated from this area to Europe and America. Cantonese cooking is regarded by many as the *haute cuisine* of China. Some people attribute this to the influence of the brilliant chefs of the Imperial Court who fled to Guangzhou (Canton) when the Ming dynasty was overthrown in 1644. The Cantonese are especially interested in exotic delicacies such as snake, frog's legs and turtle. The area is famous for its sweet and sour dishes, such as Sweet and Sour Pork, for its *dim sum*— a range of delicious snacks which are served as a light lunch or afternoon tea—and for its widespread use of soy, hoisin and oyster sauces.

The Cantonese prefer their food slightly undercooked so that the natural flavors and colors are preserved, and for this reason stir-frying and steaming are two of the most popular methods of cooking. They also avoid the heavy use of garlic, spices and oils, and concentrate instead on achieving a subtle yet harmonious blend of colors, textures, aromas and flavors. Rice is the staple of the Cantonese diet and the area is known as one of the "rice bowls" of China.

THE NORTHERN SCHOOL

This area stretches from the Yangzi (Yangtze) River to the Great Wall of China and embraces the culinary styles of Shandong (Shantung), Henan and Beijing (Peking). A distinguishing feature of its cuisine is the use of grains, rather than rice, as the staple food, particularly wheat, corn and millet, which the northerners eat in the form of bread, noodles, dumplings and pancakes. Because of the harshness of the climate, fresh vegetables are available only at certain times of the year. To compensate for this, northerners have learned how to preserve foods to see them through their long winters. Vegetables like sweet potatoes, turnips, onions and cabbages, which store well, are widely used, and the region specializes in a range of preserved ingredients such as dried mushrooms, dried and smoked meats, and pickled fruits and vegetables. Meat is in much shorter supply than in all the other regions of China, although beef, mutton and goat are available as well as pork. This area contains many of China's four million Moslems, who shun pork, and their presence has greatly affected its cuisine.

The Imperial Court of China was based in Beijing (Peking) and its influence on the culinary style of the area is still reflected in some of its more complicated and spectacular dishes, such as the celebrated Peking Duck. Of all the elaborate banquet dishes in Chinese cuisine, this is the most glorious. Its subtlety and sophistication are a distinct contrast to other more strongly flavored dishes which characterize northern cooking, depending heavily as it does on garlic, scallions, leeks, sesame seeds and oil, and sweet bean sauce.

THE EASTERN SCHOOL

This region stretches from the eastern coast to central China. It contains the cooking styles of Fujian (Fukien), Jiangxi, Zhejiang and, most important of all, Shanghai, which is the biggest city in China and its greatest port. The region contains some of the most fertile land in China, which provides a rich variety of fresh fruit and vegetables, and the area is noted for its vegetarian cuisine. The countryside is dominated by the magnificent Yangzi (Yangtze) River, and the coastline is very long. Consequently fresh fish and shellfish are also plentiful.

Eastern cooks prefer light and delicate seasonings to maximize the natural flavors of their fresh ingredients. The preferred cooking techniques are stir-frying, steaming, red-cooking (slow simmering in a dark soy sauce) and blanching. Soy sauce from this area is reputed to be the best in China. The region is also famous for some special ingredients, notably black vinegar, which is used both for cooking and as a dipping sauce; Zhejiang ham, which is rather like Smithfield ham; and rice wine. Sugar is widely used in the cooking of meat and vegetables, as is a great deal of oil, earning this area a reputation for rich food.

The Western School

This area is entirely inland and includes the provinces of Sichuan (Szechuan) and Hunan, the birthplace of Chairman Mao. This "land of abundance," as it is sometimes called, is virtually surrounded by mountains and was almost cut off from the rest of China until this century. Nowadays Sichuan cuisine in particular is fast gaining popularity in the West. In this area summers are hot and sultry and the winters mild. Fruit and vegetables are plentiful, as are pork, poultry and fish. The distinguishing aspect of the culinary style is its reliance on very strong flavorings and hot spices, particularly red chilies, Sichuan peppercorns, ginger, onions and garlic. Outsiders used to suggest that such ingredients were used to mask the taste of the food which had deteriorated in the area's muggy heat. However, regional chefs stand by their cuisine and their command of the art of seasoning. Dishes from this area are usually artful combinations of many flavors and can be hot, sour, sweet and salty all at once.

Chinese Cooking Outside China

The revolution in China in 1949 and its aftermath had consequences for cooking as well as profound political and social effects. Within China, the great cookery tradition became for quite some time almost moribund. Revolutionaries deemed the art of cooking an elitist and reactionary enterprise, a reminder of Imperial days and therefore best repressed. Only recently has an effort been made to revive the tradition, to train young chefs and to allow small private restaurants to start up or reopen.

Countries outside China benefited from the decline in Chinese cuisine brought about by this revolutionary zeal. Relaxed immigration rules, particularly in North America, allowed the entry into Western countries of Chinese people from all parts of Mainland China. Cantonese restaurants, which had been predominant, were now joined by Sichuan (Szechuan), Hunanese and Shanghai restaurants, to the great enrichment of Western palates. Increasing familiarity with and availability of Chinese ingredients, coupled with the rapid rise in the popularity of the wok, has encouraged many non-Chinese people to experiment with Chinese cooking.

The great tradition of Chinese cookery has not only survived but has been developed to a high degree of excellence in Taiwan and Hong Kong. Many food critics and gourmets now consider Hong Kong to be the greatest center of Chinese cookery in the world. The best and most traditional ingredients of Chinese cooking flow over the Chinese border into Hong Kong, and China is Hong Kong's chief food supplier. In its eagerness to earn foreign currency, China has fostered a trade which has ensured the maintenance of traditional Chinese cooking in Hong Kong, and Hong Kong's economic prosperity has supported the preservation of the best of this cuisine. In this bustling, energetic place there are over 40,000 restaurants and food stalls, all competing for the attention of the inhabitants, many of whom eat most of their meals out. Perhaps no other people in the world are so food-conscious. Even the smallest food stall sells delicious dishes of excellent quality, and the top restaurants are regarded as being among the best in the world.

Clockwise from left: Braised Cauliflower with Oyster Sauce (page 155), Hot and Sour Soup (page 68), Five-Spice Red Braised Squabs (page 116), Sichuan Shrimp in Chili Sauce (page 133).

This book contains recipes from all the cooking traditions of China as well as some from Hong Kong. It also has a chapter on techniques (page 39), which covers a range of the cooking methods used, such as braising, deep-frying, steaming and stir-frying. If you are new to Chinese cooking, do not feel that you have to prepare a meal which consists entirely of dishes from one particular region. Instead, select dishes that will provide a variety of colors, textures and tastes. On pages 51-54, I have given advice on how to put together a Chinese meal, and have suggested menus of varying complexity. Start with some of the simple ones, which will give you experience in the basic cooking methods. At first try just one or two Chinese dishes at a time, perhaps incorporating them into a European meal. Chinese snacks and soups, for example, make wonderful starters for any meal, and there are many Chinese dishes that can be successfully combined with Western-style meats and salads.

When you prepare your first entirely Chinese meal, select just two or three dishes and serve them with some plain steamed rice. Never select dishes that are all stir fried or you will have a traumatic time in the kitchen trying to get everything ready at the same time, and you will arrive at the table hot and flustered. Choose instead to do one braised dish, a cold dish, or something that can be prepared ahead of time and then warmed through, and limit your stir-frying to just one dish. This way not only will you gain the confidence needed to try more ambitious recipes, but your meal will be all the more authentic for embracing a harmonious blend of cooking techniques.

The Chinese diet is a very healthy one since it depends upon cooking methods which preserve vitamins and use small quantities of meat and no dairy products. Underlying all Chinese cooking is the ancient *yin yang* theory of food science, which is closely related to Chinese beliefs about health. In China, all foods are divided into one of three groups: *yin*, for cooling foods; *yang*, for heating foods; and *yin yang* for neutral foods. To the foreigner there is little obvious logic in the way foodstuffs are assigned to these categories. *Yin* foods include items as diverse as beer, crab, duck and soda water. *Yang* foods include brandy, beef, coffee and smoked fish. Neutral foods include bread, steamed rice, carrots, squab and peaches. Not only are all foods subdivided in this way, but people are too. A *yin* person is quiet and introverted, while a *yang* person is a more active, outgoing type. The effect of different foods on an individual will depend upon the way they conflict with or complement his or her personality type. The idea is to construct a meal and one's whole diet to achieve the right balance or harmony. Most Chinese have some knowledge of the *yin yang* food science, as the idea is instilled into them from a very young age.

Apart from a sensible mixture of *yin* and *yang* foods, the art of Chinese cookery also lies in achieving a harmonious blend of color, texture, aroma and flavor. A typical Chinese meal consists of two parts—the *fan*, which is the staple grain, be it rice, noodles or dumplings, and the *cai*, which covers the rest of the dishes: meat, poultry, fish and vegetables. The average meal comprises three to four *cai* dishes, one *fan* dish and a soup. The *cai* dishes should each have a different main ingredient; for example, one meat, one fish and one vegetable. A variety of techniques will be used to cook these dishes. A fish may be steamed, a meat braised, while the vegetables may be stir-fried. The meal will also be designed so that each dish varies and yet complements the others in terms of appearance, texture and flavor. One dish will be spicy and another mild; one may be chewy and another crisp. The total effect should appeal to all the senses. All these dishes will be placed in the center of the table and shared among the diners who help themselves and each other to a little of this, and then a little of that. Eating for the Chinese is a communal experience, and a shared meal is regarded as the visible manifestation of the harmony which should exist between family and friends.

The subtle and distinctive taste of Chinese food depends in part on the use of some special Chinese ingredients. Of the recipes I have given here, some use more complicated ingredients than others. Where possible I have suggested suitable Western alternatives, but I'm afraid that if you want to cook authentic Chinese food there is ultimately no alternative but to track down a reliable source of the key Chinese ingredients. Fortunately it is becoming easier to find some of these in supermarkets, and Chinese grocers are proliferating. The chapter on ingredients (pages 17 to 31) lists all the special ingredients I have used in the recipes, and it will help you to know what to look or ask for. You may find it useful to refer to this before embarking on a shopping trip to your nearest Chinese grocery.

Your Chinese grocery may also be a good place to buy a wok. Although it is perfectly possible to cook Chinese food successfully using ordinary Western kitchen utensils, you will probably want to invest in a wok eventually, to use for stir-frying at least. The beauty of the wok is that its shape ensures that heat is evenly distributed all over the pan, making for fast cooking, and its depth allows you to stir and toss foods rapidly when they need to be fried quickly. Equally important, you need use far less oil for deep-frying than you would with a deep-fat fryer. Woks usually work better on gas, although it is possible to get a flat-bottomed variety which is more suitable for electric burners. I have given some advice on choosing and seasoning a wok on pages 33 and 34.

There is an old Chinese proverb which says "To the ruler, people are heaven; to the people, food is heaven." Once you have embarked on the exciting road to discovering the mysteries and pleasures of Chinese cooking, you will soon find how sublime Chinese food can be. I wish you happy cooking and happy eating.

Ingredients—dried red chili, fresh chili, Chinese dried straw mushrooms. Sichuan peppercorns, sesame oil, chili oil

用 料

Chinese cooking would not be Chinese without the use of a number of special ingredients which give the foods their distinctive flavors. All the ingredients used in the recipes in this book can be obtained in this country, if not from your local supermarket then certainly from a Chinese grocery. There are now many Chinese grocers throughout the US that offer a mail-order service. It is well worth the effort to find your nearest Chinese grocery and to build up a stock of the most frequently used ingredients. Many, particularly soy sauce, vary enormously in quality, but most Chinese groceries stock good authentic brands at reasonable prices.

The following is a list of the special ingredients that I have used in this book. There are also some notes on vegetables in the introduction to the vegetable chapter on page 139 and information on rice, noodles and flour in the introduction to that chapter on page 157. One ingredient commonly used in China which you will *not* find mentioned here is monosodium glutamate (also known as MSG, Accent, or seasoning or taste powder). This is a white crystalline extract of grains and vegetables widely used to tenderize and enhance the natural flavor of certain foods, particularly meat, in Japan and China and in Western food processing. Some people have an adverse reaction to it, experiencing symptoms such as headaches, excessive thirst and palpitations. This allergic response is sometimes known as "Chinese restaurant syndrome." I believe that the freshest and finest ingredients need no enhancing and I therefore never use it.

BAMBOO SHOOTS

Bamboo shoots are the young edible shoots of some kinds of bamboo. Unfortunately in this country they are only available canned. Pale yellow with a crunchy texture, they come peeled and either whole or thickly sliced. They can be bought in most supermarkets, gourmet shops and in Chinese groceries. Rinse them thoroughly before use and transfer any unused shoots to a jar, cover them with fresh water and keep in the refrigerator. If the water is changed daily they will keep for up to a week.

BEAN CURD

Bean curd is also known by its Chinese name, *doufu*, or by its Japanese name, *tofu*. It has played an important part in Chinese cookery for over 1000 years since it is highly nutritious, being rich in protein. Bean curd has a distinctive texture but a bland taste. It is made from yellow soybeans, which are soaked, ground, mixed with water and then cooked briefly before being solidified. In this country it is usually sold in two forms: firm cakes, or as a thickish custard, but it is also available in several dried forms and fermented. The soft custard-like variety (sometimes called silken *tofu*) is used for soups, while the solid type is used for stir-frying, braising and poaching. Solid bean curd cakes are white in color and are sold in Chinese groceries and in many health-food shops. They are packed in water in plastic containers and may be kept in this state in the refrigerator for up to five days, providing the water is changed daily. To use solid bean curd, cut the amount required into cubes or shreds using a sharp knife. Do this with care as it is delicate. It also needs to be cooked carefully, as too much stirring can cause it to disintegrate.

BLACK BEANS

These small black soybeans, also known as salted black beans, are preserved by being fermented with salt and spices. They have a distinctive, slightly salty taste and a pleasantly rich smell, and are used as a seasoning, often in conjunction with garlic or fresh ginger. They are inexpensive and can be obtained from Chinese groceries, usually in cans, as "Black Beans in Salted Sauce," but you may also see them packed in plastic bags. Rinse them before use; I prefer to chop them slightly too. Transfer any unused beans and liquid to a sealed jar and the beans will keep indefinitely if stored in the refrigerator.

CHILIES

Chilies are used extensively in western China and somewhat less frequently in the south. They are the seed pods of the capsicum plant and can be obtained fresh, dried or ground.

Fresh Chilies
Fresh chilies can be distinguished by their small size and elongated shape. They should look fresh and bright, with no brown patches or black spots. There are several varieties. Red chilies, which are riper, are generally milder than green ones because they sweeten as they ripen.

To prepare fresh chilies, first rinse them in cold water. Then, using a small sharp knife, slit them lengthwise. Remove and discard the seeds. Rinse the chilies well under cold running water, and then prepare them according to the instructions in the recipe. Wash your hands, knife and chopping board before preparing other foods, and be careful not to touch your eyes until you have washed your hands thoroughly with soap and water.

Dried Red Chilies

Dried red chilies are thin and about 1 inch long. They are used to season oil for stir-fried dishes, sauces and for braising. They are normally left whole or cut in half lengthwise and the seeds left in. The Chinese like them to blacken and be left in the dish during cooking, but as they are extremely hot and spicy you may choose to remove them after using them to flavor the cooking oil. They can be found in most supermarkets and in Chinese and Asian groceries, and will keep indefinitely in a tightly covered jar.

Chili Powder

Chili powder is made from dried red chilies. It is pungent, aromatic, and ranges from hot to very hot; it is thus widely used in many spicy dishes. You will be able to buy it in any supermarket.

CINNAMON STICKS OR BARK

Cinnamon sticks are curled, paper-thin pieces of the bark of the cinnamon tree. Chinese cinnamon comes as thicker sticks of this bark. It is highly aromatic and more pungent than the more common cinnamon sticks, but the latter are an adequate substitute. They add a robust taste to braised dishes and are an important ingredient of five-spice powder. Store cinnamon sticks or bark in a tightly sealed jar to preserve their aroma and flavor. Ground cinnamon is not a satisfactory substitute.

CITRUS PEEL

Dried citrus peel made from tangerines or oranges is used extensively in Chinese cookery to flavor braised and smoked dishes. It also adds an intense aroma and taste to stir-fried dishes. Drying the peel concentrates the flavor but you can use fresh peel instead. Chinese dried citrus peel can be found in Chinese groceries, usually in cellophane or plastic packages. It is, however, simple to make your own dried peel.

To make dried citrus peel

Peel the skin off a tangerine or an orange, scraping away as much of the white pith as possible. Lay the peel on paper towels and dry it in the sun, on a drying rack, or in a warm but switched-off oven until it is dry and very hard. Store in a cool dry place in a well-sealed container.

To use dried citrus peel

Soak the required amount of peel in warm water until it softens, then chop or slice it according to the recipe.

CORIANDER (CHINESE PARSLEY, CILANTRO)

Fresh coriander is one of the relatively few herbs used in Chinese cookery. It looks like flat parsley but its pungent, musky, citrus-like flavor gives it a distinctive character which is unmistakable. Its feathery leaves are often used as a garnish, or it can be chopped and then mixed into sauces and stuffings. Parsley may be used as a substitute but for an authentic Chinese flavor it is well worth trying to obtain the real thing. Many Asian and Chinese grocers stock it, as do some greengrocers and supermarkets now.

When buying fresh coriander, look for deep green, fresh-looking leaves. Yellow or limp leaves indicate age and should be avoided.

To store coriander, wash it in cold water, drain it thoroughly and wrap in paper towels. Store it in the vegetable compartment of your refrigerator; it should keep for several days.

MUSHROOMS

Mushrooms are a popular ingredient in Chinese cookery. There are many varieties and they are used both fresh and dried. The most common are:

Chinese dried mushrooms

There are many varieties of these which add a particular flavor and aroma to Chinese dishes. They can be black or brown in color. The very large ones with a lighter color and a highly cracked surface are the best, and so they are usually the most expensive. They can be bought in boxes or plastic bags from Chinese grocers, and are fairly expensive. Keep them stored in an airtight jar.

To use Chinese dried mushrooms

Soak the required amount of dried mushrooms in hot water for about 25 minutes, until they are soft. Squeeze out any excess liquid and remove the tough, inedible stem. The mushrooms are now ready for use.

Straw mushrooms

These are among the tastiest mushrooms found in China. When fresh they have deep brown caps which are molded around the stem. In this country they are only available in cans, and can be bought in Chinese groceries and in some supermarkets and gourmet shops. Drain them and rinse in cold water before use.

CORNSTARCH

In China there are many flours and types of starch, such as water chestnut powder, taro starch and arrowroot, which are used to bind and thicken sauces and to make batter. These exotic starches and flours are difficult to obtain, but I have found that cornstarch works just as well in my recipes. As part of a marinade it helps to coat the food properly, and it gives dishes a velvety texture. It also protects food during deep-frying by helping to seal in the juices, and it can be used as a binder for stuffings. Cornstarch is invariably blended with cold water until it forms a smooth paste before it is used in sauces.

FIVE-SPICE POWDER

Five-spice powder is less commonly known as five-flavored powder or five-fragrance spice powder, and is available in many supermarkets (in the spice section) and in Chinese groceries. This brownish powder is a mixture of star anise, Sichuan peppercorns, fennel, cloves and cinnamon. A good blend is pungent, fragrant, spicy and slightly sweet at the same time. The exotic fragrance it gives to a dish makes the search for a good mixture well worth the effort. It keeps indefinitely in a well-sealed jar.

Dry Ingredients. Top row, left to right: Sichuan preserved vegetable, Chinese dried mushrooms, straw mushrooms, dried straw mushrooms. Row 2, left to right: chilies, ginger, rock sugar, Chinese sausage. Row 3, left to right: dried citrus peel, black beans, water chestnuts, wonton skins.
Bottom row, left to right: cinnamon bark, fresh coriander, Sichuan peppercorns, star anise.

GARLIC

Garlic has been an essential seasoning in Chinese cookery for thousands of years. Chinese food would be inconceivable without its distinctive, highly aromatic smell and taste. The Chinese use garlic in numerous ways: whole, finely chopped, crushed and pickled. It is used to flavor oils as well as spicy sauces, and is often paired with other equally pungent ingredients such as scallions, black beans or ginger root.

Select fresh garlic which is firm and preferably pinkish in color. It should be stored in a cool, dry place but not in the refrigerator, where it can easily become mildewed or begin sprouting.

GINGER

Fresh ginger root is indispensable in Chinese cookery. Its pungent, spicy and fresh taste adds a subtle but distinctive flavor to soups, meats and vegetables. It is also an important seasoning for fish and shellfish since it neutralizes fishy smells. Ginger root looks rather like a gnarled Jerusalem artichoke and can range in size from 4 to 6 inches long. It has pale brown, dry skin which is usually peeled away before use. Select fresh ginger which is firm with no signs of shriveling. It will keep in the refrigerator, well wrapped in plastic wrap, for up to two weeks. Ginger root can now be bought at many greengrocers and supermarkets and in most Chinese and Asian groceries. Dried powdered ginger has quite a different flavor and cannot be substituted for fresh ginger root.

A "slice" in these recipes means a very thin slice, about 2 inches by ½ inch. A "large" slice would be about 3 inches long. After some experimenting, use more or less ginger root according to your own taste preference.

HAM

Chinese ham has a rich salty flavor and is used primarily as a garnish or seasoning to flavor soups, sauces, stir-fried dishes, noodles and rice. One of the most prized Chinese smoked hams comes from Zhejiang Province. Unfortunately Chinese hams are not available in this country, but a good substitute is either Smithfield or Westphalian ham, or Italian prosciutto, which can be found in gourmet shops and good supermarkets.

OILS

Oil is the most commonly used cooking medium in China. The favorite is peanut oil. Animal fats, usually lard and chicken fat, are also used in some areas, particularly in north China. I prefer always to use oil since I find animal fats too heavy.

Throughout this book I have indicated where oils can be reused. Where this is possible, simply cool the oil after use and filter it through cheesecloth or a fine strainer into a jar. Cover it tightly and keep in a cool, dry place. If you keep it in the refrigerator it will become cloudy, but it will clarify again when the oil returns to room temperature. I find oils are best reused just once, and this is healthier since constantly reused oils increase in saturated-fat content.

Peanut oil

This is also known as arachis oil. I prefer to use this for Chinese cookery because it has a pleasant mild taste which is unobtrusive. Although it has a higher saturated-fat content than some oils, its ability to be heated to a high temperature makes it perfect for stir-frying and deep-frying. Many supermarkets stock it, but if you cannot find it, use corn oil instead.

Corn oil

Corn oil is also quite suitable for Chinese cooking. It has a high heating point but I find it rather bland, and it has a slightly disagreeable smell. It is high in polyunsaturates and is therefore one of the healthier oils.

Other vegetable oils

Some of the cheaper vegetable oils available include soybean, safflower and sunflower oils. They are light in color and taste, and can also be used in Chinese cooking.

Sesame oil

This is a thick, rich, golden brown oil made from sesame seeds, which has a distinctive nutty flavor and aroma. It is widely used in Chinese cookery as a seasoning but is not normally used as a cooking oil because it heats rapidly and burns easily. It is often added at the last moment to finish a dish. It is sold in bottles, available in many supermarkets and in Chinese groceries.

PEANUTS

Raw peanuts are used in Chinese cooking to add flavor and a crunchy texture and are especially popular when marinated or added to stir-fry dishes. They can be bought at health-food shops, good supermarkets and Chinese groceries. The thin red skins must be removed before you use the nuts. To do this simply immerse them in a pot of boiling water for about 2 minutes. Drain them and let them cool and the skins will come off easily.

RICE WINE

This wine is used extensively for cooking and drinking throughout China, and the finest variety is believed to be that from Shaoxing, in Zhejiang Province in eastern China. It is made from glutinous rice, yeast and spring water. Available from Chinese grocers, it should be kept at room temperature, tightly corked. A good-quality pale dry sherry can be substituted but cannot equal the rich, mellow taste of Chinese rice wine.

SAUCES AND PASTES

Chinese cookery involves a number of thick tasty sauces or pastes. They are essential to the authentic taste of Chinese cooking and it is well worth making the effort to obtain them. Most are sold in bottles or cans in Chinese groceries and some supermarkets. Canned sauces, once opened, should be transferred to screw-top glass jars and kept in the refrigerator, where they will last indefinitely.

Bean sauce

This thick, spicy, aromatic sauce is made with yellow beans, flour and salt, which are fermented together. It is quite salty but adds a distinctive flavor to Chinese sauces. There are two forms: whole beans in a thick sauce, and ground or puréed beans (sold as crushed yellow bean sauce). I prefer the whole bean variety because it is slightly less salty and has a better texture.

Chili bean sauce

This is a thick dark sauce or paste made from soybeans, chilies and other seasonings, and it is very hot and spicy. Widely used in cooking in western China, it is usually available here in jars in Chinese groceries. Be sure to seal the jar tightly after use and store on a cool shelf or in the refrigerator. Do not confuse it with chili sauce (see below), which is a hot, red, thinner sauce made without beans and used mainly as a dipping sauce for cooked dishes.

Chili sauce

Chili sauce is a bright red, hot sauce which is made from chilies, vinegar, sugar and salt. It is sometimes used for cooking, but it is mainly used as a dipping sauce. There are various brands available in many supermarkets and Chinese groceries, and you should experiment with them until you find the one you like best. If you find it too strong, dilute it with hot water. Do not confuse this sauce with the chili bean sauce mentioned above, which is a much thicker, darker sauce used for cooking.

Hoisin sauce

This is a thick, dark, brownish red sauce made from soybeans, vinegar, sugar, spices and other flavorings. It is sweet and spicy and is widely used in southern Chinese cookery. In the West it is often used as a sauce for Peking Duck instead of the traditional sweet bean sauce. Hoisin sauce is sold in cans and jars (it is sometimes also called barbecue sauce) and is available in Chinese groceries and some supermarkets. I find it keeps best in the refrigerator.

Sesame paste

This rich, thick, creamy brown paste is made from sesame seeds. It is used in both hot and cold dishes, and is particularly popular in northern and western China. It is sold in jars at Chinese groceries. If you cannot obtain it, use peanut butter, which resembles it in taste and texture.

Soy sauces

Soy sauce is an essential ingredient of Chinese cooking. It is made from a mixture of soybeans, flour and water, which is then naturally fermented and aged for some months. The liquid which is finally distilled is soy sauce. There are two main types:

Light soy sauce　As the names imples this is light in color, but it is full of flavor and is the best one to use for cooking. It is saltier than dark soy sauce. It is called Superior Soy.

Liquid Ingredients.
Left row from top to bottom: sesame oil, chili oil, rice wine, oyster sauce.
Center row from top to bottom: chili bean sauce, hoisin sauce, whole yellow bean sauce, sesame paste.
Right row from top to bottom: light soy sauce, dark soy sauce, white rice vinegar, black rice vinegar.

Dark soy sauce This sauce is aged for much longer than light soy sauce, hence its darker, almost black color. It is slightly thicker and stronger than light soy sauce and is more suitable for stews. I prefer it to light soy as a dipping sauce. It is called Soy Superior Sauce.

Most soy sauces sold in supermarkets are dark soy. Chinese grocers sell both types, and their quality is superior. Be sure you buy the right one as the names are very similar.

SAUSAGES

Chinese sausages look exactly like salami and are about 6 inches long. They are made from duck or pork liver, or from pork meat, and are cured. They are dark red in color with white flecks of fat. Their tasty flavor varies according to type, but they are sweet rather than spicy. They must be cooked before they can be eaten and are most commonly used to season chicken and rice dishes. They are obtainable from Chinese grocers.

SHERRY

If you cannot get rice wine you can use a good-quality pale, dry sherry instead. Do not use sweet or cream sherries.

SICHUAN PEPPERCORNS

Sichuan peppercorns are known throughout China as "flower peppers" because they look like flower buds opening. They are reddish brown in color with a strong pungent odor which distinguishes them from the hotter black peppercorns. They are actually not peppers at all, but are the dried berries of a shrub which is a member of the citrus family. I find their smell reminds me of lavender, while their taste is sharp and mildly spicy. They can be ground in a conventional peppermill and are very often roasted before they are ground to bring out their full flavor. They are sold wrapped in cellophane or in plastic bags in Chinese groceries and are inexpensive. They will keep indefinitely if stored in a well-sealed container.

To roast Sichuan peppercorns
Heat a wok or heavy skillet over medium heat. Add the peppercorns (you can cook up to about ⅔ cup at a time) and stir-fry them for about 5 minutes until they brown slightly and start to smoke. Remove the wok from the heat and let them cool. Grind the peppercorns in a peppermill, a clean coffee grinder or with a mortar and pestle. Seal the ground pepper tightly in a screw-top jar until you need it. Or keep the whole roasted peppercorns in a well-sealed container and grind them as required.

SICHUAN PRESERVED VEGETABLE

There are many types of Chinese pickled vegetables. One of the most popular is Sichuan preserved vegetable, a specialty of Sichuan Province. This is the root of the mustard green which is pickled in salt and hot chilies. It is sold in cans in Chinese groceries, and gives a pleasantly crunchy texture and spicy taste to dishes. Before using it, rinse in cold water and then slice or chop as required. Any unused vegetable should be transferred to a tightly covered jar and stored in the refrigerator, where it will keep indefinitely.

SPRING-ROLL SKINS

These are the paper-thin pastry wrappers which are filled with bean sprouts and other vegetables to make spring rolls. They are about 6 inches square, white in color, and are made from a soft flour and water dough. They are very thin and probably too tricky to make at home, so I suggest you buy them frozen in packages of 20, available from Chinese grocers. Keep them in the freezer, well sealed in plastic wrap.

STAR ANISE

The star anise is a hard, star-shaped spice and is the seedpod of the anise bush. (It is also known as Chinese anise or whole anise.) It is similar in flavor and fragrance to common aniseed but is more robust and licorice-like. Star anise is an essential ingredient of five-spice powder and is widely used in braised dishes, to which it imparts a rich taste and fragrance. It is sold in plastic packs by Chinese grocers, and should be stored in a tightly covered jar in a cool, dry place.

SUGAR

Sugar has been used in the cooking of savory dishes in China for a thousand years. Properly employed, it helps balance the various flavors of sauces and other dishes. Chinese sugar comes in several forms: as rock or yellow lump sugar, as brown sugar slabs, and as maltose or malt sugar. I particularly like to use rock sugar, which is rich and has a more subtle flavor than that of refined granulated sugar. It also gives a good luster or glaze to braised dishes and sauces. You can buy it in Chinese groceries, where it is usually sold in packages. You may need to break the lumps into smaller pieces with a wooden mallet or rolling pin. If you cannot find it, use white sugar instead.

TEA

Chinese black tea is a full-bodied, fragrant and smooth tea with a rich aroma and a superb bouquet. There are various kinds, of which Keemun is one of the most well known. Tea is used in smoked dishes or for simmering, as in the Marbled Tea Eggs (page 182). You can purchase Chinese black teas in Chinese groceries, gourmet shops and in many supermarkets. I prefer to store tea in tins since these keep the tea in the freshest possible condition.

VINEGAR

Vinegars are widely used in Chinese cooking. Unlike Western vinegars they are usually made from rice, and there are many varieties, ranging in flavor from the spicy and slightly tart to the sweet and pungent.

White rice vinegar

White rice vinegar is clear and mild in flavor. It has a faint taste of glutinous rice and is used for sweet and sour dishes.

Black rice vinegar

Black rice vinegar is very dark in color and rich though mild in taste. It is used for braised dishes, sauces, and as a dipping sauce for crab.

Red rice vinegar

Red rice vinegar is sweet and spicy in taste and is usually used as a dipping sauce for seafood.

All these vinegars can be bought from Chinese grocers. They are sold in bottles and will keep indefinitely. If you cannot get Chinese vinegars I suggest you use cider vinegar instead. Malt vinegar can be used but its taste is stronger and more acidic.

WATER CHESTNUTS

Water chestnuts do not actually belong to the chestnut family at all, but are a sweet root vegetable or bulb about the size of a walnut. They are white and crunchy. In China they are eaten as a snack, having first been boiled in their skins, or peeled and simmered in rock sugar.

Fresh water chestnuts can sometimes be obtained from Chinese groceries or good supermarkets. They are tastier than canned ones and will keep, unpeeled, in a paper bag in the refrigerator for up to 2 weeks. Peel them before use, and if you have any left over, put them back in the refrigerator, covered with cold water. Canned water chestnuts are sold in many supermarkets and Chinese groceries. They have a good texture but little taste. Rinse them well in cold water before you use them, and store any unused ones in a jar of cold water. They will keep for several weeks in the refrigerator if you change the water daily.

WONTON SKINS

Wonton skins are made from egg and flour and can be bought fresh or frozen from Chinese grocers. They are thin pastry-like wrappings which can be stuffed with minced meat and fried, steamed or used in soups. They are sold in little piles of 3¼-inch or larger squares, wrapped in plastic. The number of squares, or skins, in a package varies from about 30 to 36, depending upon the supplier. Fresh wonton skins will keep for about 5 days if stored in plastic wrap or a plastic bag in the refrigerator. If you are using frozen wonton skins, just peel off the number you require and thaw them thoroughly before you use them.

DIPPING SAUCES AND MIXTURES

Many Chinese dishes and snacks are dipped into a variety of dipping sauces before being eaten. The most popular of these are chili sauce, which can be bought ready-made, and chili oil, which can easily be made at home. Soy sauce and red and black Chinese rice vinegars are also widely used as dips. The following recipes are for some of my favorite dipping sauces, most of which will keep for several months.

Ken Hom in his kitchen. Berkeley, California.

For those who like hot and spicy food, chili oil is a must. It can be purchased ready-made from Chinese grocers, but it is also easy to make yourself. Chili oil can be added as a final spicy touch to dishes during cooking, or it can be used as a dipping sauce either on its own or combined with vinegar and soy sauce, as for the Potsticker Dumplings (page 170).

Region: western

Makes about ⅔ cup
⅔ cup oil, preferably peanut
1 tablespoon chopped dried red chilies
2 teaspoons unroasted Sichuan peppercorns (optional)

Heat a wok or skillet over high heat and add the oil. Continue to heat until the oil begins to smoke. Remove the wok from the heat and add the chilies and peppercorns. Allow the mixture to cool undisturbed, and then pour it into a jar. Let the mixture sit for 2 days, covered, and then strain the oil. It will keep indefinitely.

Ingredients **29**

Ginger and Scallion Sauce

Region: southern

3 tablespoons finely chopped
  scallions
2 teaspoons finely chopped ginger
  root
2 teaspoons salt
1 teaspoon light soy sauce
3 tablespoons oil, preferably peanut

In this simple sauce the oil is heated and then poured over the seasonings to bring out their full taste and fragrance. It is a dipping sauce best used with poultry and meat dishes, such as Twice-cooked Chicken (page 105) and Braised Chicken with Leeks (page 103).

Put all the ingredients except the oil in a small heatproof bowl and mix them well. Heat a wok or skillet and add the oil. Continue to heat until the oil is almost smoking. Remove the wok from the heat and pour the hot oil into the bowl with the other ingredients. The sauce should sizzle for a few seconds and then is ready for use.

Sweet and Sour Sauce

Region: southern

2 tablespoons ginger marmalade
2 tablespoons orange marmalade
¼ teaspoon salt
1 tablespoon Chinese white rice
  vinegar or cider vinegar
1 tablespoon hot water

This is my version of a subtle and tasty sweet and sour sauce which can be used for any deep-fried foods, such as the Fried Wonton (page 179). It keeps well in a tightly sealed jar in the refrigerator.

Combine all the ingredients in a small bowl. Be sure to mix them thoroughly. Transfer the mixture to a small dish if it is to be used at once, or put it in a jar and refrigerate until needed.

Ginger Rice Wine or Sherry

Region: all

Makes about ⅓ cup
3 tablespoons finely chopped ginger
  root
⅓ cup rice wine or dry sherry

This is simply rice wine or sherry flavored with fresh ginger. The mixture works very well as a variation in recipes that call for rice wine or sherry. Putting fresh ginger in rice wine or sherry is also a good method of preserving it, and the ginger can then be eaten as a snack.

Combine the ginger and the rice wine or sherry in a jar and put the mixture into the refrigerator until you are ready to use it. It will keep for at least 2 months.

Five Spice Salt

This dipping mixture is similar to the Sichuan peppercorn and salt mixture but has the distinctive fragrance of five-spice powder. It is best served with fried meat like chicken and squab, or with fried fish.

Heat a wok or skillet until it is hot. Then add the salt and stir-fry for a minute or so until it is quite hot. Remove the wok from the heat and stir in the five-spice powder. Mix well and allow to cool, then store the mixture in a sealed jar until needed.

Region: northern and western

3 tablespoons salt
1 teaspoon five-spice powder

Roasted Salt and Pepper

This roasted salt and pepper mixture, which is made with Sichuan peppercorns, is used throughout China as a dip for deep-fried foods. The dry-roasting method releases all the flavors of the peppercorns.

Heat a wok or heavy skillet over medium heat. Add the peppercorns and the salt and stir-fry them until the mixture begins to smoke slightly and brown a little. Remove the wok from the heat and let the mixture cool. Then grind it using a grinder, clean coffee mill or mortar and pestle. Seal the mixture tightly in a jar until you are ready to use it.

Region: all

Makes about 1/2 cup
1/4 cup Sichuan peppercorns
1/3 cup kosher salt

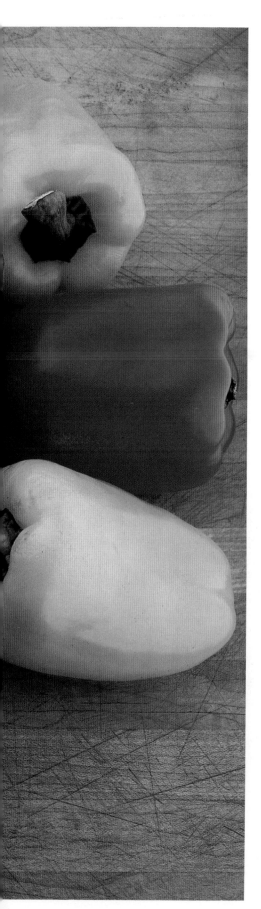

Traditional Chinese utensils are not essential for cooking Chinese food, but there are a few that will make it very much easier. Most items can be bought very cheaply, especially if you seek out authentic implements from a Chinese grocer rather than the more expensive versions sold in many department stores.

WOK

The most useful piece of equipment is the wok, which is easier to use than a large skillet because its depth makes it easier to toss foods quickly without spilling them. It also requires far less oil for deep-frying than a deep-fat fryer, although you may find the latter easier and safer to use. Another advantage is that the shape of the wok allows the heat to spread evenly over its surface, thus making for the rapid cooking which is fundamental to stir-frying.

There are two types of wok: the Cantonese wok, which has a short, rounded handle on either side, and the *pau* wok, which has one long handle. The Cantonese wok is best for steaming and deep-frying since it can be set steadily onto a stand over the heat and is easier to move when it is full of liquid. The *pau* wok is better for stir-frying since it is easier to shake it over the heat with one hand while your free hand wields a long-handled spoon or spatula. It also distances you from the heat and hot oil and makes for more comfortable, safer frying. Woks with rounded bases should be used only on gas burners. It is now possible to buy woks with flattish bottoms which are specifically designed for electric burners. Although these really defeat the purpose of the traditional design, which is to concentrate intense heat at the center, they do have the advantage of having deeper sides than a skillet.

Choosing a wok

Choose a large wok—preferably about 14 inches in diameter, with good deep sides. Some woks on the market are too shallow and are no better than a large skillet. It is easier to cook a small quantity in a large wok than to try to accommodate a large quantity in a small one. Select one which is heavy and if possible made of carbon steel rather than a light stainless steel or aluminum. The latter types tend to scorch. I do not like nonstick woks; not only are they more expensive, but they cannot be seasoned like an ordinary wok, which detracts from the flavor of the food. I also dislike electric woks because I find they do not heat up to a sufficiently high temperature and tend to be too shallow.

Seasoning a wok

All woks (except nonstick ones) need to be seasoned. Many must be scrubbed first as well to remove the machine oil which is applied to the surface by the manufacturer to protect it in transit. This is the *only* time you will ever scrub your wok—unless you let it get rusty. Scrub it with a powder cleanser and water to remove as much of the machine oil as possible. Then dry it and put it on the burner over low heat. Add 2 tablespoons of cooking oil and rub this over the inside of the wok with paper towels until the entire surface is lightly coated with oil. Heat the wok slowly for about 10 to 15 minutes, and then wipe it thoroughly with more paper towels. The paper will become blackened. Repeat this process of coating, heating and wiping until the paper towel wipes clean. Your wok will darken and become well seasoned with use.

Cleaning a wok

Do not scrub a seasoned wok. Just wash it in plain water without detergent. Dry it thoroughly, preferably by putting it over a low heat for a few minutes before putting it away. This should prevent the wok from rusting, but if it does rust, scrub the rust off with powder cleanser and repeat the seasoning process.

WOK ACCESSORIES

Wok stand

This is a metal ring or frame designed to keep a conventionally shaped wok steady on the burner and is essential if you want to use your wok for steaming, deep-frying or braising. The most common stand is a solid metal ring punched with about 6 ventilation holes. You may also be able to find a type that is a circular thin wire frame; these are preferable for gas stoves because they allow for more ventilation.

Wok lid

A wok lid is a domelike cover, usually made from aluminum, which is used for steaming. It may come with the wok or it can be purchased separately at a Chinese grocery, but any large domed lid which fits snugly over the wok can be used instead. Alternatively you could use aluminum foil.

Spatula

A long-handled metal spatula shaped rather like a small shovel is ideal for scooping and tossing food in a wok. Any good long-handled spoon can be used instead.

Rack

If you use your wok or a large pot as a steamer, you will need a wooden or metal rack, or trivet, to stand above the water level and support the plate of food to be steamed. Some woks are sold with a metal stand, but most Chinese groceries, department stores and hardware shops stock triangular wooden stands or round metal stands which can be used for this purpose. You can improvise a stand by using an empty inverted tin can of suitable height.

Bamboo brush

This bundle of stiff split bamboo is used for cleaning a wok without scrubbing off the seasoned surface. It is an attractive, inexpensive implement but not essential. A soft dish-washing brush will do just as well.

DEEP-FAT FRYERS

These are very useful and you may find them safer and easier to use for deep-frying than a wok. The quantities of oil given in the recipes are based on the amount required for deep-frying in a wok. If you are using a deep-fat fryer instead, you will need about double that amount, but *never* fill it more than half full with oil.

CLEAVERS

No self-respecting Chinese cook would be seen with a knife instead of a cleaver. These heavy, lethal-looking choppers serve many purposes. They are used for all kinds of cutting, ranging from fine shredding to chopping up bones. A Chinese cook would usually have three types: a lightweight one with a narrow blade for cutting delicate foods including vegetables; a medium-weight one for general cutting, chopping and crushing purposes; and a heavy one for heavy-duty chopping. Of course you can prepare Chinese food using good sharp knives, but if you decide to invest in a cleaver you will be surprised at how easy it is to use. Choose a good-quality stainless steel one and keep it sharp.

CHOPPING BOARD

The Chinese traditionally use a soft wood block for chopping. Not only is this difficult to maintain but it accumulates bacteria. I prefer to use a hardwood or white acrylic board. Both are strong, easy to clean and last indefinitely. There is so much chopping and slicing to be done when preparing food for Chinese cooking that it really is essential to have a large, steady cutting board. (For hygiene reasons never cut cooked meat on a wood board which you have also used for chopping raw meat or poultry. Keep a separate board for this purpose.)

STEAMERS

Bamboo steamers are among the most ancient of Chinese cooking utensils. These attractive round boxes come in several sizes, of which the 10-inch size is the most suitable for home use. Bamboo steamers are filled with food and placed on top of a pot or over a wok of boiling water. Clean damp cheesecloth is sometimes placed over the open slats under the food to prevent sticking. A tight-fitting bamboo lid is put on top to prevent the steam escaping. One of the advantages of the design is that several steamers can be stacked one on top of the other for multiple cooking. Bamboo steamers can be bought at Chinese groceries. (Alternatively, any kind of wide metal steamer can be used.) Before using a bamboo steamer for the first time, wash it and then steam it, empty, for about 5 minutes.

Ken Hom working in Berkeley, California kitchen.

Rice Cookers

Electric rice cookers are increasing in popularity. They cook rice perfectly and keep it warm throughout a meal. A rice cooker also has the advantage of freeing a burner, making for a less cluttered stove top. They are relatively expensive, however, so unless you eat rice frequently I do not think they are worth the investment.

Sand or Clay Pots

These attractive lightweight clay pots are also known as sand pots because their unglazed exteriors have a sandy texture. They come in a variety of shapes and sizes, equipped with matching lids, and are sometimes encased in a wire frame. The pots are designed to be used on the burner (since most Chinese do not have ovens) and are used for braised dishes, soups and for cooking rice. Never put an empty sand pot onto the heat or put a hot sand pot onto a cold surface. In both cases the pot will crack. Any good casserole or cast-iron pot can be used as a substitute.

Chopsticks

Chopsticks are not just used for eating. They are also used when cooking, for stirring, beating and whipping. Specially long chopsticks are available for these purposes, but it is perfectly all right to use Western cooking implements instead.

Table chopsticks come in wood, plastic and, most luxurious of all, ivory. They can be bought at many department stores, Chinese groceries and from many Chinese restaurants or takeouts. For instructions on how to eat with chopsticks, see page 56.

Wok, cooking chopsticks, Chinese oil can.

方法

The preparation of food for cooking is probably more important and more time-consuming in Chinese cookery than in any other cuisine. Although many dishes are cooked rapidly, this presupposes that every ingredient has been properly prepared beforehand and has been chopped into small, well-shaped pieces to ensure even and quick cooking. This allows food to be cooked for a minimum of time so that it retains its natural texture and taste. The other reason for careful cutting is to enhance the visual appeal of a dish. This is why most Chinese cooks are so specific about cutting techniques, particularly where vegetables are concerned. The Chinese always use a cleaver for these tasks, wielding it with skill and dexterity. Of course a sharp knife can be used instead.

Chinese cookery is a sophisticated cuisine which involves a number of cooking methods that are relatively uncommon in the West. Sometimes several different techniques are used in the preparation of a single dish. Most can be easily mastered with a little practice. When you are planning a meal, be sure to select dishes that involve a range of techniques, and limit yourself to one stir-fried dish per meal until you have become used to this important method of cooking.

CUTTING TECHNIQUES

Slicing

This is the conventional method of slicing food. Hold the food firmly on the chopping board with one hand and slice the food straight down into very thin slices. Meat is always sliced across the grain to break up the fibers and to make it more tender when it is cooked. If you use a cleaver rather than a knife for this, hold the cleaver with your index finger over the far side of the top of the cleaver and your thumb on the side nearest you to guide the cutting edge firmly. Hold the food with your other hand, turning your fingers under for safety. Your knuckles should act as a guide for the blade.

Horizontal, or flat, slicing

This is a technique for splitting food into two thinner pieces while retaining its overall shape. It is often used for cutting kidneys. The cleaver, with its wide blade, is particularly suitable for this. Hold the blade of the cleaver or knife parallel to the chopping board. Place your free hand on top of the piece of food to keep it steady. Using a gentle cutting motion, slice sideways into the food. Depending on the recipe, you may need to repeat this process, cutting the two halves into further thin flat pieces.

Diagonal slicing

This technique is used for cutting vegetables such as asparagus, carrots or scallions. The purpose is to expose more of the surface of the vegetable for quicker cooking. Angle the knife or cleaver at a slant and cut.

Shredding

This is the process by which food is cut into thin, fine, matchstick-like shreds. First cut the food into slices, and then pile several slices on top of one another and cut them *lengthwise* into fine strips. Some foods, particularly meat and chicken breast, are easier to shred if they are first stiffened slightly in the freezer for about 20 minutes.

Dicing

This is a simple technique of cutting food into small cubes, or dice. The food should first be cut into slices. Stack the slices and cut them again *lengthwise* into sticks, just as you would for shredding (above). Stack the strips or sticks and cut *crosswise* into evenly sized cubes or dice.

Roll cutting

This is rather like diagonal slicing but is used for larger vegetables such as zucchini, eggplant, large carrots, and Chinese white radish (*mooli*). As with diagonal slicing, this technique allows more of the surface of the vegetable to be exposed to the heat, thereby speeding up the cooking time. Begin by making one diagonal slice at one end of the vegetable. Then turn the vegetable 180° and make the next diagonal slice. Continue in this way until you have chopped the entire vegetable into evenly sized, diamond-shaped chunks.

Mincing

This is a fine-chopping technique. Chefs use two cleavers to mince, rapidly chopping with them in unison for fast results. One cleaver or knife is easier for the less expert, although the process will of course take a little longer! First slice the food and then, using a sharp knife or cleaver, rapidly chop the food until it is rather spread out over the chopping board. Scrape it into a pile and chop again, and continue chopping until the food reaches the desired state. You may find it easier to hold the knife or cleaver by the top of the blade (rather than by the handle) with two hands, as though you were chopping parsley. A food processor may also be used for this, but be careful not to overmince the food or you will lose out on texture and taste.

Chopping

This is a term which is used for any technique that requires food to be completely cut through. Usually this applies to whole birds or to cooked food with bones that need to be cut into smaller pieces. The food to be chopped should be placed on a firm cutting surface. Use a straight, sharp, downward motion with the cleaver or knife. To chop through bones, hit down with the blade and then finish off the blow with the flat of your other hand on the top edge of the cleaver or knife. A heavy-duty cleaver or knife is best for these tasks.

Scoring

This is a technique used to pierce the surface of foods to help them cook faster and more evenly. It also gives them an attractive appearance. Use a cleaver or a sharp knife and make cuts into the food at a slight angle to a depth of about ⅛ inch. Take care not to cut all the way through. Make cuts all over the surface of the food, cutting crisscross to give a wide diamond-shaped pattern.

OTHER PREPARATION TECHNIQUES

Marinating

This is a process in which raw meat or poultry is steeped for a time in a liquid such as soy sauce, rice wine or sherry and cornstarch to improve its flavor and to tenderize it. Sometimes other spices or seasonings, such as sugar, chilies, five-spice powder or Sichuan peppercorns, are added. The marinating time is usually at least 20 minutes in order to infuse the meat or poultry properly with the flavors of the marinade. Once marination is complete, the food is usually lifted out of the marinade with a slotted spoon before it is cooked.

Thickening

Cornstarch blended with an equal quantity of water is frequently used in Chinese cookery to thicken sauces and glaze dishes. Always make sure the mixture is smooth and well blended before adding it.

Velveting

Velveting is used to prevent delicate foods like chicken breasts from overcooking. The food is coated with a mixture of unbeaten egg white, cornstarch and sometimes salt. It is then put into the refrigerator for about 20 to 30 minutes to ensure that the coating adheres to the food. This protects the flavor and texture of the food when it is put into oil or hot water.

COOKING TECHNIQUES

Blanching

This involves putting food into hot water or into moderately hot oil for a few minutes to cook it briefly but not entirely. It is a sort of softening-up process to prepare the food for final cooking. Chicken is often blanched in oil or water after being velveted (see above). Meat is sometimes blanched to rid it of scum in order to ensure a clean taste and appearance. Blanching in water is common with harder vegetables such as broccoli or carrots. The vegetable is plunged into boiling water for several minutes. It is then drained and plunged into cold water to arrest the cooking process. In such cases blanching usually precedes stir-frying to finish the cooking.

Poaching

This is a method of simmering food until it is partially cooked. It is then put into soup or combined with a sauce and the cooking process continued.

Stir-frying

This is the most famous of all Chinese cooking techniques and it is possibly the most tricky since success depends upon having all the required ingredients prepared, measured out and immediately at hand, and on having a good source of fierce heat. Its advantage is that, properly executed, stir-fried foods can be cooked in minutes in very little oil, so they retain their natural flavors and textures. It is very important that stir-fried foods are not overcooked or greasy. Once you have mastered this technique you will find that it becomes almost second nature. Using a wok is definitely an advantage when stir-frying, as its shape not only conducts the heat well but its high sides enable you to toss and stir ingredients rapidly, keeping them constantly moving while cooking. Having prepared all the ingredients for stir-frying, the steps are:

● Heat the wok or skillet until it is very hot *before* adding the oil. This prevents food sticking and will ensure an even heat. Add the oil and, using a metal spatula or long-handled spoon, distribute it evenly over the surface. It should be very hot indeed—almost smoking—before you add the next ingredient, unless you are going on to flavor the oil (see next point).

- If you are flavoring the oil with garlic, scallions, ginger, dried red chili or salt, do not wait for the oil to get so hot that it is almost smoking. If you do, these ingredients will burn and become bitter. Toss them quickly in the oil for a few seconds. In some recipes these flavorings will then be removed and discarded before cooking proceeds.

- Now add the ingredients as described in the recipe and proceed to stir-fry by tossing them over the surface of the wok with the metal spatula or long-handled spoon. If you are stir-frying meat, let each side rest for just a few seconds before continuing to stir. Keep moving the food from the center of the wok to the sides. Stir-frying is a noisy business and is usually accompanied by quite a lot of splattering because of the high temperature at which the food must be cooked.

- Some stir-fried dishes are thickened with a mixture of cornstarch and cold water. To avoid getting a lumpy sauce be sure to remove the wok from the heat before you add the cornstarch mixture, which must be thoroughly blended before it is added. The sauce can then be returned to the heat and thickened.

Deep-frying

This is one of the most important techniques in Chinese cooking. The trick is to regulate the heat so that the surface of the food is sealed but does not brown so fast that the food is uncooked inside. Although deep-fried food must not be greasy, the process does require a lot of oil. The Chinese use a wok for deep-frying, which requires considerably less oil than a deep-fat fryer, but I think you should avoid using the wok unless you are very sure of it. If you do, be certain that it is fully secure on its stand before adding the oil, and on no account leave the wok unsupervised. Most people will find a deep-fat fryer easier and safer to use. Be careful not to fill this more than half full with oil.

Some points to bear in mind when deep-frying are:

- Wait for the oil to get hot enough before adding the food to be fried. The oil should give off a haze and almost produce little wisps of smoke when it is the right temperature, but you can test it by dropping in a small piece of food. If it bubbles all over, the oil is sufficiently hot. Adjust the heat as necesary to prevent the oil from actually smoking or overheating.

- Be sure to dry food to be deep-fried thoroughly with paper towels, as this will prevent splattering. If the food is in a marinade, remove it with a slotted spoon and let it drain before putting it into the oil. If you are using batter, make sure all the excess batter drips off before adding the food to the hot oil.

- Oil used for deep-frying can be reused. Cool it, and then strain it into a jar through several layers of cheesecloth or through a fine-mesh strainer to remove any particles of food which might otherwise burn if reheated and give the oil a bitter taste. Label the jar according to what food you have cooked in the oil and reuse it only for the same thing. Oil can be used up to three times before it begins to lose its effectiveness.

Shallow-frying

This technique is similar to sautéing. It involves more oil than stir-frying but less than for deep-frying. Food is fried first on one side and then on the other. Sometimes the excess oil is then drained off and a sauce added to complete the dish. A skillet is ideal for shallow-frying.

Slow-simmering and steeping

These processes are very similar. In slow-simmering food is immersed in liquid which is brought almost to a boil, and then the temperature is reduced so that it simmers, cooking the food to the desired degree. This is the technique used for making stock. In steeping, food is similarly immersed in liquid (usually stock) and simmered for a time. The heat is then turned off and the remaining heat of the liquid finishes off the cooking process.

Braising and red-braising

This technique is most often applied to tougher cuts of meat and certain vegetables. The food is usually browned and then put into stock which has been flavored with seasonings and spices. The stock is brought to the boil, the heat reduced and the food simmered gently until it is cooked. Red-braising is simply the technique by which food is braised in a dark liquid such as soy sauce. This gives food a reddish brown color, hence the name. This type of braising sauce can be saved and frozen for reuse. It can be reused many times and becomes richer in flavor.

Steaming

Steaming has been used by the Chinese for thousands of years. Along with stir-frying and deep-frying it is the most widely used technique. Steamed foods are cooked by a gentle moist heat which must circulate freely in order to cook the food. It is an excellent method for bringing out subtle flavors and so is particularly wonderful for fish. Bamboo steamers are used by the Chinese but you could use any one of several utensils:

● *Using a bamboo steamer in a wok*   For this you need a large bamboo steamer about 10 inches wide. Put about 2 inches of water in a wok. Bring it to a simmer. Put the bamboo steamer containing the food into the wok, where it should rest safely, perched on the sloping sides. Cover the steamer with its matching lid and steam the food until it is cooked. Replenish the water as required.

● *Using a wok as a steamer*   Put about 2 inches of water into a wok. Then put a metal or wooden rack into the wok. Bring the water to a simmer and put the food to be steamed onto a plate. Lower the plate onto the rack and cover the wok tightly with a lid. Check the water level from time to time and replenish it with hot water when necessary.

● *Using a large roasting pan or pot as a steamer*   Put a metal or wooden rack into the pan or pot and pour in about 2 inches of water. Bring it to a simmer and put the food to be steamed onto a plate. Lower the plate onto the rack and cover the pan or pot with a lid or with aluminum foil. Replenish the water as necessary.

● *Using a metal steamer*   If you have a metal steamer which is wide enough to take a plate of food, this will give you very satisfactory results. Keep an eye on the level of the water in the base.

If you do not have a metal or wooden rack, you can use a small empty tin can to support the plate of food. Remember that the food needs to remain above the water level and must not get wet. The water level should always be at least 1 inch below the edge of the food plate. (Be sure to use a heat-proof plate.)

Roasting

In China roasting is done only in commercial establishments since most homes do not have ovens. The Chinese roast food in large metal drum-shaped ovens which stand about 5 feet high and are fueled by charcoal. The food is hung on hooks inside the oven over intense heat. The idea is to expose all the surface of the food to the heat to give it a crisp outer surface and a moist interior. You can approximate the Chinese method by putting food onto a rack in a roasting pan so that the hot air of the oven can circulate around it.

Barbecuing

This is a variation on roasting and it is not very common. Marinated meat is placed over a charcoal fire and the meat constantly basted to keep it moist. Today modern grills and outdoor barbecues produce much the same result.

Twice-cooking

As the name implies, this is a two-step process involving two quite different techniques, such as simmering and stir-frying. It is used to change the texture of food, to infuse it with flavor and to render foods which are difficult to cook into a more manageable state. It is especially useful for removing fat from meat before final cooking.

Reheating foods

Steaming is one of the best methods of reheating food since it warms it without cooking it further and without drying it out. To reheat soups and braised dishes, bring the liquid slowly to a simmer but do not boil. Remove it from the heat as soon as it is hot to prevent overcooking.

GARNISHES

The Chinese pay much attention to the presentation of their cuisine. This is why cutting techniques are so important, since the size and shape of individual ingredients should harmonize with each other. We also like to decorate dishes with various kinds of garnish ranging from the simple scallion brush to the elaborate tomato rose. Here are instructions for making some simple, attractive garnishes.

Carrot flowers

1. Peel the carrots and cut them into 3-inch chunks.

2. Cut a V-shaped slice down the length of each chunk. Repeat, making 3 or 4 more lengthwise cuts around each.

3. Now slice the carrots crosswise to form thin flower shapes. Soak them in cold water until required.

Scallion brushes

1. Cut off the green part of the scallion and trim off the base of the bulb. You should have a 3-inch white segment left.

2. Make a lengthwise cut about 1 inch long at one end of the scallion. Roll the scallion 90° and cut again. Repeat this process at the other end.

3. Soak the scallions in ice water and they will curl into flower brushes. Spin or pat them dry before use.

Tomato roses

1.   Select firm tomatoes and, using a very sharp knife, peel off the skin from the top in one piece as though you were peeling an apple. Do not break the strip.

2.   Roll the strip of tomato skin into a tight coil.

3.   Turn the coil over and you should have a tomato rose.

Radish roses

1.   Remove any leaves, and trim the top and the root end of the radish.

2.   Make thin, rounded cuts to form petals.

3.   Soak the radishes in ice water for about an hour.

Cucumber fans

1. Using a sharp knife, cut off the rounded end of half a cucumber. Then cut it in half *lengthwise*.

2. Turn each cucumber piece so that the skin side is uppermost. Make a horizontal slice to reduce the thickness of each cucumber piece, so that you end up with a slice which is mainly skin with just a little flesh.

3. Now make parallel cuts down the length of the slice, as shown in the illustration. The cuts will have to curve slightly so that you will be able to splay the slices out like a fan.

4. Starting with the second slice, bend every other slice in toward the base of the cucumber piece, tucking them in so that they stay securely in place.

5. Keep the cucumber fans in cold water until you are ready to use them.

Fresh chili flowers

1.   Trim the tip of the chili but do not remove the stem.

2.   Make 4 cuts lengthwise from the stem of the chili to the tip, to form 4 sections. Remove and discard any seeds.

3.   Soak the chilies in cold water. They will "flower" in the water.

Remember to wash your hands after handling chilies (page 18).

*Crab with Black Bean Sauce, Deep-fried
Green Beans and plain rice.*

CHINESE MEALS AND MENUS

菜譜

Chinese meals always consist of a soup, a rice, noodle or bread dish, a vegetable dish and at least two other dishes which may be mainly meat, fish or chicken. The meal may be preceded and concluded with tea, but during the meal itself soup will be the only beverage. Soup is drunk not as a first course as it is in the West but throughout the meal. The exception to this is a banquet when soup, if it is served at all, comes at the end of the meal or as a palate-cleanser at several points during the dinner. On such occasions, wine, spirits, beer or even fruit juice will be drunk with the food. At banquets (which are really elaborate dinner parties) dishes are served one at a time so that the individual qualities of each dish can be properly savored. There may be as many as eight to twelve courses. Rice will not be served except at the end of the meal, when fried rice might be offered to anyone who has any appetite left.

At ordinary family meals all the dishes are served together, including the soup. The food is placed in the center of the table. Each person has his own rice bowl into which he puts a generous amount of steamed rice. Then, using his chopsticks, he helps himself to a little of one dish, transferring this to his rice bowl. Once he has eaten this together with some rice, he will have a chopstick-full of another dish. No Chinese would dream of heaping his rice bowl with what he regarded as his full share of any dish before proceeding to eat. Eating is a communal affair and each diner will take care to see that everyone else at the table is receiving a fair share of everything.

Of course you can eat Chinese food any way you like. I think it blends deliciously with many Western dishes, and when you are new to Chinese cooking you may find it easier to familiarize yourself with the cuisine by trying out just one or two dishes at a time and incorporating them into a non-Chinese menu. Chinese soups, for example, make excellent starters, and stir-fried vegetables are delicious with broiled meats and roasts.

When you do devise an all-Chinese meal, try to see that you have a good mix of textures, flavors, colors and shapes. Apart from a staple dish, such as steamed rice, you should opt for a variety of meat, poultry and fish. It is better to serve one meat and one fish dish rather than two meat dishes, even if the meats are different. It will also be a better-balanced meal (and easier to prepare) if you use a variety of cooking methods. Serve a stir-fried dish with a braised, steamed or cold dish. It's important to try to select one or two things that can be prepared in advance. Avoid doing more than two stir-fried dishes, which will make for frantic activity at the last minute.

SUGGESTED MENUS

EASY FAMILY FARE FOR 4
(pictured on page 69)

Tomato Egg-Flower Soup
Steamed Fish with Garlic, Scallions and Ginger
Stir-fried Beef with Orange
Lettuce with Oyster Sauce
Steamed Rice

AUTUMN OVERTURE FOR 4
(pictured on page 147)

Kidney and Bean-Curd Soup
Stir-fried Ground Pork
Cold Marinated Bean Sprouts
Steamed Rice

STYLISH FALL SUPPER
FOR 4–6
(pictured on page 52)

Wonton Soup
Curried Chicken with Peppers
Peking Braised Lamb
Braised Spicy Eggplant
Steamed Rice

SPICY FAVORITES FOR 4
(pictured on page 65)

Curried Corn Soup with Chicken
Five-Spice Spareribs
Fried Fish with Ginger
Cold Spicy Noodles
Stir-fried Snow Peas with Water Chestnuts

SUMMER ENTERTAINING
FOR 6
(pictured on page 109)

Sesame Shrimp Toast
Chinese Chicken Salad
Stir-fried Pork with Scallions
Stir-fried Spinach with Garlic
Steamed Rice
Fruit Compote

Clockwise from the bottom: Curried Chicken with Peppers (page 95), Wonton Soup (page 67), Braised Spicy Eggplant (page 143), Peking Braised Lamb (page 90).

SUGGESTED MENUS

SUMMER PICNIC FOR 4
(pictured on page 185)

Cold Spicy Noodles
Chicken Pieces in Black Bean Sauce
Stir-fried Scallops with Pork Kidneys
Cold Sweet-and-Sour Chinese Cabbage
Fresh Fruit

ELEGANT DINNER ON A WINTER EVENING FOR 4
(pictured on page 13)

Hot and Sour Soup
Sichuan Shrimp in Chili Sauce
Five-Spice Red Braised Squab
Braised Cauliflower with Oyster Sauce
Steamed Rice

RELAXED SUPPER FOR 4
(pictured on page 55)

Beef Noodle Soup
Fried Wonton
Stir-fried Cucumbers with Hot Spices
Peaches in Honey Syrup

INFORMAL WINTER PARTY FOR 4–6
(pictured on page 89)

Shrimp Crackers
Mongolian Hot Pot
Stir-fried Pork with Scallions
(optional)

CELEBRATION DINNER FOR 6–8
(pictured on page 112)

Caramel Walnuts
Corn Soup with Crabmeat
Rainbow Beef in Lettuce Leaves or
Peking Duck with Chinese Pancakes
Stir-fried Snow Peas with Water Chestnuts
Braised Pork with Bean Curd
Fresh Fruit

This is an ambitious menu to
embark on only after you've
mastered the individual
dishes. The menu is
designed so that each dish
is served as a
separate course.

*Clockwise from lower left: Beef Noodle
Soup (page 168), Stir-fried Cucumbers
with Hot Spices (page 149), Peaches
in Honey Syrup (page 184), Fried Wonton
(page 179) with Sweet and Sour Sauce
(page 30).*

TABLE-SETTING

You don't need any special dishes or cutlery for serving Chinese food, although I think it tastes infinitely better when it is eaten with chopsticks rather than a fork. Knives are definitely unnecessary since Chinese food is always cut into bite-size pieces before it is served. Each person will need a rice bowl, a soup bowl, a teacup if you are serving tea, and a small plate for any bones or debris. A small dish or saucer each will also be needed if you are having any dipping sauces. Soup or cereal bowls will do for the rice and soup. Chopsticks are usually set to the right of the rice bowl, where a knife would normally be put. A spoon, metal or china, will be needed for soup and as an adjunct to chopsticks for noodles.

The Chinese always help themselves (and others) to the food using their own chopsticks. Some people provide separate serving chopsticks but these are usually abandoned in the enthusiasm of eating.

USING CHOPSTICKS

Using chopsticks just takes a little practice, and the hungrier you are the quicker you learn!

1.   Put one chopstick into the crook of your hand between your thumb and first finger, holding the chopstick about two-thirds the way up from the thinner end. Let it rest on your third finger.

2.   Put the second chopstick between your thumb and forefinger so that its tip is level with the first chopstick below.

3.   Keep the lower chopstick steady and move the top one to pick up food.

When eating rice and other tricky morsels it is perfectly acceptable to lift your rice bowl under your chin and "shovel" rice into your mouth with your chopsticks. The Chinese do this all the time.

WHAT TO DRINK

If you want to be authentic, serve soup with your Chinese meals. If you prefer you could serve tea, preferably Chinese tea, which is drunk without milk or sugar. There are three different types of Chinese tea. Green, or unfermented, tea is made from green leaves which, when infused, result in a pale yellowish tea with a refreshing astringent taste. Black tea is made from fermented black leaves and is red when infused. It has a hearty, robust flavor. Oolong tea is made from partially fermented leaves and is strong and dark. Of all these I think green jasmine tea is the nicest with food. (Do not confuse any of these teas with "China tea" which is a tea blended for the western market.)

Chinese wines are usually made from fermented rice, the most famous being Shaoxing, which is also used for cooking. It has a very different flavor from wine made from grapes and is rather an acquired taste. Many European wines go very well with Chinese food, particularly dry whites and light reds. In recent years whiskey and cognac have become very popular with the more affluent Hong Kong Chinese, who drink these neat with their meals.

MENUS AND SERVINGS

Throughout this book I have given suggestions about what accompanying dishes would go with a particular recipe. There is of course no need to stick rigidly to these ideas. Although most Chinese meals consist of at least three dishes, rice and soup, I recommend that you concentrate on achieving success with relatively few dishes until you become more familiar with the cooking techniques and with the recipes. Chefs apart, the Chinese themselves would not expect to be proficient in cooking the real delicacies of their cuisine. These they would order in a restaurant and would not attempt at home. (The Chinese who live in towns and cities eat out a great deal, although many restaurants are very humble, simple places.)

Chinese cooking can be very time-consuming. The recipes in this book are based on the expectation that you will cook two meat, chicken or fish dishes per meal. (This is in addition to a vegetable dish, rice or noodles and, probably, a soup.) This way the total meat, chicken and fish allowance per head will be about 6 to 8 ounces. If you prefer to cook just one such dish, you will probably have to double the quantities given in the recipe. Doing this at least means you will have a chance to try the authentic taste of Chinese food without quite so much work. Once you gain confidence you will be able to cope with preparing more dishes and be able to serve a more authentic Chinese meal.

湯

In China soups are rarely served as a separate course except at banquets. During some formal banquets light soups are served at various stages of dining. They signal the end of a course and are used to cleanse the palate in preparation for the next one. Most commonly a thin clear soup will be served at the end of the dinner but before the dessert. At family meals soup is served at the same time as all the other dishes. In this case it complements the various tastes and textures of the meal and also serves as a beverage.

There are two basic types of soup in Chinese cookery: light and heavy. Light soups are clear broths garnished with a little meat, fish, shellfish or vegetable. Such soups are a liquid accompaniment to other dishes. (Drinks such as water, wine and tea are rarely served with a meal in China.) I remember family gatherings when a large tureen of clear soup would dominate the center of the table, with all the other dishes arranged round it. It was considered good form always to drink a good helping of it during the meal.

The heavy soups are more like separate courses, or meals in their own right. They are substantial in texture, more like stews than soups, and are made from a rich stock with the addition of meat, fish or shellfish, chopped vegetables and seasonings. These soups are generally thickened with a starch such as cornstarch or water-chestnut flour. They are made in a heatproof casserole and simmered slowly until all the flavors marry. Shark's Fin is one of the most famous Chinese thick soups. It is a classic gourmet soup. Its essential ingredient (shark's fin) is expensive to obtain, and it is time-consuming to make, so it is not really suitable for the domestic kitchen and is best enjoyed in a restaurant.

The key to a good Chinese soup, as to any soup, is good stock. I learned about stock first by watching my mother making it with meticulous care in her kitchen. These lessons were reinforced for me in my uncle's restaurant, where a large pot of stock was the heart of the kitchen. All the world's great cuisines emphasize the importance of stock. The French call it the *fonds de cuisine*, the basis or foundation of cooking. In China stock is essential in many recipes, and it is indispensable in soup. In Chinese cuisine stock is generally made from chicken, with pork bones sometimes added to enrich the broth. Beef is rarely used because it is expensive and also because it is considered too strong for the Chinese palate.

All of the soups in the following chapter are easy to make, particularly if you have already made stock ahead of time. They can be served, Chinese-style, with other dishes, or as a separate course, or on their own as a light meal. You need not limit your enjoyment of these soups to an all-Chinese meal, as Chinese soups blend deliciously with European food.

Chicken Stock

Region: all

This recipe makes about 3 quarts
  4½ pounds uncooked chicken bones
    (backs, feet, wings, etc.)
  1½ pounds uncooked chicken, cut
    into pieces
  3½ quarts cold water
  2 slices ginger root
  2 scallions
  2 garlic cloves, unpeeled
  ½ teaspoon salt

Chicken stock is an all-purpose base, not only for soups but also for sauces and glazes. It is light and delicious, its chief ingredient is fairly cheap, and it is easy to make. With such attributes it is small wonder that chicken stock is essential in Chinese cookery. Your first step on the path to success with Chinese cooking must be to prepare and maintain an ample supply of good chicken stock. I prefer to make large quantities of it at a time and freeze it. Once you have a supply available, you will be able to prepare any number of soups or sauces very quickly. Never ever use bouillon cubes for Chinese cooking. They contain too much salt and too little flavor and will never produce the sort of rich, thick stock on which so many Chinese dishes depend for their subtle taste. Here are several points to remember:

● *Good stock requires meat to give it richness and flavor. It is therefore necessary to use at least some chicken meat, if not a whole bird.*
● *The stock should never boil. If it does it will be undesirably cloudy and the fat will be incorporated into the liquid.*
● *Simmer slowly and skim the stock regularly.*
● *Strain the finished stock well through several layers of cheesecloth or a fine-mesh strainer.*
● *Let the stock cool thoroughly before freezing it.*

The classic Chinese method to ensure a clear stock is to blanch the meat and bones before simmering. I find this is unnecessary. My method of careful skimming achieves the same result with far less work. Remember to save all your uncooked chicken bones and carcasses for stock. They can be frozen until you are aready to make it. (Be sure to wrap the bones well before freezing them.) (If you find the portions in this recipe too large for your needs, cut the amounts in half.)

Put the chicken bones and chicken pieces into a very large pot. (The bones can be put in either frozen or defrosted.) Cover them with the cold water and bring it to a simmer. Remove the green tops of the scallions. Lightly crush the garlic cloves, leaving the skins on.

Using a large, flat spoon, skim off the scum as it rises from the bones. Watch the heat; the stock should never boil. Keep skimming until the stock looks clear. This can take from 20 to 40 minutes. Do not stir or disturb the stock.

Add the ginger, scallions, garlic cloves and salt. Simmer the stock over a very low heat for about 4 hours, skimming any fat off the top at least twice during this time. The stock should be rich and full-bodied, which is why it needs to be simmered for such a long time. This way the stock (and any soup you make with it) will have plenty of flavor.

Strain the stock through several layers of dampened cheesecloth or through a very fine mesh strainer, and then let it cool thoroughly. Remove any fat which has risen to the top. It is now ready to be used or transferred to containers and frozen for future use.

Pork and Chicken Stock

Pork is used extensively in Chinese cookery, and pork bones, when added to chicken stock, make for a richer, tastier and sweeter soup or broth. It was a favorite in our house not only as a beverage but as a "rinse" for our rice bowls between courses. I also loved chewing on the cooked bones and looking for morsels of pork to dip in soy sauce.

Trim the green tops off the scallions, leaving the white part. Put the pork bones into a heavy pot or casserole together with the chicken stock. (Thaw the pork bones beforehand if they are frozen; otherwise you will get a cloudy stock.) Bring the liquid to a simmer and skim off any scum that rises to the surface. Then add the ginger, scallions and salt. Simmer over very low heat for 1½ hours.

Strain the stock through dampened cheesecloth or through a fine-mesh strainer, and then leave it to cool. When the stock is cold, remove any fat that has risen to the surface. It is now ready to be used as soup or as a stock for other soups such as Ham and Zucchini Soup (page 64). You can also freeze it for future use.

Region: all

Makes about 2 quarts
   2 scallions
   1½ pounds uncooked pork bones
   2 quarts Chicken Stock (page 60)
   1 slice ginger root
   ½ teaspoon salt

Corn Soup with Crabmeat

My mother often made this soup using fresh corn. For convenience, canned or frozen corn may be substituted, but I think fresh is quite superior. It reheats well and has a rich, thick texture which goes well with Beef in Oyster Sauce (page 82) and Stir-fried Ginger Broccoli (page 146).

If you are using fresh corn, wash the cobs and, with a sharp knife or cleaver, remove the kernels. (You should end up with about 1½ cups of corn). Mix the egg white and sesame oil together in a small bowl and set it aside.

Bring the stock to a boil in a large pot and add the corn. Simmer for 15 minutes, uncovered, and then add the rice wine or sherry, ginger, salt, sugar and cornstarch mixture. Bring it back to a boil, then lower the heat to a simmer. Now add the crabmeat and then slowly pour in the egg white mixture in a steady stream, stirring all the time. Transfer the soup to a tureen and garnish.

Region: southern

Serves 4 to 6
   4 ears fresh corn on the cob, or 10
       ounces canned or frozen corn
   1 egg white
   1 teaspoon sesame oil
   1 quart Chicken Stock (page 60)
   1 tablespoon rice wine or dry sherry
   2 teaspoons finely chopped ginger
       root
   1 teaspoon salt
   1 teaspoon sugar
   2 teaspoons cornstarch, blended
       with 2 teaspoons water
   6 ounces fresh cooked, canned or
       frozen crabmeat

Garnish
   2 tablespoons finely chopped
       scallions

(pictured on page 112)

Chicken and Spinach Soup

Region: eastern

Serves 4 to 6

   6 ounces fresh spinach
   6 ounces boneless chicken breasts
   1 quart Chicken Stock (page 60)
   2 tablespoons light soy sauce
   2 teaspoons sugar
   2 tablespoons finely chopped
      scallions

Spinach, with its distinctive taste and deep green color, is a favorite of the Chinese. This soup is a thin one and is very attractive to look at. Its ingredients are blanched separately before they are combined with the stock. This way each ingredient retains its unique taste. This is an easy soup to make and many of the steps can be done in advance.

Remove the stems of the spinach and wash the leaves well. Blanch the leaves for a few seconds in a pot of boiling water until they are just wilted. Then freshen them in cold water to prevent further cooking.

Cut the chicken into thin slices about 2 inches long. In a separate pot of boiling water blanch the chicken slices for 2 minutes until they are slightly firm and white. Now drain both the spinach and the chicken slices. The soup can be prepared up to this point several hours ahead.

Just before you are ready to eat, bring the chicken stock to a simmer and season it with the soy sauce and sugar. Add the blanched spinach and chicken slices. Bring the soup back to the simmering point and then add the scallions. Serve at once.

Chicken and Spinach Soup.

This soup combines two classic southern Chinese ingredients: chicken and dried mushrooms. Dark chicken meat from the legs and thighs is most often used for this soup to give it a rich, strong flavor and a good texture. Fresh button mushrooms can be used instead of dried ones, but you should try to use the dried Chinese mushrooms if you can get them as their smoky flavor enhances the total effect of the soup.

There are two techniques involved here. The chicken is first stir-fried to give it a rich flavor. Then all the other ingredients are simmered together with the fried chicken. The result is a good soup which would also go well with French bread and butter for a non-Chinese meal. It reheats nicely, tasting even better when made one day and eaten the next.

Cut the chicken into ½-inch cubes, retaining any bones. Put them into a bowl together with the rice wine or sherry and 1 tablespoon of soy sauce and let the mixture stand for 10 minutes. Soak the mushrooms in warm water for 20 minutes. Then drain them and squeeze out the excess liquid. Remove and discard the stems and finely shred the caps into thin strips.

Bring the stock to a simmer in a large pot. Drain the marinade into the stock, reserving the chicken cubes. Add the mushrooms, scallions, ham and soy sauce. Continue to simmer the soup, and meanwhile heat the oil in a wok or large skillet. When it is hot, stir-fry the chicken cubes over high heat until they are nicely brown. This should take about 5 minutes. Drain them on paper towels and then add them to the soup. Simmer together for 5 minutes, and the soup is ready to serve.

Region: southern

Serves 4 to 6

¼ pound chicken thighs or legs, skinned
1 tablespoon rice wine or sherry
1 tablespoon light soy sauce
1 ounce Chinese dried mushrooms (about 10 large)
1 quart Chicken Stock (page 60)
1 tablespoon finely chopped scallions
1 ounce Smithfield ham or prosciutto, shredded (about 3 tablespoons)
1 tablespoon light soy sauce
2 teaspoons oil

This is a simple soup which typifies the fresh, light cooking of the south. Like many good soups, it takes a little effort to prepare, but it is worth it. It is best to use bean sprouts which are really fresh to give your soup a good crunchy texture. Chinese ham is traditionally used to produce the distinctive smoky flavor, but since it cannot be obtained here, Smithfield ham or prosciutto is a satisfactory substitute.

Soak the noodles in a bowl of warm water for about 20 minutes or until they are soft. Drain them thoroughly in a colander and cut them into 2-inch pieces. If you have time, remove both ends of the bean sprouts. This will give the soup a cleaner look.

Bring the chicken stock to a simmer in a large pot. Add the drained noodles and soy sauce and simmer for 2 minutes. Then add the ham, coriander and scallions, and simmer for 30 seconds. Finally, add the bean sprouts and simmer for another 30 seconds. Serve at once.

Region: southern

Serves 4 to 6

2 ounces bean thread (transparent) noodles (1½ small packages)
3 ounces fresh bean sprouts (about ¼ cup)
1 quart Chicken Stock (page 60)
1 tablespoon light soy sauce
3 ounces Smithfield ham or prosciutto, shredded (about ¼ cup)
2 tablespoons finely chopped fresh coriander
2 tablespoons finely chopped scallions

Curried Corn Soup with Chicken

Region: southern

Serves 4 to 6

4 ears fresh corn or 1 can (12 ounces) whole corn kernels, drained, or cream-style corn
½ pound boneless chicken breasts, skinned
1 egg white
1 teaspoon cornstarch
1 teaspoon salt
1 egg
1 teaspoon sesame oil
1 quart Chicken Stock (page 60)
1 tablespoon rice wine or dry sherry
1 tablespoon curry powder or paste
1 teaspoon salt
1 teaspoon sugar
2 teaspoons cornstarch blended with 2 teaspoons water

Garnish

2 tablespoons finely chopped scallions

(pictured opposite)

Curry is especially popular in southern China, which has a long history of contact with India. The Chinese favor curry powder or paste from Madras, but unlike Indians, Chinese cooks use curry only as a light addition to the usual Chinese seasonings, a subtle touch rather than a dominant tone.

This is not a traditional Chinese soup but is my version of corn soup, which has become popular in the West. It is easy to make and is delicious. If you use canned creamed corn, which is already quite thick, you could leave out the cornstarch mixture. The rich golden sheen of the curried soup makes it a good, bright dish for a dinner which might include Stir-fried Pork with Scallions (page 73), a green vegetable such as spinach, and plain steamed rice.

Clean the corn and remove the kernels with a sharp knife or cleaver. You should end up with about 1½ cups. If you are using canned corn, empty the contents into a bowl and set it aside. Using a cleaver or a sharp knife, thinly slice the chicken breasts into fine shreds about 3 inches long. Mix the chicken shreds together with the egg white, 1 teaspoon cornstarch and salt in a small bowl and set it aside. Beat the whole egg and sesame oil together in another small bowl and set it aside.

Bring a small pot of water to the boil. Quickly blanch the chicken shreds in it until they just turn white. (This should take about 20 seconds.) Remove them with a slotted spoon and drain them in a colander or sieve. Now bring the stock to a boil in a large pot and add the corn. Simmer for 10 minutes, uncovered, and then add the rice wine or sherry, curry powder, salt, sugar and, if you are using it, the cornstarch mixture. Bring it back to the boil, then lower the heat and simmer for another 5 minutes. Now add the blanched chicken shreds, and then slowly pour in the egg and sesame oil mixture in a steady stream, stirring all the time. Transfer the soup to a tureen, garnish with scallions and serve.

Clockwise from left: Cold Spicy Noodles (page 168), Five-Spice Spareribs (page 81), Curried Corn Soup with Chicken (page 64), Snow Peas with Water Chestnuts (page 153), Fried Fish with Ginger (page 121).

Ham and Zucchini Soup

Region: western

Serves 4 to 6

½ pound zucchini
1 quart Pork and Chicken Stock (page 61)
2 ounces Smithfield ham or prosciutto, finely shredded (about ¼ cup)
½ teaspoon chili bean sauce or chili powder
1½ tablespoons light soy sauce
½ teaspoon salt

Garnish

1 teaspoon sesame oil

Although zucchini is not available in China, there are many similar members of the same family which are used in Chinese cookery. This is an adaptation of a traditional recipe which calls for "hairy melon," or Chinese squash, which is much more appetizing than it sounds. The exterior of Chinese squash is fuzzy and hairy, rather like a peach—hence its name. I think that zucchini tastes very similar and makes an excellent alternative. This is basically a clear soup. It goes well with Sweet and Sour Pork (page 75) and Stir-fried Spinach with Garlic (page 151).

Trim the ends of the zucchini and, if you are using large ones, remove the seeds. Cut into ½-inch cubes. Bring the stock to a boil in a large pot. Add the ham, zucchini and all the other ingredients. Simmer the soup, uncovered, for 15 minutes. Add the sesame oil and give it a good stir. Serve the soup immediately in individual bowls or in a large soup tureen.

Watercress Soup

Region: southern

Serves 4 to 6
  1 quart Chicken Stock (page 60)
  2 tablespoons light soy sauce
  1 teaspoon sugar
  ½ pound watercress leaves (about 3
    bunches)
  1 teaspoon finely chopped ginger
    root
  1 tablespoon finely chopped
    scallions

Here is a soup from my childhood. My mother used to make it with pork pieces, and its delightful fragrance emanating from the kitchen signified good things to come. I would remove the pork pieces from the soup and dip them in soy sauce before eating them. Then I would pour some of the soup into my rice bowl to flavor the rice. In our family restaurant, this soup was a favorite at staff meals because of its wonderfully delicate flavor and because it is so easy to make. Nowadays I prefer it plain, without any meat added. Use only the leaves of the watercress; the leftover stalks can be stir-fried and served as a vegetable. Spinach or Swiss chard can be used instead of watercress.

Bring the stock to a simmer in a large pot. Add the soy sauce and sugar and simmer for 3 minutes. Then add the watercress leaves, ginger and scallions and continue to simmer the soup for another 4 minutes. Serve at once.

Ham and Squab Steamed in Soup

Region: eastern

Serves 4 to 6
  4 squabs, about 1 pound each
  1 ounce Smithfield ham or
    prosciutto
  4 slices ginger root
  1 quart Pork and Chicken Stock
    (page 61)
  4 scallions
  2 tablespoons rice wine or dry
    sherry
  ½ teaspoon salt

This unusual technique for making soup is not difficult to master. It is called double-steaming, a process in which rich ingredients are steamed for hours in a covered casserole which is filled with soup. This extracts all the flavors from the ingredients and is a technique often used for making the classic Shark's Fin and Bird's Nest soups. The result is a distinctive soup, clear and rich but also light. Game birds other than squab, such as partridge, snipe, woodcock or quail, would work equally well. This soup is particularly suitable for a dinner party. For easy planning, I would make it in advance and freeze it, as it reheats well.

Using a sharp, heavy knife or cleaver, cut the squabs into quarters. Bring a pot of water to a boil, turn the heat down and add the squabs. Simmer them in the water for 10 minutes. (This blanching rids the squabs of some of their fat and impurities.) Remove them with a slotted spoon and discard the water. Cut the ham into very fine shreds. Cut the ginger into long ¼-inch strips.

Set a rack into a wok or deep pan. Fill it with 2½ inches of water and bring it to a boil. Bring the stock to a boil in another large pot and then pour it into a heatproof glass or china casserole. Add the squabs, ham, scallions, ginger, rice wine or sherry and salt to the casserole, and cover it with a lid or foil. Put the casserole on the rack and cover the wok or pan tightly with a lid or foil. You now have a casserole within a steamer, hence the name "double-steaming." Turn the heat down and steam gently for 2 to 3 hours or until the squabs are tender. Replenish the hot water from time to time. An alternative method is simply to simmer the soup very slowly in a conventional pot, but the resulting taste will be quite different.

When the soup is cooked, remove all the ingredients with a slotted spoon and discard the scallions, ginger and ham. Serve the soup together with the squab pieces. The soup can be served immediately or cooled and stored in the refrigerator or freezer to be reheated when required.

Kidney and Bean-Curd Soup

My mother often made kidney soup for our family dinner because it was tasty and inexpensive. Sometimes she added watercress or spinach to it. In this recipe the kidneys are cleaned in baking soda and quickly blanched before being added to the stock. This prevents the kidney juices from clouding the soup. It is a light and nutritious soup which reheats well. Serve it with Cashew Chicken (page 99) and Spicy Stir-fried Mushrooms (page 150).

Using a sharp knife, remove the thin outer membrane of the kidney. Then, with a sharp cleaver or knife, cut each kidney in half, cutting horizontally to keep the shape of the kidney. Now cut away the small knobs of fat and any tough membrane that surrounds them. Put the kidney halves flat on the cutting surface and score the top of each half, making light cuts in a crisscross pattern all over the surface. Then cut the halved kidneys into thin slices. Toss the kidney slices with the baking soda and let them sit for about 20 minutes. Then rinse them thoroughly with cold water and toss them in the vinegar and salt. Put them into a colander and let them drain for at least 30 minutes.

Bring a pan of water to a boil. Blot the kidney slices dry with paper towels and blanch them in the water for about 2 minutes. Drain them in a colander or sieve and set aside. Cut the bean curd into ½-inch cubes.

In a separate pot, bring the stock to a simmer and add the rest of the ingredients. Simmer for about 5 minutes and then add the kidney slices to the soup. Give the soup several stirs and simmer another 2 minutes. Serve at once, or allow to cool and reheat gently when required.

Region: eastern

Serves 4 to 6
  1 pound pork kidneys
  1 teaspoon baking soda
  2 teaspoons Chinese white rice
     vinegar or cider vinegar
  1 teaspoon salt
  14 ounces fresh bean curd (2 cakes)
  1 quart Pork and Chicken Stock
     (page 61)
  1 teaspoon finely chopped ginger
     root
  2 teaspoons finely chopped scallions
  2 tablespoons light soy sauce
  1 teaspoon salt

(pictured on page 147)

Wonton Soup

This is one of the most popular soups in southern China, and it is equally popular in Chinese restaurants in the West. Ideally, soup wonton should be stuffed savory dumplings poached in clear water and then served in a rich broth. Unfortunately in many restaurants the soup often arrives with wonton skins but very little filling. This recipe will enable you to make a simple but authentic wonton soup, perfect for any family meal. Wonton skins can be obtained from Chinese grocers and in some supermarkets. They are beige in color, square, and are packaged in small stacks. They can be bought fresh or frozen and can be found on the shelf or in the freezer. (Be sure to thaw them thoroughly if they are frozen.)

Combine the filling ingredients in a large bowl and mix them well. Using a small spoon, put a small amount of filling in the center of each wonton skin. Bring up the sides of the skin around the filling and pinch them together at the top so that the wonton is well sealed. It should look like a small filled bag.

Bring a large pot of water to a boil and place the wonton in the water for 1 minute, until they float to the top. This poaching rids the wonton of any excess flour and starch and will ensure that the soup itself is clear and has a clean texture. Remove the wonton with a slotted spoon and put them on a plate.

Now bring the chicken stock to a boil in a large pot. Add the cooked wonton and the garnish ingredients. Turn the heat down and simmer for 2 minutes. Although this soup can be reheated, it is best eaten right away.

Region: southern

Serves 4 to 6
  1 package wonton skins (about 30
     to 35)
  1 quart Chicken Stock (page 60)

Filling
  ¾ pound ground pork
  1 tablespoon light soy sauce
  2 teaspoons rice wine or dry sherry
  1½ tablespoons finely chopped
     scallions
  1 teaspoon sesame oil
  1 egg white
  ½ teaspoon cornstarch
  1 teaspoon granulated sugar
  ½ teaspoon salt

Garnish
  1 tablespoon light soy sauce
  1 tablespoon finely chopped
     scallions
  1 teaspoon sesame oil

Hot and Sour Soup

Region: northern and western

Serves 4 to 6

  3 ounces lean boneless pork
  1 ounce dried Chinese mushrooms
    (about 10 large)
  1 ounce bean thread (transparent)
    noodles (about ½ package)
  10 ounces fresh bean curd (1 cake)
  2 small eggs
  1 teaspoon sesame oil
  1 quart Chicken Stock (page 60)
  2 teaspoons sugar
  3 tablespoons Chinese red vinegar
    or cider vinegar
  ½ teaspoon ground white pepper
  2 tablespoons dark soy sauce
  1 tablespoon cornstarch blended
    with 1 tablespoon water
  2 tablespoons finely chopped
    scallions
  2 tablespoons finely chopped fresh
    coriander
  1 teaspoon sesame oil
  1 teaspoon Chili Oil (page 29)
    (optional)

This Chinese soup has become quite popular in the Western world, perhaps because it is a heavy soup, suited to cold climates. It combines sour and spicy elements in a rich, tasty stock, and reheats very well. The list of ingredients may be daunting but the recipe is, in fact, quite easy to make. I have suggested cider vinegar as a substitute for Chinese red vinegar, which may be hard to find.

Cut the pork into thin shreds. Bring some water to a boil in a pot and blanch the pork in it for 2 minutes. Drain the meat and set it aside. Soak the mushrooms in warm water for 20 minutes, then drain them and squeeze out any excess liquid. Discard the stems and finely shred the caps. Soak the noodles for 5 minutes in warm water, and then drain them. Cut them into 5-inch lengths and set them aside. Drain the bean curd and shred it into thin strips. Beat the eggs and sesame oil together in a small bowl.

  Bring the chicken stock to a simmer in a large pot. Add the prepared pork, mushrooms, noodles and bean curd together with the sugar, vinegar, white pepper and dark soy sauce. Simmer for 3 minutes, and then thicken it with the cornstarch mixture. Simmer for 2 minutes with the heat as low as possible.

  Next pour the beaten egg mixture into the soup in a steady stream, and pull the egg into strands with a fork or chopsticks. Stir in the scallions, fresh coriander, sesame oil and chili oil. Pour the soup into a large tureen or individual bowls and serve at once.

Clockwise from lower left: Steamed Fish with Garlic (page 125), Stir-fried Beef with Orange (page 82), Steamed Rice (page 159), Lettuce with Oyster Sauce (page 152), Tomato Egg-Flower Soup (opposite).

Tomato Egg-Flower Soup

Region: southern

Serves 4 to 6

  1 quart Chicken Stock (page 60)
  2 medium-sized fresh or 1 cup
    drained canned tomatoes
  2 small eggs
  ½ teaspoon sesame oil
  2 teaspoons light soy sauce
  1 teaspoon salt
  1 tablespoon finely chopped
    scallions, white part only

Optional garnish
  1 tablespoon finely chopped scallion
    tops

  (pictured opposite)

Tomatoes were introduced into China only 100 years ago. They were gradually adopted into southern Chinese cuisine and have become one of its most popular ingredients. Their intense, sweet flavor, brilliant color and versatility adapt perfectly to Chinese cookery. Here they are used to enhance my adaptation of the traditional egg drop soup. The egg "flowers" are simply strands of lightly beaten eggs which float on the surface of the soup like lilies on a pond. This effect is created by gently guiding the eggs over the soup in strands instead of dropping the mixture in all at once, which would cause the egg to lump together. The egg mixture slightly thickens the soup, which nevertheless remains very light.

  This is an impressive-looking soup but it is very easy to make. It is especially delightful in summer when fresh tomatoes are at their most plentiful. Although canned tomatoes are acceptable, fresh ones are always preferable.

Put the chicken stock into a pot and bring it to a simmer. If you are using fresh tomatoes, peel, seed and cut them into 1-inch cubes. If you are using canned tomatoes, chop them into small chunks. Lightly beat the eggs and then combine them with the sesame oil in a small bowl.

  Add the light soy sauce and salt to the simmering stock, and stir to mix them in well. Then add the tomatoes and simmer for 5 minutes. Next stir in the scallions, and then add the egg mixture in a very slow, thin stream. Using a chopstick or fork, pull the egg slowly into strands. (I have found that stirring the egg in a figure eight works quite well.) Garnish with the finely chopped scallion tops.

肉類

Whenever my family talked about meat we invariably meant pork. On rare occasions we ate beef and even less frequently, lamb. This was probably because although I was brought up in the U.S. my family came from southern China, where beef and lamb are less commonly eaten. Beef, mutton and goat are more popular in northern China, a reflection of the Moslem and Mongolian influence in this area. In the main, however, most Chinese think of meat as being pork, so, as you might expect, there are innumerable pork dishes in Chinese cuisine. It is an extremely versatile meat which can be prepared in many different ways, and its subtle flavor lends itself to many complementary ingredients, seasonings and sauces. Pork fat is also highly prized, and it is cooked in various ways which render it not only edible but delicious.

This chapter contains some recipes for beef and lamb although their flavor is less familiar to Chinese palates. If you like you can substitute beef for pork in some of the recipes. Stir-fried Pork with Scallions (page 73) and Stir-fried Ground Pork (page 74) will work just as well with beef, for instance.

The same Chinese character is used for both "sheep" and "goat." Goat is more widely available in north China, but is also eaten in other areas. I prefer to use lamb instead. A Chinese poet once wrote, "There are seventy-two ways of cooking lamb; of these only eighteen or nineteen are palatable." The recipes here are within the latter category!

The American cuts of meat which are most suitable for Chinese cooking are:

PORK

For stir-frying, use boneless loin, loin chops with the bones and all the fat removed, or pork steaks or tenderloin. Fresh side pork (uncured bacon) is best for braising. The best ground pork comes from the butt, which is a reasonably priced cut.

BEEF

I prefer tenderloin for stir-frying since it is lean and tender and full of flavor. Although it is expensive, a little goes a long way. Porterhouse, flank and sirloin steak are also suitable. My favorite cut for braising is brisket. Although it is fatty, its taste and ability to absorb the flavors of a sauce are unbeatable. The Chinese love the texture of braised brisket. Shin and chuck steak or roast are also suitable for slow-cooking.

LAMB

Loin or rib chops with the bones and all the fat removed are perfect for stir-frying, as are lamb steaks, also known as shoulder-blade chops. The best cuts for braising are breast and lamb shank.

Lack of refrigeration means that various meats which are preserved by drying or curing are also popular in Chinese cuisine. Dried beef is often eaten as a snack, and cured ham is used in cooking. The regions of Zhejiang and Yunnan are famous for their hams, which unfortunately are unobtainable here. I frequently use Smithfield ham or prosciutto as acceptable substitutes for Zhejiang ham. In Chinese cookery nothing is ever wasted. Every part of the animal is utilized. Variety meats (innards) are extremely popular and are usually braised, except for liver which is commonly stir-fried.

I prefer to use meat which has not been frozen since it contains less water and I think it has a better flavor. This is particularly important when selecting meat for stir-frying, which needs to be as dry as possible so that it will fry rather than steam in its own juices. Although the Chinese are very fond of meat, they eat it in small quantities. This is one reason Chinese food is so healthful.

Pork with Black Bean Sauce

Pork goes particularly well with black beans, the salty and spicy flavor of which is so distinctively Chinese. This simple, homely, stir-fried dish is one I often ate as a child. Sometimes my mother would vary the taste by adding an extra spicy touch of chili powder. It is very quick to cook and goes well with plain rice and any stir-fried vegetable.

Cut the pork into thin slices 2 inches long. Put the slices into a small bowl and mix them well with the rice wine or dry sherry, soy sauce and cornstarch. Let them marinate for about 20 minutes.

Heat a wok or large skillet until it is hot. Add about ½ tablespoon of the oil and, when it is almost smoking, lift the pork out of the marinade with a slotted spoon and quickly stir-fry it for about 2 to 3 minutes. Then transfer it at once to a bowl.

Wipe the wok clean, reheat it and add the rest of the oil. Then quickly add the black beans, garlic and scallions. A few seconds later add the rest of the ingredients. Bring the mixture to a boil and then return the pork to the wok. Stir-fry the entire mixture for another 5 minutes. Turn it onto a platter and serve.

Region: southern
Method: stir-frying

Serves 4
¾ pound lean boneless pork
2 teaspoons rice wine or dry sherry
2 teaspoons light soy sauce
½ teaspoon cornstarch
1 tablespoon oil
1½ tablespoons coarsely chopped black beans
1½ teaspoons finely chopped garlic
1 tablespoon finely chopped scallions
2 teaspoons light soy sauce
1 teaspoon sugar
2 teaspoons Chicken Stock (page 60) or water

Stir-fried Pork with Scallions

This is a simple stir-fried dish in the southern Chinese tradition. The key to success is not to overcook the pork.

Cut the pork into thin slices 2 inches long. Put the sliced pork into a bowl and mix in the rice wine or dry sherry, soy sauce and cornstarch. Let the mixture sit for 10 to 15 minutes so that the pork absorbs the flavors of the marinade. Cut the scallions on the diagonal into 2-inch lengths.

Heat a wok or skillet over very high heat. Add the oil. When it is almost beginning to smoke, add the pork slices and stir-fry them until they are brown. Add the scallions, salt and sugar. Continue to stir-fry until the pork is cooked and slightly firm. This should take about 5 minutes. Remove and arrange the pork on a warm serving platter. Pour any juices over and serve at once.

Region: southern
Method: stir-frying

Serves 3 to 4
¾ pound lean boneless pork
2 teaspoons rice wine or dry sherry
2 teaspoons light soy sauce
½ teaspoon cornstarch
4 scallions
2 teaspoons oil
½ teaspoon salt
½ teaspoon sugar

(pictured on page 109)

Sweet and Sour Pork (facing page).

Stir-fried Ground Pork

Region: northern
Method: stir-frying

Serves 4
    4 ounces Sichuan or Tianjin
      preserved vegetable, or Cold
      Sweet and Sour Chinese Cabbage
      (page 149)
    1½ tablespoons oil, preferably
      peanut
    1 pound ground pork
    2 tablespoons dark soy sauce
    1 tablespoon rice wine or dry sherry
    2 teaspoons sugar

Garnish
    3 tablespoons finely chopped
      scallions

    (pictured on page 147)

This is tasty, quick and inexpensive. The secret of its delicious flavor lies in the use of preserved vegetables, which are typical of the cuisine in the north of China, where winters are long and cold and vegetables must be preserved by salting or pickling. You can use the Cold Sweet and Sour Chinese Cabbage (page 149) instead of the Sichuan or Tianjin preserved vegetable, but it is worth the effort to get the latter from a Chinese grocer. I like to serve this as a stuffing for fresh lettuce leaves or Chinese pancakes (page 173). Plain steamed rice and a simple stir-fried vegetable dish such as Stir-fried Spinach with Garlic (page 151) would also go well with it.

Rinse the preserved vegetable or Cold Sweet and Sour Chinese Cabbage well in cold water. Drain in a colander and then blot dry with paper towels. Chop fine and set aside.

    Heat a wok or large skillet over high heat. Add the oil. When it is almost smoking, add the pork and stir-fry it for 2 minutes. Stir constantly to break up any lumps. Then add the preserved vegetable or Chinese Cabbage and the rest of the ingredients. Continue to stir-fry for another 5 minutes or until the pork is cooked. Turn it onto a warm serving platter.

    If you are serving it with Chinese pancakes or lettuce leaves, each person piles a little of the meat mixture into a pancake or lettuce leaf, wraps it up well and eats it with his or her fingers.

Of all Chinese dishes, Sweet and Sour Pork is probably one of the best known in the West. Unfortunately for Westerners, it is rarely properly made, often consisting of heavy, doughy balls containing a scrap of pork drenched in a hideously sweet red sauce. Properly prepared, sweet and sour Chinese dishes are so delicately balanced that one is hard pressed to describe them as either strictly sweet or sour. In my version of this classic dish, you will find that balance. This dish is best served with plain steamed rice and a simple blanched vegetable such as Chinese Cabbage in Soy Sauce (page 148).

Cut the pork into 1-inch cubes. Put the cubes into a bowl together with the rice wine or sherry, 1 tablespoon of light soy sauce and ½ teaspoon salt, and marinate for 20 minutes. Meanwhile, cut the green and red peppers into 1-inch squares. Peel and cut the carrots and scallions into 1 inch chunks. (The uniform size of meat and vegetables adds to the visual appeal of the dish.) Bring a pot of water to a boil and blanch the carrots in it for 4 minutes; drain and set aside.

Mix the egg and cornstarch in a bowl until they are well blended into a batter. Lift the pork cubes out of the marinade, put them into the batter and coat each piece well. Heat the oil in a deep-fat fryer or large wok until it is almost smoking. Remove the pork pieces from the batter with a slotted spoon, and deep-fry them. Drain the deep-fried pork cubes on paper towels.

Combine the chicken stock, soy sauce, salt, vinegar, sugar and tomato paste in a large saucepan. Bring it to a boil. Add all the vegetables, but not the lychees or oranges, and stir well. In a small bowl, blend together the cornstarch and water. Stir this mixture into the sauce and bring it back to a boil. Turn the heat down to a simmer. Add the lychees or oranges and pork cubes. Mix well, and then turn the mixture onto a deep platter. Serve at once.

Region: southern
Method: deep-frying and braising

Serves 4
¾ pound lean boneless pork
1 tablespoon rice wine or dry sherry
1 tablespoon light soy sauce
½ teaspoon salt
1 small green bell pepper
1 small red bell pepper
1 carrot
2 scallions
1 egg, beaten
2 tablespoons cornstarch
2 cups oil, preferably peanut (see Deep-fat fryers, page 35)
3 ounces canned lychees, drained, or 1 fresh orange in segments

Sauce
⅔ cup Chicken Stock (page 60)
1 tablespoon light soy sauce
½ teaspoon salt
1½ tablespoons Chinese white rice vinegar or cider vinegar
1 tablespoon sugar
1 tablespoon tomato paste
1 teaspoon cornstarch
1 teaspoon water

Cold Peking Pork

Region: northern
Method: braising

Serves 4 to 6
  1½ pounds fresh ham or pork
    shoulder, in one piece

Braising liquid
  1 quart Chicken Stock (page 60)
  3 slices ginger root
  3 scallions
  2 star anise
  2 tablespoons rice wine or dry
    sherry
  2 teaspoons five-spice powder
  5 tablespoons Chinese rock sugar,
    or 3 tablespoons granulated
  2 tablespoons dark soy sauce
  1 teaspoon salt
  2 teaspoons whole Sichuan
    peppercorns, roasted (page 26)
    (optional)

Top: Cold Sesame Broccoli (page 145).
Bottom: Cold Peking Pork.

This dish is a little like a European pâté and has a very good flavor. It should be prepared a day in advance and then served cold. The pork is first blanched for a few minutes to rid it of any impurities, and is then slowly simmered in a rich liquid infused with Chinese spices. The cooked meat is removed and the braising liquid reduced. This is then poured over the pork, which is left to marinate overnight. This tasty cold dish is ideal for a picnic.

Remove the rind from the pork but do not discard it. Bring a pan of water to a boil and blanch the rind and the pork in it for about 3 to 5 minutes. Remove them with a slotted spoon, discard the liquid and chop the rind into small pieces. Rinse the pot clean and return the pork to the pot. Add all the braising liquid ingredients and the pieces of rind. Bring the mixture to a boil, then turn the heat down to a very low simmer. Cover the pot and simmer for about 2 hours.

Remove the cooked pork from the pot with a slotted spoon and skim off as much fat as possible. Turn the heat back to high and reduce the liquid to about half. Put the pork into a bowl or deep dish. Strain the reduced liquid and pour it over the meat. Allow it to cool and put it into the refrigerator. Let it sit in the refrigerator for at least 8 hours, covered, before serving. Just before serving, remove the pork and slice it as thinly as possible. If the juice has jelled, cut it into cubes and arrange it as a garnish around the sliced pork; otherwise simply pour some of the cooled liquid over the pork slices and serve.

This is my adaptation of a famous Chinese dish called Honey Ham with Lotus Seed, in which Chinese ham is braised in sugar, rice wine and lotus seeds until the mixture is reduced to a syrup which glazes the ham like honey. This process usually takes about 4 hours, but I have found that the method can be applied to thick pork chops, taking considerably less time and with excellent results. Serve this with plain steamed rice and a simple green vegetable dish.

Lightly salt the meat and set it aside. Cut the scallions into 3-inch lengths. Cut the ginger into long ½-inch strips.

Heat the oil in a wok or large skillet. Reduce the heat and then add the scallions and ginger. After a few seconds add the meat and cook it until it browns. Bring the braising sauce ingredients to a boil in a heavy pot or casserole, and then turn the heat down to a simmer. Add the pork mixture. Turn the heat as low as possible, cover, and simmer for about 40 minutes or until the pork is tender.

When the chops are cooked, remove them from the liquid and let them cool slightly before you slice them, cutting them diagonally. Remove any surface fat from the braising liquid, and spoon some of the liquid over the pork slices. Serve immediately. The rest of the braising liquid can be cooled and frozen for future use. (Remove any surface fat before transferring it to the freezer.)

Region: western
Method: braising

Serves 4 to 6
　1 pound boned pork chops, at least
　　　1½ inches thick
　¼ teaspoon salt
　2 scallions
　2 large slices ginger root
　1 tablespoon oil

Braising sauce
　2 cups rice wine, or ⅔ cup dry
　　　sherry mixed with 1¼ cups
　　　Chicken Stock (page 60)
　4 ounces Chinese rock sugar, or ⅓
　　　cup granulated
　1½ teaspoons roasted Sichuan
　　　peppercorns (page 26) or black
　　　peppercorns

This is one of the most famous family dishes in China. It is sometimes known as "Ma Po's" bean curd, which means Mother Po's method of braising. My mother used to make a wonderful version of this simple peasant dish, using a range of spices to transform fresh but rather bland bean curd into truly delicious fare. This recipe is typical of the Chinese flair for stretching scarce meat, and it makes an economical, tasty and very nutritious dish. You can buy fresh bean curd from good health-food shops and Chinese grocers.

Cut the bean curd into ½-inch cubes and put them into a sieve to drain.

Heat a wok or large skillet. Add the oil, and then add the garlic and ginger. A few seconds later add the pork and stir-fry it for 2 minutes. Then add all the other ingredients except the bean curd. Bring the mixture to a boil and then turn the heat down to low. Add the bean curd and mix it in well but gently, taking care not to break up the chunks. Let the mixture simmer slowly, uncovered, for about 15 minutes. If necessary add a little more chicken stock during this time. Garnish with the chopped fresh coriander. (This dish may be cooked ahead of time and then gently reheated.)

Region: western
Method: braising

Serves 6
　8 ounces fresh bean curd (1 cake)
　2 teaspoons oil
　2 teaspoons finely chopped garlic
　2 teaspoons finely chopped fresh
　　　ginger root
　½ pound ground pork
　1½ tablespoons finely chopped
　　　scallions
　1 teaspoon chili bean sauce or chili
　　　powder
　½ teaspoon sugar
　2 teaspoons rice wine or dry sherry
　1 tablespoon dark soy sauce
　1 tablespoon bean sauce
　½ teaspoon roasted Sichuan
　　　peppercorns, freshly ground
　　　(page 26) (optional)
　⅓ cup Chicken Stock (page 60)

Optional garnish
　1 tablespoon finely chopped fresh
　　　coriander

(pictured on page 112)

Chili Pork Spareribs

Region: western
Method: deep-frying and braising

Serves 2 to 4
2 cups oil, preferably peanut (see
    Deep-fat fryers, page 35)
1½ pounds pork spareribs,
    separated into individual ribs

Braising sauce
3½ cups Chicken Stock (page 60)
1 tablespoon chili bean sauce, or
    2 teaspoons chili powder
2 teaspoons sugar
⅓ cup rice wine or dry sherry
1 tablespoon dark soy sauce
1 tablespoon light soy sauce
2 teaspoons finely chopped garlic
1 tablespoon finely chopped
    scallions
1 tablespoon bean sauce
1½ tablespoons hoisin sauce

Here is a spicy and delicious way of preparing pork spareribs. Although the recipe involves a series of techniques, much of the work can be done ahead of time and the dish can be quickly completed at the last moment. The combination of spices and sauces is the hallmark of dishes from western China. It is worthwhile getting the chili bean sauce for an authentic taste, although chili powder is a reasonably acceptable substitute. The spareribs can be finished in the oven, under a grill or on a barbecue.

Heat the oil in a deep-fat fryer or large wok, and deep-fry the spareribs until they are brown and crisp. Do this in several batches, draining each cooked batch well on paper towels.

Combine all the sauce ingredients in a large pot and bring it to a boil. Add the deep-fried spareribs and simmer them, covered, for about 40 minutes or until they are tender. Drain off the sauce and remove any remaining fat. This sauce can now be frozen and reused the next time you want to make this dish. The dish may be prepared up to this point the day before.

Preheat the oven to 350°F. Put the spareribs onto a rack in a roasting pan and bake them in the oven for 15 to 20 minutes, until they are nice and brown. Baste them from time to time with the braising sauce if you like. You can also cook the spareribs under a boiler or on a barbecue, until they are brown. Using a cleaver or a sharp, heavy knife, chop the spareribs into pieces 1½ inches long and serve.

Steamed Pork with Spicy Vegetables

Region: western
Method: steaming

Serves 3 to 4
5 ounces Cold Sweet and Sour
    Chinese Cabbage (page 149), or
    2½ ounces Sichuan preserved
    vegetable
¾ pound ground pork
1 tablespoon rice wine or dry sherry
1 teaspoon chili bean sauce or chili
    powder
1 teaspoon dark soy sauce
½ teaspoon light soy sauce
1 tablespoon finely chopped
    scallions
½ tablespoon finely chopped ginger
    root

Preserved vegetables are often used to flavor meats in China. This dish can be made with Cold Sweet and Sour Chinese Cabbage or with Sichuan preserved vegetable, which can be bought canned from Chinese grocers and which has a pleasant crunchy texture. This recipe employs the technique of steaming, which keeps the dish moist and hot without any risk of overcooking the pork. It is a tasty and homely dish and it reheats well. It goes well with Stir-fried Rice Noodles with Vegetables (page 169).

Rinse the preserved vegetable or Cold Sweet and Sour Chinese Cabbage thoroughly under running water and drain it in a sieve or colander. Then chop fine and put into a bowl. Add the pork and all the other ingredients and mix everything together very well. Put the mixture onto a deep heat-proof plate, and make a well in the center where the juices can collect during cooking.

Set up a steamer or fill a wok or deep casserole with at least 2½ inches of water. Put a rack into the wok or casserole and bring the water to a boil. Now lower the plate of meat into the steamer or onto the rack and cover the pot tightly. Gently steam on a low heat for 50 minutes or until the pork is done. Serve this dish on the plate in which it is steamed.

Chili Pork Spareribs (facing page).

Braised Fresh Bacon

Region: eastern
Method: braising

Serves 6
1½ pounds fresh bacon (side pork)
1 tablespoon salt
1 tablespoon oil, preferably peanut

Braising liquid
3 large slices ginger root
2 cups Chicken Stock (page 60)
1¼ cups rice wine or dry sherry
⅔ cup light soy sauce
3 ounces Chinese rock sugar, or
　⅓ cup granulated sugar
1 teaspoon five-spice powder
3 scallions

Uncured bacon (side pork) is an inexpensive cut which is very popular in Chinese cuisine and has always been a favorite of mine. At first glance it might look rather fatty and unappetizing, but its gelatinous texture is highly prized by the Chinese and when it is properly cooked the taste is unbeatable. In this recipe the long simmering process renders down most of the fat, leaving a juicy, delicious dish which goes very well with plain steamed rice.

Rub the side pork with the salt and let it stand for 1 hour. Then carefully rinse the salt off. This helps to clean the pork and to firm it up by drawing out some of the moisture from the meat. Dry the meat with paper towels.

Heat a wok or large skillet. Add the oil, and in it brown the pork, rind side only, until it is crisp and brown. Add more oil if necessary. Cut the ginger into long ¼-inch strips. Put all the braising liquid ingredients into a large pot or casserole. Bring the liquid to a simmer and then add the browned pork. Cover the pot and simmer it slowly for 1½ to 2 hours.

When the pork is cooked, remove it from the pot and let it cool slightly. (The braising sauce liquid can now be cooled and frozen for reuse. Remove any surface fat before transferring it to the freezer.) Then slice the meat thin. The Chinese would serve the pork rind and fat as well as the meat, but do remove it if you prefer. If you like, some of the braising liquid may be thickened with a little cornstarch and served as a sauce over the sliced pork. If you do this, be sure to remove all traces of fat from the sauce before thickening it.

Braised Fresh Bacon.

This is a delightful meat dish which engages the senses with many contrasting tastes. The spareribs are first marinated, next deep-fried in oil, and then slowly braised in an unusual piquant sauce. This works especially well in a clay pot. It can be easily reheated and the taste improves if it is cooked the day before it is eaten.

Have your butcher cut the spareribs into individual ribs, and then into chunks approximately 3 inches long. Or do this yourself, using a heavy sharp cleaver which can cut through the bones. Mix the marinade ingredients together in a bowl and steep the spareribs in the marinade for about 25 minutes at room temperature.

Heat the oil in a deep-fat fryer or large wok. Slowly cook the marinated spareribs in several batches until they are brown. Drain each cooked batch on paper towels. (Leave the cooking oil to cool. Strain it once it has cooled if you want to keep it for reuse when cooking pork.)

Put the sauce ingredients into a clean wok, skillet or clay pot. Bring the sauce to a boil and then reduce the heat to very low. Add the spareribs and simmer them slowly, uncovered, for about 40 minutes, stirring occasionally. There is very little liquid, so you may want to add a little water to the sauce to prevent it from drying out. Only the fat will remain, so pour it off and then serve.

Region: northern
Method: deep-frying and braising

Serves 2 to 4
> 1½ pounds pork spareribs
> 2 cups oil, preferably peanut (see Deep-fat fryers, page 35)

Marinade
> 1 tablespoon rice wine or dry sherry
> 1 tablespoon light soy sauce
> 1 tablespoon Chinese white rice vinegar or cider vinegar
> ½ teaspoon sesame oil

Sauce
> 1 tablespoon finely chopped garlic
> 1 tablespoon five-spice powder
> 1½ tablespoons finely chopped scallions
> 1 tablespoon sugar
> 1 tablespoon light soy sauce
> 2 teaspoons finely chopped fresh orange peel
> ⅓ cup Chinese black rice vinegar or cider vinegar

(pictured on page 65)

This typically Cantonese dish is one of the quickest and tastiest ways to cook beef. The ginger adds a subtle and fragrant spiciness. Serve it with Ham and Bean Sprout Soup (page 63) and Lettuce with Oyster Sauce (page 152).

Put the beef in the freezing compartment of the refrigerator for 20 minutes. This will allow the meat to harden slightly for easier cutting. Then cut it into thin slices 1½ inches long. Put the beef slices into a bowl and add the salt, soy sauce, rice wine or sherry, sesame oil and cornstarch. Mix well, and let the slices steep in the marinade for about 15 minutes. Meanwhile, finely shred the ginger slice and set it aside.

Heat a wok or large skillet and add the oil. When it is very hot, remove the beef from the marinade with a slotted spoon and stir-fry it for about 2 minutes. When all the beef is cooked, remove it, wipe the wok clean and reheat it. Add a little oil and stir-fry the ginger for a few seconds. Then add the stock or water and sugar. Quickly return the meat to the pan and stir well. Turn the mixture onto a platter and serve at once.

Region: southern
Method: stir-frying

Serves 4
> ¾ pound boneless lean beef
> ¼ teaspoon salt
> 2 teaspoons light soy sauce
> 2 teaspoons rice wine or dry sherry
> ½ teaspoon sesame oil
> 1 teaspoon cornstarch
> 1 slice ginger root
> 1 tablespoon oil
> 1 tablespoon Chicken Stock (page 60) or water
> ½ teaspoon sugar

Beef in Oyster Sauce

Region: southern
Method: stir-frying

Serves 4
    ¾ pound boneless lean beef
    2 teaspoons light soy sauce
    2 teaspoons rice wine or dry sherry
    1 teaspoon cornstarch
    1½ tablespoons oil
    ⅓ cup Chicken Stock (page 60)
    1½ tablespoons oyster sauce
    1 teaspoon cornstarch, blended
        with 1 teaspoon water

Garnish
    1½ tablespoons finely chopped
        scallions

This was one of the most popular dishes in our family's restaurant. A good brand of oyster sauce does not taste at all fishy. Rather, it has a meaty flavor and goes very well with beef or pork. This dish is easy to make and is delicious served with plain steamed rice and Chinese Cabbage in Soy Sauce (page 148).

Cut the beef into thin slices 2 inches long and put them into a bowl. Add the soy sauce, rice wine or sherry and cornstarch. Let the mixture marinate for 20 minutes.

Heat the oil in a wok or large skillet until it is very hot and almost smoking, and then stir-fry the beef slices. Remove them and drain them. Wipe the wok or pan clean and reheat it over high heat. Add the chicken stock and oyster sauce. Bring the liquid to a boil, and then add the cornstarch mixture and simmer for 2 minutes. Return the drained beef to the pan and coat all the slices thoroughly with the sauce. Turn the mixture onto a serving platter and garnish it with the scallions. Serve at once.

Stir-fried Beef with Orange

Region: northern
Method: stir-frying

Serves 4
    ¾ pound boneless lean beef
    2 teaspoons dark soy sauce
    2 teaspoons rice wine or dry sherry
    1 teaspoon finely chopped ginger
        root
    1 teaspoon cornstarch
    1 teaspoon sesame oil
    ⅓ cup oil, preferably peanut
    2 dried red chilies, cut in half
        lengthwise
    1 tablespoon coarsely chopped fresh
        orange peel, or 2 teaspoons
        soaked and coarsely chopped
        dried citrus peel (page 19)
    ½ teaspoon finely ground roasted
        Sichuan peppercorns (page 26)
        (optional)
    2 teaspoons dark soy sauce
    ¼ teaspoon salt
    1 teaspoon sugar
    ½ teaspoon sesame oil

(pictured on page 69)

This is a northern Chinese beef specialty. I have adapted it by substituting fresh orange peel for the dried tangerine peel, which is sometimes hard to get. The Chinese always use peel which has been dried. The older the skin, the more prized the flavor. It's quite easy to make your own dried peel (see page 19), but I find the tartness of the fresh orange peel works just as nicely to balance the robust taste of the beef. This is an easy dish to make and is a pleasant change of flavor from the usual stir-fried beef recipes. Serve it with rice and Corn Soup with Crabmeat (page 61).

Cut the beef into thin slices 2 inches long, cutting against the grain. Put the beef into a bowl together with the soy sauce, rice wine or sherry, ginger, cornstarch and 1 teaspoon of sesame oil. Mix well, and then let the mixture marinate for about 20 minutes.

Heat the oil in a wok or large skillet until it is very hot. Remove the beef from the marinade with a slotted spoon. Add it to the pan and stir-fry it for 2 minutes until it browns. Remove it and leave to drain in a colander or sieve. Pour off most of the oil, leaving about 1 teaspoon. Reheat the pan over a high heat and then add the dried chilies. Stir-fry them for 10 seconds, and then return the beef to the pan. Add the rest of the ingredients and stir-fry for 4 minutes, mixing well. Serve the dish at once.

Beef in Oyster Sauce (facing page).

Stir-fried Pepper Beef with Snow Peas.

Stir-fried Pepper Beef with Snow Peas

Region: southern
Method: stir-frying

Serves 4

¾ pound boneless lean beef
2 teaspoons light soy sauce
2 teaspoons rice wine or dry sherry
1 teaspoon cornstarch
2 red or green bell peppers
1½ tablespoons oil, preferably
   peanut
2 ounces snow peas, trimmed
⅓ cup Chicken Stock (page 60) or
   water
1 tablespoon dark soy sauce

This is my adaptation of a stir-fried beef dish which is popular in Chinese restaurants in the U.S. What makes this recipe so adaptable is that any fresh vegetable can be substituted for the snow peas. It is extremely simple to make and is perfect for a quick but delicious, wholesome family meal. Try it with plain steamed rice and Steamed Fish with Garlic (page 125).

Cut the beef into thin slices 2 inches long. Put the slices into a bowl and add the light soy sauce, rice wine or sherry, and cornstarch. Mix well with the beef and allow the mixture to marinate for 15 minutes. Cut the pepper into 2-inch strips.

Heat a wok or large skillet until it is very hot. Add 1 tablespoon of the oil and when it is almost smoking, stir-fry the beef for 3 minutes. Remove the beef slices and drain them in a colander or sieve. Clean the wok or pan, add the remaining ½ tablespoon of oil and reheat. When it is hot, stir-fry the pepper and snow peas for 2 minutes. Then add the chicken stock and dark soy sauce. Bring the mixture to a boil. Return the cooked beef to the pan and give the mixture a few quick stirs to mix it well. Serve immediately.

Some have speculated that this dish is not traditionally Chinese but an invention of some Hong Kong restaurant. Whatever the truth, it doesn't hide the fact that it is a truly delightful dish to eat. Various colorful vegetables constitute the "rainbow," and they are stir-fried with beef and garnished with crispy bean thread noodles and hoisin sauce to create a delicious combination of tastes and textures.

This dish makes a good starter for a dinner party or festive occasion. The rainbow beef mixture, crispy noodles and lettuce leaves are served on individual platters, and the hoisin sauce in a small bowl. Each guest puts a helping of each ingredient into a hollow lettuce leaf (rather like stuffing a pancake) and eats the filled leaf with his or her fingers.

Region: southern
Method: stir-frying

Serves 4 to 6
¾ *pound boneless lean beef*
2 teaspoons rice wine or dry sherry
2 teaspoons light soy sauce
1 large carrot
2 ounces canned bamboo shoots
1 small zucchini
1 small red or green bell pepper
½ *ounce Chinese dried mushrooms*
(5 to 6 large) (optional)
small head of iceberg lettuce
1¼ cups oil (see Deep-fat fryers,)
page 35)
1 ounce bean thread (transparent)
noodles (½ package)
1 tablespoon oil
1 teaspoon light or dark soy sauce
2 teaspoons rice wine or dry sherry
2 to 3 tablespoons hoisin sauce

Put the beef in the freezer for 20 minutes if possible, as this will allow the meat to harden slightly for easier cutting. Then cut it into thin slices 2 inches long. Put the beef slices into a small bowl together with the rice wine or dry sherry and light soy sauce and let them marinate for about 20 minutes.

Meanwhile peel and cut the carrots into 2-inch fine shreds. Cut the bamboo shoots, zucchini and pepper into 2-inch fine shreds also. If you are using the dried mushrooms, soak them in warm water for 20 minutes, drain them and squeeze out any excess liquid. Trim off the stems and shred the caps into 2-inch strips. Separate and wash the lettuce leaves, wiping off any excess water, and set them aside.

In a deep-fat fryer or large wok, heat 1¼ cups of oil until it is almost smoking. Deep-fry the noodles until they are crisp and puffed up. Drain them on paper towels. (Leave the oil to cool; it can be saved for future use.)

Put 1 tablespoon of the oil in which you have fried the noodles into a wok or skillet and heat it. Then stir-fry the beef for about 1 minute. Remove the beef and put it into a bowl. Wipe the wok clean. Reheat the wok and when it is hot, add 1 tablespoon of fresh oil. When it is smoking slightly, stir-fry the carrots for 1 minute, and then add the rest of the vegetables (except the lettuce), together with the soy sauce and rice wine or sherry. Stir-fry the mixture for 3 minutes and then return the beef to the wok. Mix well and continue to stir-fry for 1 more minute. Turn the mixture onto a platter. Arrange the lettuce and noodles each on separate platters, put the hoisin sauce into a small bowl, and serve at once.

Steamed Beef Meatballs

Region: southern
Method: steaming

Serves 4
¾ pound ground beef
1 egg white
1 tablespoon very cold water
½ teaspoon salt
1 tablespoon light soy sauce
1 teaspoon freshly ground black
    pepper
2 teaspoons sesame oil
1 tablespoon finely chopped fresh
    coriander
1½ tablespoons finely chopped
    scallions
1 teaspoon cornstarch
1 teaspoon sugar

Since my days as an apprentice in our family restaurant I have always enjoyed these steamed meatballs. The secret of making them light and fluffy lies in the egg white and cornstarch. We used to mince the beef by hand with two cleavers, one in each hand, adding egg white and cornstarch as we chopped until it was all fully incorporated into the meat. Then we added the seasonings and continued to chop until the meat was almost a light paste. Such chopping requires concentration! But when that stage was over we all sat about chatting as we rolled the meat into balls. Today with a blender or food processor, this long process takes only a few minutes. The texture will be smoother, of course, but it does mean a lot less work. The meatballs reheat well by steaming and are perfect for dinners, for parties or with drinks.

Mix the beef in a blender or food processor for a few seconds. Slowly add the egg white and cold water and mix for a few more seconds until they are fully incorporated into the meat. Then add the rest of the ingredients and mix for about a minute, until the meat mixture has become a light paste.

Using your hands, form the mixture into 1½-inch balls—about the size of a golf ball. (This recipe makes about 10 balls.) Put the meatballs on a plate and set it into a steamer. (Or put a rack into a wok or deep pan filled with simmering water.) Cover, and steam the meatballs gently for about 20 minutes. Pour off any liquid that has accumulated on the plate. Put the steamed meatballs on a clean platter and serve.

Stir-fried Liver in Spicy Sauce

Region: southern
Method: stir-frying

Serves 4
½ pound fresh liver, preferably pork
3 scallions
⅓ cup oil, preferably peanut

Marinade
1 egg white
1 tablespoon rice wine or dry sherry
2 teaspoons salt
2 teaspoons finely chopped ginger
    root
2 teaspoons cornstarch

Sauce
2 teaspoons light soy sauce
2 teaspoons rice wine or dry sherry
1 teaspoon sugar
1½ tablespoons bean sauce
½ teaspoon chili bean sauce or chili
    powder

Pork liver is another Chinese specialty which is delicious when it is properly prepared. My uncle used to make a delectable pork liver dish with vegetables. His secret was to cut the liver into thin slices, to stir-fry them quickly and then to drain them to get rid of any bitter juices.

This recipe has a robust and tasty sauce containing spices which help to balance the rich flavor of the liver. Cooked this way, the liver tastes a little like beef. (You could also use beef or calf's liver for this recipe.) I like to serve this dish with plain steamed rice and some green vegetables.

Cut the liver into thin slices 3 inches long. Mix the marinade ingredients together in a bowl, add the liver slices and coat them thoroughly with marinade. Cover the bowl tightly with plastic wrap and let it sit in the refrigerator for at least 20 minutes. Meanwhile cut the scallions into 2-inch diagonal segments. In a separate bowl mix together the sauce ingredients.

Heat the oil in a wok or large skillet until it is almost smoking. Lift the liver out of the marinade with a slotted spoon and stir-fry it in the oil for 2 minutes. Drain the cooked liver in a colander or sieve, leaving about 2 teaspoons of the oil in the pan. (Discard the rest of the oil.)

Reheat the wok and add the scallions. Stir-fry them for 1 minute and then add the sauce ingredients. When the sauce comes to a boil, return the liver to the wok and toss it well, coating it with the sauce. Stir-fry for 30 seconds and then serve.

Beef in China is often tough, and braising is therefore the preferred method of cooking it. Chinese cooks long ago learned to make a virtue of this necessity by using spices and seasonings during the long braising process to imbue the meat with subtle and complex flavors. This recipe is really a Chinese version of a beef stew and uses many of the favorite seasonings of northern China. Be sure to use an inexpensive cut of beef such as brisket or shin. One of the ingredients is Chinese white radish, sometimes called daikon. *If you cannot find it you could use turnips or carrots instead. Plain steamed rice is a perfect accompaniment.*

Cut the meat into 1-inch cubes. Slice the scallion at a slight diagonal into 2-inch segments. Heat the oil in a wok or large skillet, and when it is hot add the beef. Stir-fry until it is brown. (This should take about 10 minutes.) Then pour off any excess fat, leaving 1 tablespoon of oil in the pan. Add the scallion, ginger, garlic and chili and stir-fry with the beef for about 5 minutes.

Transfer this mixture to a large casserole or pot. Add the braising sauce ingredients. Bring the liquid to a boil, skim off any fat from the surface and turn the heat as low as possible. Cover and braise for 1½ hours. Peel the Chinese white radish and cut it at a slight diagonal into 2-inch chunks, or roll cut the radish. Add these to the meat and continue to cook for another 30 minutes or until the beef is quite tender. Then uncover, turn the heat up to high and rapidly reduce the liquid for about 15 minutes. The sauce should thicken slightly. It can be served immediately or be cooled and reheated later.

Region: northern
Method: braising

Serves 4 to 6
¾ pound stewing beef, such as
  brisket or shank
1 scallion
2 teaspoons oil, preferably peanut
1 slice ginger root
1 clove garlic, lightly crushed
1 dried red chili (optional)
½ pound Chinese white radish

Braising sauce
1¼ cups Chicken Stock (page 60)
2 teaspoons sugar
1½ teaspoons light soy sauce
1 tablespoon dark soy sauce
2 teaspoons rice wine or dry sherry
2 teaspoons five-spice powder
2 tablespoons hoisin sauce
2 teaspoons bean sauce

Stewed Beef Northern Style.

Mongolian Hot Pot

Region: northern
Method: simmering

Serves 4 to 6

2 to 3 pounds boneless lean lamb
4 ounces bean thread (transparent)
   noodles (2½ packages)
½ pound spinach
½ pound Chinese cabbage
1 quart Chicken Stock (page 60)
1 teaspoon finely chopped ginger root
2 tablespoons finely chopped scallions
1 teaspoon minced garlic
1 tablespoon finely chopped fresh
   coriander

Dipping sauce

2 tablespoons sesame paste or peanut
   butter
1 tablespoon light soy sauce
1 tablespoon rice wine or dry sherry
2 teaspoons chili bean sauce
1 tablespoon sugar
1 tablespoon hot water

This northern dish is similar in style to a European fondue. It was introduced into China after the Mongolian conquest in the thirteenth century, and soon could be found throughout China with regional touches added. Beef was sometimes substituted for the traditional lamb and the Cantonese developed their "Chrysanthemum Fire Pot," which includes edible flower petals. In this recipe, which follows the traditional method, thin slices of lamb and vegetables are simmered in a broth. Each diner cooks his own food at the table in the pot of stock. The cooked food is then dipped into various sauces before being eaten. Toward the end of the meal, bean thread noodles are cooked in the remaining broth, which is then drunk as a soup. The Chinese use a special charcoal-burning "fire pot" for this dish, but you could use either a large fondue pot or a small portable electric hot plate and heatproof or clay pot instead. (If you have an authentic Chinese fire pot, use it only in a well-ventilated room with the windows open, or use it out of doors. Otherwise the carbon monoxide fumes arising from the charcoal can be dangerous.)

Using a cleaver or sharp knife, slice the lamb into very thin slices. Soak the noodles in warm water for 5 minutes, then drain them and cut them into 5-inch lengths. Separate the spinach leaves from the stalks and wash them well. Discard the stalks. Cut the Chinese cabbage into 3-inch pieces. Combine all the ingredients for the dipping sauce in a small bowl and mix them well.

Each guest should have his or her own small portion of dipping sauce and a plate containing lamb, spinach and Chinese cabbage. When you are ready to begin, bring the stock to a boil and light the fondue. Ladle the stock into the fondue pot and put the ginger, scallions, garlic and coriander into the stock.

Each person selects a piece of food and cooks it quickly in the pot. When all the meat and vegetables have been eaten, add the noodles to the pot, let them heat through, then ladle the soup into soup bowls.

This dish also works successfully with other foods such as steak, fish balls, oysters, shrimp, squid, mushrooms and lettuce, although it will no longer be a Mongolian hot pot, but more like the Cantonese Chrysanthemum Pot.

Mongolian Hot Pot.

Stir-fried Lamb Kidneys

Region: western
Method: stir-frying

Serves 4
½ pound lamb or pork kidneys
½ teaspoon baking soda
1 teaspoon Chinese white rice
  vinegar or cider vinegar
½ teaspoon salt
1 tablespoon oil, preferably peanut
1 dried red chili
1 tablespoon finely chopped garlic
1 tablespoon dark soy sauce
2 teaspoons rice wine or dry sherry
½ teaspoon finely ground roasted
  Sichuan peppercorns (page 26)
  (optional)
½ teaspoon sugar
¼ teaspoon salt
1 teaspoon sesame oil

Garnish
2 teaspoons finely chopped scallions

Lamb kidneys are delicious when they are simply stir-fried. As a young cook I was taught a wonderful technique for cleaning kidneys which I use to this day. First the kidneys should be scored and tossed in baking soda; this helps to tenderize them and to neutralize their acidity. Then the baking soda is rinsed off and they are tossed in a mixture of vinegar and salt to remove any remaining bitterness. The result is a clean and fresh-tasting kidney. This dish can also be made with pork kidneys. Serve it with Corn Soup with Crabmeat (page 61) and plain steamed rice.

Using a sharp knife, remove the thin outer kidney membrane. Then, with a sharp cleaver or knife, slit the kidneys in half by cutting horizontally. Now cut away the small knobs of fat and any tough membrane surrounding them. Next, score the kidneys in a crisscross pattern and cut them into thin slices. Toss the kidney slices with the baking soda and let them sit for about 20 minutes. Then rinse them thoroughly with cold water and toss them with the vinegar and salt. Put them into a colander and let them drain for at least 30 minutes, preferably longer.

Blot the kidney slices dry with paper towels. Heat a wok or large skillet over a high heat until it is very hot. Add the oil and the dried chili. Stir-fry to flavor the oil for about 20 seconds. Then add the kidney slices and stir-fry, coating the kidneys with the oil, for about 1 minute. Now add the rest of the ingredients and toss them well with the kidneys. Continue to stir-fry the mixture for about 2 minutes or until the kidney edges begin to curl. Turn the mixture onto a warm serving platter, garnish with the scallions, and serve at once.

Peking Braised Lamb

Region: northern
Method: braising

Serves 4
1 pound boned shoulder of lamb
2 scallions
2 large slices ginger root
1 tablespoon oil
½ small onion, finely chopped

Braising sauce
2 cups Chicken Stock (page 60)
2 whole star anise (optional)
2 ounces Chinese rock sugar, or
  ¼ cup granulated
1½ tablespoons dark soy sauce
1 tablespoon rice wine or dry sherry
½ piece Chinese cinnamon bark or
  cinnamon stick
2 teaspoons sesame paste or peanut
  butter
1 tablespoon hoisin sauce

(pictured on page 52)

The Chinese usually cook mutton and goat rather than lamb, which is scarce, and have many exciting ways of braising both these meats with spices which help to mask their strong taste. This tasty and filling family dish is perfect for the winter. It goes well with plain steamed rice and Chinese Cabbage in Soy Sauce (page 148).

Cut the meat into 2-inch cubes. Next, blanch the lamb by plunging it into boiling water for 5 minutes. Then remove the meat and discard the water. Slice the scallions at a slight diagonal into 3-inch pieces. Slice the ginger into long ¼-inch strips.

Heat the oil in a wok or large skillet, and when it is hot, add the pieces of lamb. Stir-fry them until they are brown, then remove any excess fat, leaving just 1 tablespoon. Now add the scallions, ginger and onion and continue to stir-fry for 5 minutes. Transfer this mixture to a large casserole or pot and add the braising sauce ingredients. Bring the liquid to a boil, skim off any fat from the surface, and turn the heat down as low as possible. Cover and braise for 1½ hours or until the lamb is quite tender. (The leftover liquid can be frozen and reused another time to braise lamb.) Arrange the cooked meat on a platter and serve.

Hot and Sour Kidneys

Pork kidneys are tender and tasty when stir-fried in this hot and sour sauce. The contrasting flavors of the sauce perfectly complement the robust taste of the kidneys. As in the preceding recipe, I suggest you marinate the kidneys in baking soda and then toss them in vinegar and salt. This dish is inexpensive to make and goes well with plain steamed rice and any stir-fried vegetable.

Follow the instructions on page 90 for preparing the kidneys, marinating them, and tossing them in vinegar and salt.

Blot the kidney slices dry with paper towels. Heat a wok or large skillet over high heat. Add the oil and the ginger. Stir-fry to flavor the oil for about 20 seconds. Then add the kidney slices and stir-fry them for about 1 minute. Now add the sauce ingredients and toss them together well with the kidneys. Continue to stir-fry the mixture for about 2 minutes or until the kidney edges begin to curl. Turn the mixture onto a warm serving platter and serve at once.

Region: western
Method: stir-frying

Serves 4
½ pound pork kidneys
½ teaspoon baking soda
1 teaspoon white rice vinegar or cider vinegar
½ teaspoon salt
1 tablespoon oil, preferably peanut
1 slice ginger root
1 teaspoon finely chopped garlic
1 teaspoon finely chopped ginger root
1 teaspoon chili powder
1 teaspoon Chinese white rice vinegar or cider vinegar
½ teaspoon sugar
2 teaspoons dark soy sauce
¼ teaspoon ground roasted Sichuan peppercorns (page 26) (optional)
1½ tablespoons Chicken Stock (page 60) or water

Stir-fried Lamb with Garlic

Lamb is especially delicious when it is stir-fried. This way of preparing it, with lots of garlic and scallions to balance its strong taste, is a popular one. The tenderest parts of the lamb, such as steaks or chops, are best for this dish. Serve it with rice and Braised Spicy Eggplant (page 143).

Cut the lamb into thin slices and put it into a bowl. Mix in the rice wine or sherry, soy sauces and sesame oil and let the meat marinate for 20 minutes. Then drain off the marinade liquid.

Heat a wok or large skillet. When it is very hot, add the oil. Then add the marinated lamb pieces with just a little of the marinade. Stir-fry for 2 minutes. Now add the scallions, garlic and ginger, and continue to stir-fry for another 4 minutes. Serve immediately.

Region: northern
Method: stir-frying

Serves 3 to 4
¾ pound boneless lean lamb
2 teaspoons rice wine or dry sherry
2 teaspoons dark soy sauce
2 teaspoons light soy sauce
½ teaspoon sesame oil
2 teaspoons oil
1½ teaspoons finely chopped scallions
3 garlic cloves, peeled and thinly sliced
½ teaspoon finely chopped ginger root

CHICKEN, DUCK & GAME BIRDS

雞鴨

Chicken is the most highly regarded of all poultry in China. To impress a guest a Chinese hostess might announce that she has killed a chicken in his honor. It is frequently served on special occasions, on birthdays, and at festivals and banquets. At our family gatherings chicken was always the centerpiece. Early every Sunday morning my mother would bring home a live chicken from the market in Chinatown in Chicago, where we lived. Its noisy clucking would usually wake me up. The chicken would be quickly dispatched and then prepared in one of many ways. One of my favorites was when it was slowly poached and then served with a soy sauce and scallion dipping sauce.

In China most homes do not have ovens, and poultry is usually roasted only by professional cooks. Home-cooked chicken is braised, stir-fried, deep-fried, steamed or simmered. One of the virtues of chicken is that its distinctive but mild flavor blends well with other seasonings, spices and sauces. It is a very versatile bird and is almost as popular in China as pork.

The Chinese prefer to buy their chickens live, to ensure that they are at their freshest when cooked. Obviously this is almost impossible in the West! In Europe and North America there are plentiful supplies of relatively inexpensive chicken, but because of modern farming methods, commercially produced chickens tend to lack taste. Frozen chicken is especially bland. Try to buy a fresh chicken for Chinese cooking. It should have a healthy pinkish color, a fresh smell, and be firm in texture. If possible buy free-range chickens. Not only have they been raised by more humane methods but their taste is far superior.

Whole cooked chickens are never carried to the table to be carved, but are always chopped into bite-size pieces before being arranged on a platter. However, many of the recipes in this chapter can be made with chicken pieces rather than with a whole chicken. All parts of the chicken are used in China. The dark meat from the thighs and drumsticks is especially prized for its superior flavor. Roasting chickens are the most suitable for frying, steaming and braising. If possible use stewing fowl for stock to give you a rich liquid with a good flavor. Cornish game hens are also suitable for stir-fried dishes.

Fresh chicken should be cooked as soon as possible. Keep it cold until you are ready to use it. If you wish to store the chicken, first remove any wrapping and the giblets. Rinse it carefully in cold water and blot it completely dry with paper towels. Wrap it loosely in plastic wrap and put it in the refrigerator, where it will keep for two days. If you are using frozen chicken be sure to thaw it thoroughly before proceeding with the recipe.

Duck is also popular in Chinese cookery, with Peking Duck being one of the most famous of all Chinese dishes. Like chicken, it is never roasted at home. In domestic kitchens duck is cut up and then braised or stir-fried. It is also steamed and then deep-fried, a process which results in a very tender fat-free duck. Fresh duck is always preferable to frozen and should be stored in the same way as chicken. If you use frozen duck, be sure to defrost it thoroughly first.

Game birds are widely used in Chinese cookery, but because their flavor tends to be strong they are frequently stewed or put into soups together with medicinal herbs and seasonings. Squab and quail are two birds which are readily available here and which are ideal for Chinese cooking. Squabs can be found frozen, as well as fresh. As a substitute, Rock Cornish game hens can be used in some recipes, but they do not have as much flavor as squabs.

Peking Duck fresh out of the oven (page 113).

This recipe is a favorite one for me because it evokes childhood memories of the fragrance of black bean sauce mixed with garlic, which often used to greet me at the door when I came home from school. My mother used to make this dish with chicken wings, the tender and juicy flesh of which is among the tastiest parts of the chicken. Wings are ideal for stir-frying because they cook quickly, but other parts of the chicken work just as well. Serve this dish with plain rice and Stir-fried Spinach with Garlic (page 151).

If you are using chicken wings, cut them in half at the joint. If you are using chicken pieces, cut them into 2-inch chunks. Mix the soy sauce and rice wine or sherry together and pour it over the chicken pieces. Let the chicken marinate for about 1 hour, then drain the chicken and discard the marinade.

 Heat a wok or large skillet. Add the oil, and when it is hot add the ginger. Stir-fry it for a few seconds and then add the garlic, scallions and black beans. A few seconds later add the chicken wings or pieces and stir-fry them for 2 to 5 minutes over high heat until they are brown. Then add the stock. Bring the mixture to a boil and then reduce the heat. Simmer for 15 minutes or until the chicken is cooked. (If you are using boneless chicken breasts, cook for just 5 minutes.) This dish can be cooked ahead of time and reheated, and it is also delicious served cold.

Region: southern
Method: stir-frying and braising

Serves 4
 1 pound chicken wings or chicken
  pieces, with the skin on
 1 tablespoon light soy sauce
 1 tablespoon rice wine or dry sherry
 2 teaspoons oil, preferably peanut
 1 tablespoon finely chopped ginger
  root
 1 tablespoon finely chopped garlic
 1½ tablespoons finely chopped
  scallions
 1½ tablespoons coarsely chopped
  black beans
 ⅔ cup Chicken Stock (page 60)

(pictured on page 185)

Curry blends well with chicken, especially when used in the style of southern Chinese cuisine, namely as a light and subtle sauce which does not overpower the delicate chicken meat. Peppers provide the dish with a crunchy texture but carrots, if blanched first, can be used instead. Serve this with Tomato Egg-Flower Soup (page 68) and plain steamed rice.

Cut the chicken breasts into 1-inch cubes. Combine them with the egg white, salt and 1 teaspoon of cornstarch in a small bowl, and put the mixture into the refrigerator for about 20 minutes. Wash and seed the peppers and cut them into 1-inch pieces.

 Heat the oil in a wok or large skillet until it is moderately hot. Add the chicken mixture and stir-fry it quickly in the oil to keep it from sticking. Cook it until it turns white, which should take about 2 minutes. Put the chicken immediately into a colander or sieve and drain off the remaining oil. (This oil, once cooled, may be saved for future stir-fried dishes using chicken.)

 Clean the wok and add about 1 tablespoon of the drained oil. Reheat it until it is very hot. Add the peppers and stir-fry them for 2 minutes. Then add the rest of the ingredients and cook the mixture for another 2 minutes. Return the chicken to the pan and stir-fry for another 2 minutes, coating the chicken pieces thoroughly with the sauce. Serve at once.

Region: southern
Method: stir-frying

Serves 3 to 4
 ½ pound boneless chicken breasts,
  skinned
 1 egg white
 1 teaspoon salt
 1 teaspoon cornstarch
 ½ pound red, yellow or green bell
  peppers, or a combination (3 to 4)
 ⅔ cup oil, preferably peanut
 ⅓ cup Chicken Stock (page 60)
 2 teaspoons good curry powder or
  paste
 1 teaspoon granulated sugar
 2 teaspoons rice wine or dry sherry
 1 tablespoon light soy sauce
 1 teaspoon cornstarch, blended
  with 1 teaspoon water

(pictured on page 52)

Spicy Chicken with Peanuts (facing page).

Spicy Chicken with Peanuts

This is a classic western Chinese dish which is better known in China as Gongbao chicken. According to one expert, the dish was named after a Chinese official, Ding Baozhen, who was governor of Sichuan province in the nineteenth century. There are many versions of this recipe; this one is close to the original and is also quick and easy to make. Rice and Stir-fried Bok Choi (page 148) would go well with it.

Cut the chicken into 1-inch cubes. Split the dried chili in half lengthwise. Heat the oil in a wok or large skillet, and add the chili. (You may remove it when it turns black or leave it in.) Next add the chicken cubes and peanuts and stir-fry them for 1 minute. Remove the chicken, peanuts and chili from the pan.

Put all the sauce ingredients, except the sesame oil, into the pan. Bring the sauce to a boil, and then turn the heat down. Return the chicken and peanuts to the pan and cook for about 2 minutes in the sauce. Add the sesame oil, and then serve immediately.

Region: western
Method: stir-frying

Serves 4

½ pound boneless chicken breasts, skinned
1 dried red chili
1½ tablespoons oil
3 ounces (¼ cup) raw shelled peanuts (page 23)

Sauce

1 tablespoon Chicken Stock (page 60) or water
1 tablespoon rice wine or dry sherry
2 teaspoons dark soy sauce
2 teaspoons chili bean sauce
1 teaspoon granulated sugar
1 teaspoon finely chopped garlic
2 teaspoons finely chopped scallions
½ teaspoon finely chopped ginger root
1 teaspoon Chinese white rice vinegar or cider vinegar
½ teaspoon salt
1 teaspoon sesame oil

Garlic Chicken with Cucumber

Cucumbers, never served raw in China, are delicious cooked. In this recipe they are stir-fried with delicate chicken breasts and flavored with garlic and chili. This is an uncomplicated dish which goes well with Honey-Glazed Pork (page 77) or Tomato Egg-Flower Soup (page 68).

Cut the chicken into 1-inch cubes and set aside. Peel the cucumber, halve it and remove the seeds with a teaspoon. Then cut it into cubes, sprinkle with the salt and put the cubes into a colander to drain for 20 minutes. (This removes the excess moisture from the cucumber.) Then rinse the cucumber in cold running water and blot dry with paper towels.

Heat the oil in a wok or large skillet. When it is hot, add the chicken cubes and stir-fry them for a few seconds. Add all the other ingredients except the cucumber and continue to stir-fry for another 2 minutes. Now add the cucumber cubes and keep stir-frying the entire mixture for another 3 minutes. Serve at once.

Region: western
Method: stir-frying

Serves 4

¾ pound boneless chicken breasts, skinned
½ cucumber
¼ teaspoon salt
2 teaspoons oil, preferably peanut
2 teaspoons finely chopped garlic
1 tablespoon finely chopped scallions
2 teaspoons light soy sauce
2 teaspoons rice wine or dry sherry
¼ teaspoon chili bean sauce or chili powder

Lemon Chicken

Region: southern
Method: stir-frying

Serves 3 to 4
   ½ pound boneless chicken breasts,
      skinned
   1 egg white
   2 teaspoons cornstarch
   ⅓ cup oil, preferably peanut

Sauce
   ⅓ cup Chicken Stock (page 60) or
      water
   1½ tablespoons fresh lemon juice
   2 teaspoons granulated sugar
   2 teaspoons light soy sauce
   2 teaspoons rice wine or dry sherry
   ½ teaspoon finely chopped garlic
   1 dried red chili, or ¼ teaspoon
      chili powder
   1 teaspoon cornstarch, blended
      with 1 teaspoon water

The Hong Kong Chinese have made a specialty of chicken cooked with lemon. The tart lemon sauce goes very well indeed with the delicate flavor of chicken. Unlike many versions which employ a cloyingly sweet sauce, this recipe balances tartness with sweetness. Sometimes the lemon chicken is steamed, but I think it is equally good stir-fried. Serve it with plain steamed rice and Cold Sesame Broccoli (page 145).

Cut the chicken breasts into strips 3 inches long. Combine the chicken strips with the egg white and cornstarch in a bowl, and chill it in the refrigerator for about 20 minutes.

Heat the oil in a wok or deep skillet until it is moderately hot. Add the chicken strips and stir them quickly in the oil to keep them from sticking. Cook the strips until they turn white. (This takes about 1 minute.) Drain the breasts immediately in a colander or sieve. (The oil may be saved for future stir-fried chicken dishes.)

Wipe the wok clean and reheat it. Add all the sauce ingredients except for the cornstarch mixture. Bring it to a boil over high heat and then add the cornstarch mixture. Simmer for 1 minute. Return the chicken strips to the sauce and stir-fry them long enough to coat them all well with the sauce. Turn onto a platter and serve at once.

Lemon Chicken.

This recipe pairs the crunchy texture of walnuts with the delicate flavor of chicken in a classic stir-fry dish. For a variation try this recipe with other nuts such as cashews, pine nuts or almonds, but be sure the nuts you use are very fresh. Stale nuts will ruin the flavor. I like to serve it with Fried Stuffed Cucumbers (page 152) and Corn Soup with Crabmeat (page 61).

Cut the chicken breasts into ½-inch cubes. Combine the cubes with the egg white, salt and cornstarch in a small bowl, and chill it in the refrigerator for about 20 minutes. Blanch the walnuts in a small pot of boiling water for 5 minutes; then drain them.

Heat the oil in a wok or deep skillet until it is moderately hot. Add the chicken mixture and stir-fry it quickly in the oil to keep it from sticking, until it turns white. This will take about 2 minutes. Drain the cooked chicken in a colander or sieve. (The oil, once cooled, may be saved for future stir-fried dishes with chicken.)

Put about 1 tablespoon of the oil in which you have cooked the chicken into a clean wok or skillet. Reheat it until it is very hot. Add the walnuts and stir-fry them for 1 minute. Remove and set aside. Add the garlic, ginger and scallions to the pan and stir-fry for a few seconds. Return the walnuts to the pan and then add the rest of the ingredients. Return the chicken to the pan and stir-fry the mixture for another 2 minutes. Serve at once.

Region: eastern
Method: stir-frying

Serves 3 to 4
½ pound boneless chicken breasts, skinned
1 egg white
1 teaspoon salt
2 teaspoons cornstarch
3 ounces (about ¼ cup) walnuts, shelled halves or pieces
⅔ cup oil, preferably peanut
1 teaspoon finely chopped garlic
½ teaspoon finely chopped ginger root
1 tablespoon finely chopped scallions
1 tablespoon rice wine or dry sherry
1 tablespoon light soy sauce

This dish exemplifies the Chinese penchant for contrasting textures. Here, tender succulent pieces of chicken are used with sweet crunchy cashew nuts. The original Chinese version would have been made with peanuts because cashew nuts are not a part of Chinese cuisine. Nevertheless this dish uses the best Chinese cooking principles: stir-frying to seal in the juices of the chicken, and then stir-frying again with spices to flavor it.

Cut the chicken breasts into ½-inch cubes. Combine them with the egg white, salt and cornstarch in a small bowl, and chill it in the refrigerator for about 20 minutes.

Heat the oil in a wok or deep skillet until it is moderately hot. Add the chicken mixture and stir-fry it quickly in the oil to keep it from sticking. Cook it until it turns white, which should take about 2 minutes. Place the chicken cubes in a colander or sieve and drain off the oil. (The oil, once cooled, may be saved for future stir-fried dishes using chicken.)

Put about 1 tablespoon of the oil in which you have cooked the chicken into a clean wok or skillet. Reheat it until it is very hot. Add the cashew nuts and stir-fry them for 1 minute. Then add the rest of the ingredients. Return the chicken to the pan and stir-fry the mixture for another 2 minutes. Garnish the dish with the scallions and serve at once.

Region: southern
Method: stir-frying

Serves 3 to 4
½ pound boneless chicken breasts, skinned
1 egg white
1 teaspoon salt
1 teaspoon cornstarch
⅔ cup oil, preferably peanut
2 ounces cashew nuts (about ¼ cup)
2 teaspoons rice wine or dry sherry
1 tablespoon light soy sauce

Garnish
1 tablespoon finely chopped scallions

Country-Style Chicken

Region: western
Method: stir-frying

Serves 3 to 4
½ pound boneless chicken breasts,
    skinned
2 small fresh green or red chilies
8 ounces canned bamboo shoots
½ pound zucchini
1 large red or green bell pepper
2 tablespoons oil, preferably peanut
2 tablespoons Chicken Stock
    (page 60)
2 tablespoons rice wine or dry
    sherry
1½ to 2 teaspoons chili bean sauce
2 teaspoons granulated sugar
2 tablespoons dark soy sauce
1 tablespoon Chinese black rice
    vinegar or cider vinegar
1 tablespoon tomato paste

Not all western Chinese cooking is hot and spicy. Many simple homely recipes like this one use relatively little chili. Rather, the accent is on seasonal vegetables. It is equally tasty without the fresh chili if you prefer. Steamed rice is a perfect accompaniment to this dish.

Cut the chicken breasts into shreds about 3 inches long. Cut the fresh chilies in half, carefully remove the seeds and shred the chilies. (Do not touch your eyes while doing this, as it will make them sting.) Then prepare all the vegetables. Rinse the bamboo shoots in clean water and shred them. Trim the zucchini and shred them. Wash the bell pepper, remove the seeds and shred this too.

Heat 1 tablespoon of the oil in a wok or large skillet. When it is almost smoking, quickly stir-fry the chicken shreds for 1 minute or until the chicken is slightly firm. Remove the cooked chicken and drain it.

Wipe the wok clean. Reheat it and add the rest of the oil. When it is hot, add the shredded chilies, bamboo shoots, zucchini and bell pepper. Stir-fry for about 2 minutes, and then add the rest of the ingredients. Mix them well and stir-fry for another minute. Return the chicken shreds and give the mixture a few quick stirs to finish cooking the chicken. Turn onto a serving platter and serve at once.

Spiced Deep-fried Chicken

Region: western
Method: deep-frying

Serves 4
¾ pound boneless chicken pieces
2 cups oil (see Deep-fat fryers,
    page 35)
⅔ cup all-purpose flour

Marinade
1 teaspoon chili bean sauce or chili
    powder
2 teaspoons rice wine or dry sherry
1 teaspoon light soy sauce
1 teaspoon dark soy sauce
2 teaspoons finely chopped ginger
    root
1 tablespoon finely chopped
    scallions
1 teaspoon granulated sugar

This is a fragrant crispy chicken dish which has always brought me compliments. It is simple to make and should be served as soon as it is cooked. I like to serve this with Watercress Soup (page 66) and Rainbow Rice (page 161).

Cut the chicken into strips 2 inches × ½ inch and put them into a large bowl. Blend the marinade ingredients together and pour the mixture over the chicken. Mix well to ensure an even distribution. Allow the chicken to marinate for 30 to 40 minutes at room temperature.

Heat the oil in a deep-fat fryer or large wok until it is quite hot. Lightly sprinkle the chicken strips with the flour and deep-fry them for 8 minutes. Remove them and drain on paper towels. Serve at once.

Shredded Chicken with Sesame Seeds.

Shredded Chicken with Sesame Seeds

This is my version of a fragrant Sichuan dish popularly known as "Strange Taste Chicken" because it incorporates so many flavors, being hot, spicy, sour, sweet and salty all at the same time. It is delicious as a hot dish but I find it an excellent cold dish as well. I simply let it cool and serve it at room temperature. The sesame seeds add a crunchy texture which contrasts nicely with the tender chicken meat. Serve this dish with Ham and Zucchini Soup (page 64) and Stir-fried Broccoli with Hoisin Sauce (page 146).

Cut the chicken breasts into fine shreds 3 inches long. Combine them with the egg white, salt and cornstarch, and chill for about 20 minutes.

Heat the oil in a wok or large skillet until it is moderately hot. Add the chicken mixture and stir-fry it quickly in the oil to keep it from sticking. Cook until it turns white, which should take about 1 minute. Drain the chicken immediately in a colander or sieve and drain off the oil.

Clean the wok and add about 1 tablespoon of the drained oil. Reheat it until it is hot. Add the sesame seeds and stir-fry them for 1 minute or until they are slightly brown. Then add the sauce ingredients and bring to a boil. Return the cooked chicken to the pan and stir-fry the mixture for another 2 minutes, coating the pieces thoroughly with the sauce and sesame seeds. Serve at once, or let it cool and serve at room temperature.

Region: western
Method: stir-frying

Serves 3 to 4
   ½ *pound boneless chicken breasts, skinned*
   1 *egg white*
   ½ *teaspoon salt*
   2 *teaspoons cornstarch*
   ⅔ *cup oil, preferably peanut*
   1 *tablespoon white sesame seeds, untoasted*

Sauce
   1 *teaspoon dark soy sauce*
   1 *teaspoon Chinese black rice vinegar or cider vinegar*
   ½ *teaspoon chili bean sauce*
   ½ *teaspoon sesame oil*
   1 *teaspoon sugar*
   2 *teaspoons rice wine or dry sherry*
   ½ *teaspoon roasted Sichuan peppercorns (page 26) (optional)*
   2 *teaspoons finely chopped scallions*

Hot Spiced Chicken

Region: western
**Method: shallow-frying and
braising**

Serves 4

3/4 to 1 pound chicken pieces (wings
or thighs)
1/2 teaspoon salt
2 scallions
2/3 cup oil, preferably peanut
1 dried red chili, halved lengthwise
1 teaspoon oil
1/2 teaspoon finely chopped ginger
root
1 teaspoon chili bean sauce, or 1/2
teaspoon chili powder
1 1/3 cups Chicken Stock (page 60)
1/2 teaspoon ground roasted Sichuan
peppercorns (page 26) (optional)
1/2 teaspoon granulated sugar
2 teaspoons dark soy sauce

This hot and spicy chicken dish can easily be made ahead of time and reheated. It is a good example of the combination of contrasting flavors which characterize the spicy cuisine of western China. The finished dish smells wonderfully fragrant and it has an equally delightful taste.

Rub the chicken pieces with the salt and let them sit for about 30 minutes. Cut the scallions into 2-inch pieces. Heat the 2/3 cup of oil in a wok or large skillet, and then add the dried chili to flavor the oil. When it turns black, turn the heat down. (At this point you may remove the chili or leave it in as the Chinese do.) Slowly brown the chicken pieces, a few at a time, skin-side down. Then turn them over and brown the other side. Drain the cooked pieces on paper towels.

Heat a clean wok or skillet and add 1 teaspoon oil. Fry in it the scallions, ginger and chili bean sauce (or chili powder), taking care not to have the heat too high or the sauce will burn. A few seconds later add the chicken stock, Sichuan peppercorns, sugar and dark soy sauce. Then turn the heat down low, and add the chicken pieces. Cover, and finish cooking the chicken in this sauce, turning the pieces from time to time. This should take about 20 to 30 minutes. Serve the chicken with the sauce, first removing any surface fat.

Stir-fried Chicken Shreds

Region: eastern
Method: stir-frying

Serves 3 to 4

1/2 pound boneless chicken breasts,
skinned
1 egg white
1/2 teaspoon salt
1/2 teaspoon cornstarch
6 ounces fresh bean sprouts (about
2 cups)
4 ounces snow peas, trimmed
6 fresh water chestnuts, or
1/2 8-ounce can, drained
2/3 cup oil, preferably peanut
1 teaspoon salt

This is a simple recipe which is quick and easy to make and is very suitable for family meals. The secret of cooking the chicken shreds without drying them out is to stir-fry them quickly in oil until they turn opaque and then remove them at once. You can substitute other vegetables such as asparagus, carrots or green peas for the ones I have used, if you prefer. This dish goes nicely with rice and Ham and Zucchini Soup (page 64).

Cut the chicken into very thin shreds and combine these with the egg white, salt and cornstarch in a bowl. Mix well and chill in the refrigerator for about 20 minutes. Meanwhile, trim the bean sprouts, finely shred the snow peas lengthwise, and shred or slice the water chestnuts.

Heat the oil in a wok or large skillet and when it is almost smoking add the chicken. Stir-fry quickly for 1 minute. Drain the chicken in a colander or sieve immediately. Pour off the oil, leaving 1 tablespoon in the wok. (The rest of the oil may be saved when it is cooled and used for future cooking with chicken.)

Reheat the wok and stir-fry the vegetables for 2 minutes. Return the drained chicken to the pan, stir to mix well, and add the salt. Give the mixture a few more stirs and then turn it onto a warm serving platter.

Leeks are popular in northern Chinese cooking. They have a flavor which is less pronounced than that of garlic or onions and which blends well with the mild taste of chicken. Leeks need to be thoroughly washed, and I find it easier to do this after they have been chopped. This warm rich dish is perfect for cold winter days. I like to cook it in a Chinese clay pot, but any heavy casserole will do. Serve with plain steamed rice or plain boiled noodles and Ginger and Scallion Dipping Sauce (page 30).

Pat the chicken pieces dry with paper towels. Using a heavy cleaver or knife, cut them into smaller pieces about 2 inches × 1 inch and put them into a bowl. Add 2 teaspoons of rice wine or dry sherry and 2 teaspoons of light soy sauce. Mix well and set the chicken to one side.

Trim the leeks and discard any yellow parts. Cut the leeks at the point where they begin to turn green and discard the green parts. Then split the white parts in half and cut them at a slight diagonal into 2½-inch segments. Now wash them well in cold water. (You may have to do this several times until there is no trace of dirt.) Cut the scallion and ginger at a slight diagonal into 2½-inch pieces.

Heat a wok or large skillet until it is hot. Add the oil, and when it is almost smoking, add the scallion and ginger. Quickly lift the chicken pieces out of the marinade, using a slotted spoon, and add them to the pan together with the leeks. Stir-fry for about 5 minutes until they are thoroughly browned, and then remove them from the pan with a slotted spoon and discard the oil.

Bring the stock to a boil in a medium-size pot and add the rice wine or sherry and soy sauce. Then add the browned chicken and vegetables. Skim off any scum and reduce the heat to a simmer. Cover the pot tightly and braise for about 25 minutes. Before serving, skim off any fat. Serve at once or let it cool and then refrigerate. (It reheats beautifully.)

Region: northern
Method: stir-frying and braising

Serves 4
¾ to 1 pound chicken pieces (wings
　or thighs)
2 teaspoons rice wine or dry sherry
2 teaspoons light soy sauce
2 leeks
1 scallion
1 slice ginger root
1 tablespoon oil, preferably peanut
1 cup Chicken Stock (page 60)
2 teaspoons rice wine or dry sherry
2 teaspoons light soy sauce

Drunken Chicken

Region: northern
Method: steeping and marinating

Serves 4
  1 slice ginger root
  2 to 2⅓ cups water
  ½ teaspoon salt
  1 scallion
  ¾ pound chicken pieces
  ⅔ cup rice wine, or dry sherry
    mixed with ⅓ cup Chicken Stock
    (page 60)

This dish isn't called Drunken Chicken without reason! You do need quite a lot of alcohol to cover the chicken during the steeping process, but it can be reused. I think this traditional dish tastes best when it is made with Chinese rice wine rather than sherry. Because it can be prepared at least two days ahead, it makes an ideal dish for a party or a large gathering.

Cut the ginger into long ¼-inch strips. Fill a large casserole with the water. Bring it to a boil, and add the ginger, salt, whole scallion and the chicken pieces. If they are not covered by the water add some more. Bring the liquid back to the boiling point, and then turn the heat down. Simmer for 30 to 40 minutes, skimming any fat or scum off the surface as it appears. Then turn the heat off, cover the casserole tightly and let the chicken sit in the liquid for 20 to 30 minutes.

Remove the cooked chicken to a large plate and let it cool. (The cooking liquid can be saved and used for stock.) If the chicken is not already in bite-size pieces, cut it up and put it into a large bowl. Cover with the rice wine or sherry and stock mixture, and leave it for 2 days in the refrigerator, covered, turning it over from time to time.

After 2 days remove the chicken and arrange it on a serving platter. Pour some of the wine over the chicken to moisten it. The remaining wine can be kept in the refrigerator and used for cooking other dishes that call for sherry or rice wine.

Chicken with Garlic Vinegar Sauce

Region: northern
**Method: steaming and deep-
    frying**

Serves 6
  4 large slices ginger root
  4 scallions
  1 whole chicken (about 2½ pounds)
  2 teaspoons salt
  4 cups oil (see Deep-fat fryers, page
    35)

Sauce
  1 tablespoon finely chopped garlic
  2 tablespoons Chinese white rice
    vinegar or cider vinegar
  2 tablespoons light soy sauce
  2½ tablespoons finely chopped
    scallions

I remember the first time I had this dish in a northern Chinese restaurant. I liked it so much that I immediately set out to re-create it. The secret is in steaming the chicken to keep it moist and then deep-frying it without batter. The result is a juicy chicken with a crisp, parchment-like skin. The chicken is served with a piquant sauce, and goes well with plain steamed rice and Stir-fried Ginger Broccoli (page 146).

Cut the ginger into long ¼-inch strips. Cut the scallions into 3-inch pieces. Rub the whole chicken with the salt and stuff the cavity with the ginger and scallions. Let the chicken sit at room temperature for 30 minutes.

Next, set up a steamer or put a rack into a wok or deep pan and fill it with 2 inches of water. Bring the water to a boil over high heat. Put the chicken onto a heatproof plate and then carefully lower it into the steamer or onto the rack. Turn the heat to low and cover the pan tightly. Steam gently for 1 hour or until the chicken is cooked through to the bone. Remember to replenish the water from time to time.

Remove the cooked chicken and let it cool and dry. This takes at least 3 hours. Wipe the chicken completely dry and cut it in half, lengthwise. Mix the sauce ingredients together and set aside.

Heat the oil in a deep-fat fryer or large wok. Deep-fry one chicken half until it is golden and crisp. Remove and then deep-fry the other half. Drain the cooked halves on paper towels. Cut the meat into bite-size pieces, arrange them on a warm platter, and pour the sauce over the top. Serve at once.

Soy Sauce Chicken

My friends are often surprised at their first taste of Soy Sauce Chicken. Instead of the saltiness they expect, given the name of the dish, they taste tender, succulent chicken bathed in a rich and subtle sauce. The technique of steeping used here ensures that the chicken is moist and tender, and allows the rich flavors of the sauce to gently permeate the meat. The chicken may be served hot, but I think it is best cooled and served at room temperature, or refrigerated and served cold. It also makes a delicious picnic dish. The steeping liquid may be used as a sauce, and the rest may be frozen and reused for making more Soy Sauce Chicken.

First make the sauce by combining all the sauce ingredients in a very large pot and bringing the liquid to a simmer. Meanwhile, cut the ginger into long ¼-inch strips. Stuff the cavity of the chicken with the whole scallions and ginger slices. Put the chicken into the pot with the sauce mixture. If the liquid does not cover the chicken add a little more stock. Bring it back to a simmer and simmer for about 30 to 40 minutes uncovered, skimming all the while. Turn the chicken over so the breast is touching the bottom of the pot. Turn off the heat, cover the pot tightly and leave for about 20 to 30 minutes.

After this time remove the chicken from the liquid with a slotted spoon and put it on a plate to cool. It can now be put into the refrigerator or cut up into pieces and served. Remove any surface fat from the sauce and serve a little of it spooned over the chicken pieces. If you like, garnish with fresh coriander sprigs.

Region: eastern and southern
Method: simmering and steeping

Serves 4 to 6
    4 slices ginger root
    1 whole chicken (about 2½ pounds)
    4 scallions

Sauce
    3 cups Chicken Stock (page 60) or
        water
    1 pint dark soy sauce
    ⅔ cup light soy sauce
    1⅓ cups rice wine, or ⅔ cup dry
        sherry mixed with ⅔ cup
        Chicken Stock
    4 ounces Chinese rock sugar, or
        ¼ cup granulated
    3 whole star anise (optional)
    3 pieces Chinese cinnamon bark or
        cinnamon sticks

Optional garnish
    fresh coriander sprigs

Twice-Cooked Chicken

This eastern Chinese recipe involves a two-step cooking process. First the chicken is marinated and steamed. This cooks the flesh but retains the moisture and flavor of the bird. The chicken pieces are then dried and deep-fried to a golden, crispy brown.

Combine the marinade ingredients in a bowl. Next, rub the marinade mixture all over the chicken pieces and let them sit in a cool place for 1 hour or more.

Set up a steamer or put a rack into a wok or large deep pan and fill it with 2 inches of water. Bring the water to a boil. Arrange the chicken pieces on a deep heatproof plate with the breast pieces on the bottom and the joints on the top, and then gently lower the plate into the steamer or onto the rack. Cover the pan tightly and lower the heat. Gently steam the chicken for at least 1 hour. Top up the water level from time to time.

Remove the cooked chicken and let it cool and dry completely. The skin should become taut. This may take 1 hour or more. (The dish can be made a day ahead up to this point.)

Heat the oil in a deep-fat fryer or large wok until it is hot. Deep-fry the pieces of dried, steamed chicken, a few pieces at a time, until the skin is golden brown and heated right through. Drain the pieces on paper towels. Serve the chicken hot, with one of the dipping sauces on pages 28 to 30.

Region: eastern
**Method: steaming and deep-
    frying**

Serves 4 to 6
    1½ pounds chicken pieces, with the
        skin on
    2⅓ cups oil, preferably peanut (see
        Deep-fat fryers, page 35)

Marinade
    1 tablespoon rice wine or dry sherry
    1 tablespoon light soy sauce
    1 tablespoon finely chopped
        scallions
    1 teaspoon finely chopped ginger
        root
    1 teaspoon ground roasted Sichuan
        peppercorns (page 26), or
        1 teaspoon freshly ground black
        peppercorns
    2 teaspoons sugar
    ½ teaspoon salt

Crispy Chicken Dumplings

Region: northern
**Method: steaming and shallow-
    frying**

Serves 3 to 4
    *½ pound boneless chicken breasts,
        skinned*
    2 egg whites
    2 teaspoons cornstarch
    2 teaspoons rice wine or dry sherry
    *1 teaspoon finely chopped ginger
        root*
    2 teaspoons finely chopped scallions
    1 teaspoon salt
    1 cup oil, preferably peanut
    ¼ cup cornstarch, for dusting

Sauce
    *1 tablespoon Chinese white rice
        vinegar or cider vinegar*
    2 teaspoons finely chopped garlic
    1 tablespoon dark soy sauce
    *1 teaspoon Chili Oil (page 29)
        (optional)*

These doughless dumplings are similar to French chicken quenelles and are usually eaten as part of a meal and not as a snack. Instead of being poached, the chicken paste mixture is steamed, which cooks it and keeps it moist at the same time. Then it is cut into dumplings which are shallow-fried to give them a crisp exterior. A spicy cold garlic and vinegar sauce is then poured over the chicken. Although two techniques are involved here, the first step (the steaming) can be done up to a day in advance.

Chop and then blend the chicken with the egg whites, cornstarch, rice wine or sherry, ginger, scallions and salt in a blender or food processor until you have a fine paste. Alternatively, you could chop the chicken with a sharp knife or cleaver until it is very fine and then incorporate it with the other ingredients in a bowl.

Rub 1 tablespoon of the oil on a deep heatproof plate (this is to keep the mixture from sticking) and put the chicken mixture on it. Set up a steamer or put a rack into a wok or deep pan and pour in 2 inches of water. Bring the water to a boil and then set the plate of chicken mixture into the steamer or onto the rack. Cover it with a lid and steam gently for about 15 minutes or until the chicken is firm and cooked. Remove the chicken and let it cool.

Divide the chicken mixture into bite-size pieces and dust them lightly with the cornstarch. Mix the sauce ingredients together and set them aside.

Heat the oil in a pot, wok or deep skillet until it is hot, and then fry the chicken pieces for 2 minutes or until they are golden brown. Drain them on paper towels. (You may have to do this in two batches.) Arrange the chicken pieces on a warm serving platter, pour the sauce over the top and serve.

Crispy Chicken

Region: southern
**Method: simmering and deep-
    frying**

Serves 6
    *1 whole chicken (about 2½ pounds)
        cut in half lengthwise*
    *4 cups oil (see Deep-fat fryers, page
        35)*

Simmering sauce
    4⅔ cups water
    *1 piece Chinese cinnamon bark or
        cinnamon stick*
    1 cup dark soy sauce
    1 whole star anise (optional)

This is one of my favorite chicken dishes. I remember eating it at family gatherings on special occasions. Although it is usually served in restaurants, it can easily be made at home. Some of the ingredients may be difficult to obtain, but it is worth the effort to achieve the authentic taste of the dish. It also requires a bit of patience, but much of the work can be done the day before.

Combine all the ingredients for the simmering sauce in a large casserole or pot and bring the mixture to a boil. Then turn the heat down to a simmer. Lower in the chicken halves and simmer them, uncovered, for 30 to 40 minutes. Remove the chicken halves and let them cool on a rack for at least 3 hours. The skin of the chicken should be completely dried.

(continued)

In a pan or wok, heat the glaze ingredients to the boiling point. Next, baste the skins of the dried chicken halves with this glaze. Let the chicken dry again for another 2 hours, keeping it in a very cool and airy place but not in the refrigerator. The dish can be prepared up to this point the day before you want to serve it.

Heat the oil in a deep-fat fryer or large wok, and lower in one of the chicken halves, skin-side down. Deep-fry it until it is a rich, dark brown color and very crisp. Remove it and deep-fry the other half. Cut the meat into bite-size pieces, arrange on a warm platter and garnish. Serve with Roasted Salt and Pepper.

1½ teaspoons whole Sichuan peppercorns, roasted (page 26) (optional)
1 tablespoon soaked and finely chopped dried citrus peel (page 19) or finely chopped fresh orange peel
2 slices ginger root
2 scallions
½ ounce Chinese rock sugar, or 2 tablespoons granulated

Glaze
2½ tablespoons honey
1⅓ cups water
2 tablespoons Chinese white rice vinegar or cider vinegar

Garnish
1 lemon, cut in wedges
Roasted Salt and Pepper (page 31)

Crispy Chicken.

Chinese Chicken Salad

Region: western
Method: steaming

Serves 6
  1 whole chicken, uncooked, or
    1 plain roasted chicken (about
    2½ pounds)
  8 ounces fresh bean sprouts (about
    2 cups)
  2 medium cucumbers
  1 to 2 carrots

Dressing
  3 tablespoons sesame paste or
    peanut butter
  2 tablespoons finely chopped
    scallions
  2 teaspoons sesame oil
  2 tablespoons Chinese white rice
    vinegar or cider vinegar
  3 tablespoons light soy sauce
  1½ tablespoons finely chopped
    garlic
  1 teaspoon salt
  2 teaspoons sugar
  ⅔ cup Chicken Stock (page 60)
  1 tablespoon rice wine or dry sherry

I have often enjoyed serving this salad either as a first course or as a main course for dinner on a warm summer night. It has been a success at picnics too. It is easy to prepare and is served with a tasty dressing.

If you are using uncooked chicken, cut it into about 8 pieces and put them on a large heatproof plate. Set up a steamer, or put a rack into a wok or deep pan, and pour in about 2 inches of water. Bring the water to a simmer and then lower the plate of chicken into the steamer or onto the rack. Cover it with a lid and let the chicken steam for about 1 hour. Test it with a skewer to see if the juices run clear. If they are still pink, continue to steam until the juices are clear and the chicken is just cooked.

Next prepare the vegetables. Trim the bean sprouts at both ends. Peel the cucumber, split it in half lengthwise and remove the seeds with a teaspoon. Finely shred the cucumber into 3-inch lengths. Peel and finely shred the carrots into 3-inch lengths. Set the vegetables aside.

Take all the meat off the cooked chicken and shred it into fine strips using a sharp knife or cleaver. Arrange the chicken strips on a platter and surround them with the bean sprouts, cucumbers and carrots. Combine all the ingredients for the dressing and mix them thoroughly. (I find an electric blender is useful for this but you could use a screw-top jar and shake everything in it well.) Pour the dressing all over the chicken and vegetables and mix well. Serve at once.

Clockwise from bottom: Stir-fried Pork with Scallions (page 73), Stir-fried Spinach with Garlic (page 151), Fruit Compote (page 184), Chinese Chicken Salad (page 108), Sesame Shrimp Toast (page 179).

Crispy Sichuan Duck

Region: western
Method: steaming and deep-frying

Serves 4 to 6
1 whole duck (4 to 5 pounds)
2 tablespoons five-spice powder
2 tablespoons salt
4 slices ginger root
4 scallions
5 cups oil, preferably peanut (see Deep-fat fryers, page 35)

In my family, duck was a treat reserved for special occasions and family banquets. I always remembered such feasts long afterward. This duck recipe is one of my favorites. Don't be intimidated by the long preparation process. Most of the steps are quite simple and can be done up to a day ahead, and the results are well worth the labor. The technique of steaming renders out most of the fat, leaving the duck meat moist and succulent. The final deep-frying gives the duck skin a crispy texture. This is a dish for a special dinner party and should be served with Steamed Buns (page 172) and Roasted Salt and Pepper (page 31).

If the duck is frozen, thaw it thoroughly. Blot it with paper towels until it is thoroughly dry, then rub it inside and out with the five-spice powder and salt. Make sure these are rubbed on evenly. Wrap well in plastic wrap and chill in the refrigerator for at least 3 hours, preferably longer.

Cut the ginger into long ¼-inch strips. Slice the scallions into 3-inch lengths. Stuff the ginger and scallions into the cavity of the duck, and put on a heatproof china or glass plate.

Set up a steamer or put a rack into a wok or deep pan. Pour about 2 inches of water into the pan and bring to a boil. Put the plate with the duck into the steamer or onto the rack, cover it with a lid and steam gently for about 2 hours. Replenish the water from time to time to keep the steam constant. Remove the duck and pour off all the fat and liquid which may have accumulated. Discard the ginger and scallions. Keep the duck on a platter in a cool dry place for about 2 hours, until it has thoroughly dried and cooled. At this point the duck can be refrigerated.

Just before you are ready to serve it, cut the duck into quarters. Heat the oil in a deep-fat fryer or wok. When the oil is almost smoking, deep-fry the duck quarters in 2 batches until each is crisp and warmed right through. Drain the quarters on paper towels and then chop them into smaller serving pieces.

To eat Crispy Sichuan Duck, dip a piece of duck meat in the Roasted Salt and Pepper mixture and then put the meat into a split Steamed Bun and eat it rather like a sandwich.

Fried Chicken Livers in Ginger

Region: eastern
Method: shallow-frying and stir-frying

Serves 4
½ pound fresh chicken livers
¼ cup all-purpose flour, for dusting
⅔ cup oil, preferably peanut

Marinade
¼ teaspoon salt
2 teaspoons finely chopped garlic
1 teaspoon finely chopped ginger root

Chicken livers are extremely tasty when they are cooked properly and not overdone. In this recipe, the livers are marinated briefly, coated with flour and shallow-fried before being finally stir-fried in a delicious sauce. Although this process is a little elaborate, the delectable taste and velvety texture of the dish make it all worthwhile. It is surprisingly good when served cold and is perfect for picnics.

Clean the livers and discard any connecting membranes. Dry them well on paper towels. Combine the marinade ingredients with the chicken livers and let the livers marinate for 30 minutes or more.

Drain the livers in a colander and discard the marinade. Dry them with paper towels and lightly dust with the flour. Heat the ⅔ cup oil in a deep skillet or large wok until it is hot. Fry small batches of the livers at a time

(continued)

until they are crisp and brown. (Each batch should take about 2 to 3 minutes to reach this point.) Drain the cooked livers on paper towels.

Transfer about 1 tablespoon of the oil in which you have cooked the livers to a clean wok or skillet. Fry the ginger for a few seconds and then add the other sauce ingredients and bring the sauce to a simmer. Return the livers to the pan and quickly stir-fry them in this sauce for about 4 minutes, until they are thoroughly coated and are firm to the touch. Serve immediately, or if you prefer, let them cool and put them in the refrigerator. They are delicious cold and make a wonderful addition to a cold meat platter.

1 tablespoon finely chopped
　　scallions
½ teaspoon sugar
½ teaspoon sesame oil

Sauce
1½ teaspoons finely chopped
　　ginger root
1½ teaspoons light soy sauce
1 teaspoon dry sherry or rice wine
1 teaspoon Chinese white rice
　　vinegar or cider vinegar
½ teaspoon sugar
1 teaspoon sesame oil

Crispy Sichuan Duck (facing page).

The Chinese have a special reverence for duck, regarding it as a symbol of whole-someness and fidelity. Of course its delectability is its chief virtue. With Peking Duck, Chinese cooks mastered the art of making the most of the duck's rich, succulent flesh while minimizing its major flaw—its relatively large proportion of bone and fat. There is little doubt that this spectacular dish was first concocted in the Imperial kitchens. Its popularity spread as restaurants, staffed by former Imperial chefs, made it a specialty to be served at banquets. The dish can now be found in all parts of China.

The preparation and cooking of Peking Duck in China is an art form. Specially raised ducklings are fed a rich diet of corn, sorghum, barley and soybeans for 1½ months before they are ready for the kitchen. After a duck is killed and cleaned, air is pumped through the bird to separate the skin from the meat. (This allows the skin to roast separately and remain crisp while the fat melts, keeping the meat moist.) Hot water is then poured over the duck to close the skin pores and it is hung up to dry. During the drying process a solution of malt sugar is liberally brushed over the duck, which is then roasted in wood-burning ovens. The result is a shiny, crisp and aromatic duck with beautiful brown skin, moist flesh and no fat.

Preparing Peking Duck is a time-consuming task, but I have devised a simpler method which closely approximates the real thing. Just give yourself plenty of time and the results will be good enough for an emperor. Traditionally Peking Duck is served with Chinese Pancakes, scallions cut into brush shapes and sweet bean sauce. In Hong Kong and in the West hoisin sauce is used instead. It is very similar to sweet bean sauce but contains vinegar. Each guest spoons some sauce onto a pancake. Then a helping of crisp skin and meat is placed on top with a scallion brush and the entire mixture is rolled up like a stuffed pancake. It can be eaten using chopsticks or one's fingers. This makes an unforgettable dish for a very special dinner party.

If the duck is frozen, thaw it thoroughly. Rinse the duck well and blot it completely dry with paper towels. Insert a meat hook near the neck.

Using a sharp knife, cut the lemon into ¼-inch slices, leaving the rind on. Combine the lemon slices with the rest of the honey syrup ingredients in a large pot and bring the mixture to a boil. Turn the heat to low and simmer for about 20 minutes. Using a large ladle or spoon, pour this mixture over the duck several times, as if to bathe it, until all the skin of the duck is completely coated with the mixture. Hang the duck in a cool, well-ventilated place to dry for 4 to 5 hours, or hang it in front of a cold fan for about 3 hours—in either case, the longer the better. (Be sure to put a tray or roasting pan underneath to catch any drips.) Once the duck has dried, the surface of the skin will feel like parchment.

Preheat the oven to 475°F. Meanwhile, place the duck on a rack in a roasting pan, breast side up. Put ⅔ cup of water into the roasting pan. (This will prevent the fat from splattering.) Now put the duck into the oven and roast it for 15 minutes. Then turn the heat down to 350°F and continue to roast for 1 hour and 10 minutes.

Remove the duck from the oven and let it sit for at least 10 minutes before you carve it. Using a cleaver or a sharp knife, cut the skin and meat into pieces and arrange them on a warm platter. Serve at once with Chinese Pancakes, scallion brushes and a bowl of hoisin sauce.

Region: northern
Method: blanching and roasting

Serves 4 to 6
1 whole duck, fresh or frozen (4 to 5 pounds)

Honey syrup mixture
1 lemon
4 cups water
3 tablespoons honey
3 tablespoons dark soy sauce
⅔ cup rice wine or dry sherry

To serve
8 to 12 Chinese Pancakes (page 173)
4 to 6 tablespoons hoisin sauce
16 to 24 scallion brushes (page 46)

A Chinese banquet of Peking Duck (this page) with Chinese Pancakes (page 173), Braised Pork with Bean Curd (page 77), and Snow Peas with Water Chestnuts (page 153), accompanied by Corn Soup with Crabmeat (page 61), fresh fruit and Caramel Walnuts (page 183).

Braised Duck

Region: southern
Method: shallow-frying and
braising

Serves 4 to 6
1 whole duck (about 4 pounds)
1⅓ cups oil, preferably peanut

Sauce
5 cups Chicken Stock (page 60) or
water
5 cups dark soy sauce
1⅓ cups light soy sauce
2 cups rice wine, or 1 cup dry
sherry mixed with 1 cup Chicken
Stock
4 ounces Chinese rock sugar, or
¼ cup granulated
3 whole star anise (optional)
3 pieces Chinese cinnamon bark or
cinnamon sticks

Garnish
fresh coriander sprigs (optional)

The braising sauce used for this duck recipe is the same as for the Soy Sauce Chicken (page 105). The sauce can be frozen and reused. Unlike chicken, duck needs long braising to cook it thoroughly and to render out the fat in the skin. You can see this braised duck in food shops in Hong Kong (and in the US), hanging picturesquely from hooks. It is easy to make at home and reheats well, although I think it is best served at room temperature. It would go well with Hot Bean Thread Noodles (page 169) and Lettuce with Oyster Sauce (page 152).

Cut the duck into quarters. Dry these thoroughly with paper towels. Heat the oil in a wok or large skillet until it is almost smoking, and then shallow-fry 2 pieces of the duck, skin-side down. Turn the heat down and continue to fry slowly until the skin is browned. This should take about 15 to 20 minutes. Do not turn the pieces over, but baste the duck as it fries. Drain the cooked duck on paper towels. Shallow-fry the rest of the duck in the same way.

Combine all the sauce ingredients in a large pot and bring the mixture to a boil. Add the duck pieces and turn the heat down to a simmer. Cover the pot and slowly braise the duck for 1 hour, or until it is tender.

Skim off the large amount of surface fat which will be left when the duck is cooked. (This will prevent the duck from becoming greasy.) Now remove the duck pieces with a slotted spoon. Let them cool and then chop them into smaller pieces. Arrange on a warm platter, garnish with the fresh coriander and serve at once. Or you can let the duck cool thoroughly and serve it at room temperature. Once the sauce has cooled, remove any lingering surface fat. Now the sauce can be frozen and reused to braise duck or chicken.

Deep-fried Squabs (facing page).

On Sundays in Hong Kong one of the most popular outings is to Shatin, a town in the New Territories, to play the famous Chinese game Mahjong and to eat squabs. Squabs have a rich, gamy taste. The southern Chinese like to braise them quickly, let them dry and then deep-fry them just before serving. The result is a moist, highly flavored squab with crisp skin. The secret to this dish lies in the braising liquid, which is used over and over again. In some restaurants it is used for years, like a vintage stock.

This dish takes time and patience, but it is not difficult to make and much of the work can be done several hours in advance. It is an impressive dish for any special dinner party. Serve it with rice, Braised Spicy Eggplant (page 143) and Roasted Salt and Pepper (page 31).

Bring a large pot of water to a boil. Blanch the squabs in the boiling water for about 2 minutes. (This helps to rid them of impurities and tightens the skin.) Remove the squabs from the pot and discard the water.

Combine all the braising sauce ingredients in a large pot and bring it to a boil. Add the squabs. Lower the heat to a simmer and cover the pot tightly. Let it simmer for about 35 minutes, until the squabs are just tender. Remove them with a slotted spoon and let them dry on a plate, or hang them up in a cool, dry, airy place, for at least 2 hours. The braising liquid, once cooled, can be stored in a plastic container and frozen for future use.

After 2 hours the skin of the squabs should feel like parchment paper. Just before you are ready to serve them, heat the oil in a deep-fat fryer or large wok. When it is hot, lower in the squabs and deep-fry them until they are crisp and deep brown in color. Turn them over frequently with a slotted spoon so that all sides are thoroughly cooked and browned. This should take about 10 minutes. Drain the cooked squabs on paper towels and let them cool for a few minutes. Using a heavy cleaver or knife, chop them into 4 to 6 pieces and arrange on a warm serving platter. Serve at once.

Region: southern
Method: braising and deep-frying

Serves 2 to 4
2 squabs, 8 to 12 ounces each
2 large slices ginger root
3½ cups oil, preferably peanut (see Deep-fat fryers, page 35)

Braising sauce
4 cups Chicken Stock (page 60)
2 tablespoons dark soy sauce
2 tablespoons light soy sauce
⅔ cup rice wine or dry sherry
2 tablespoons honey
1 teaspoon salt
2 pieces soaked and finely chopped dried citrus peel (page 19) or finely chopped fresh orange peel
1 piece Chinese cinnamon bark or cinnamon stick
1 star anise (optional)
½ teaspoon ground white pepper
1 teaspoon sesame oil

Barbecued Quails

Region: southern
Method: roasting

Serves 4
6 quails, about 4 ounces each
1 tablespoon salt

Sauce
3 tablespoons hoisin sauce
1 tablespoon rice wine or dry sherry
1 tablespoon light soy sauce

I enjoy being in southern China or Hong Kong in autumn because this is the season for rice birds. These very small birds are caught with nets in the rice fields and then simply barbecued on skewers with a zesty sauce. Unable to find rice birds in Europe or America, I discovered an excellent alternative—quails. They are easy and quick to prepare, and as they are also delicious cold they make a wonderful dish for a picnic. If you are serving them hot, Braised Spicy Eggplant (page 143) is an excellent accompaniment.

Preheat the oven to 475°F.

If the quails are frozen, make sure you thaw them thoroughly. Dry them well with paper towels and then rub each one inside and out with a little salt.

Mix the sauce ingredients in a small bowl. Rub each of the quails inside and out with this sauce. Put the quails on a rack in a small roasting pan and put them into the oven for 5 minutes. Then turn the heat down to 350°F and continue to roast the birds for another 15 minutes. Turn off the oven and leave them there for another 5 minutes. Take them out of the oven and let them rest for another 10 minutes before serving.

Serve the quails whole, or if you wish to serve them Chinese-style, use a cleaver or heavy knife and chop each of them into 4 to 6 pieces. Arrange on a warm platter and serve.

Five-Spice Red Braised Squabs

Region: eastern
Method: blanching and braising

Serves 2 to 4
4 squabs, about 8 ounces each

Sauce
2 cups dark soy sauce
2/3 cup light soy sauce
2 tablespoons five-spice powder
2/3 cup rice wine or dry sherry
2 ounces Chinese rock sugar, or
    2 tablespoons granulated

Garnish
2 tablespoons finely chopped
    scallions
1 tablespoon finely chopped ginger
    root

(pictured on page 13)

In this recipe, the five-spice powder gives the squabs a delicious flavor, while the soy braising sauce endows them with a rich brown color. Chinese cooks often blanch squabs before braising them to rid them of any impurities. Braising is a good technique to use as it keeps the squabs moist. If you prefer you can substitute quails or other small game birds. This dish is excellent served cold and is perfect for an exotic picnic.

Blanch the squabs by immersing them in a large pot of boiling water for about 5 minutes. Remove them with a slotted spoon and discard the water.

Combine the sauce ingredients in a medium-size pot and bring to a boil. Turn the heat down to a simmer and then add the squabs. Cover the pot and braise the birds over low heat for about 45 minutes, or until they are tender. Then remove them with a slotted spoon and let them cool. (The braising sauce may be saved and frozen for the next time you cook this dish.) Chop the squabs into bite-size pieces and arrange them on a warm serving platter. Sprinkle the garnish ingredients on top and serve at once. If you want to serve the dish cold, let the pieces cool and then sprinkle them with the garnish ingredients. Refrigerate them, well wrapped in plastic wrap, until you are ready to serve them.

Quails are popular in southern China because of their excellent flavor and their suitability for stir-frying. This technique seals in the taste and juices of the game-birds and precludes overcooking. The bamboo shoots and water chestnuts provide a crunchy texture which complements the tenderness of the quail meat.

This recipe is an adaptation of a banquet dish from the Lee Gardens Rainbow Room Restaurant in Hong Kong. There, just the breast of quails are served, an extravagance possible in a high-class restaurant staffed by expert chefs. I have found that this dish works equally well without the tedious job of boning these small birds. The robust flavors and rich colors of the dish make it a perfect main course for a dinner party. Serve it with the Corn Soup with Crabmeat (page 61) and rice.

If the quails are frozen, thaw them thoroughly. Dry them inside and out with paper towels. Then, using a cleaver or heavy sharp knife, cut each quail into about 6 pieces. Put the pieces into a bowl with the marinade ingredients, mix them well and let them steep for about 20 minutes.

Next prepare the vegetables. If you are using fresh water chestnuts, peel and slice them. If you are using canned water chestnuts, rinse them thoroughly in cold water before slicing them. Rinse the bamboo shoots in cold water and slice these too. Cut the scallions at a slight diagonal into 3-inch segments.

Heat a wok or large skillet over high heat. Remove half the quail pieces from the marinade, using a slotted spoon. Add half the peanut oil to the wok and, when it is smoking slightly, stir-fry the quail pieces for about 5 minutes or until they are brown. Transfer them to a colander or sieve to drain and discard the cooking oil. Reheat the wok and stir-fry the rest of the pieces in the same manner, using the other half of the peanut oil. Again, drain the quail in a colander or sieve, but leave about 1 tablespoon of oil in the pan.

Reheat the pan over high heat. Add the scallions, fresh water chestnuts if you are using them and bamboo shoots, and stir-fry them for about 2 minutes. Then add the rest of the ingredients and bring the mixture to a boil. Return the quails to the pan and cook for about 3 minutes. Make sure you coat all the quail pieces thoroughly with the sauce. If you are using canned water chestnuts add these now and cook for 2 more minutes. Serve at once.

Region: southern
Method: stir-frying

Serves 4 to 6

6 quails, about 4 ounces each
12 fresh water chestnuts, or
   1 8-ounce can, drained
8 ounces canned bamboo shoots
6 scallions
⅔ cup oil, preferably peanut
1⅓ cups Chicken Stock (page 60)
2 tablespoons oyster sauce
2 teaspoons sugar
2 teaspoons cornstarch mixed with
   2 teaspoons water

Marinade

2 tablespoons rice wine or dry
   sherry
2 tablespoons light soy sauce
1 tablespoon cornstarch
2 teaspoons sesame oil

*Fresh seafood from Monterey Fish Market
in Berkeley, California.*

FISH AND SHELLFISH

海鮮

Of the many remarkable and fortunate food experiences I had growing up as a young Chinese I count the extensive consumption of fresh seafood as among the most pleasurable. In my family, fish and shellfish were regarded with special affection, whether as part of a simple family dinner or a large banquet. The first question always asked about fish, however, was "How fresh is it?" From this early childhood experience I learned, as do all Chinese, to value good fresh seafood.

Fish and shellfish are a major feature of Chinese cookery. China's long coastline gives it access to numerous saltwater varieties and its many rivers, lakes, streams and canals teem with freshwater fish and shellfish all year round. It is estimated that several hundred species of seafood are used in Chinese cookery. Most are caught wild but a few species, such as carp, are raised on special fish farms. We Chinese prefer that no more than a few hours elapse between the catching and cooking of fish. Indeed, in many markets in Hong Kong fish is sold live. You can select the fish of your choice while it swims around in a special glass tank, and then take it straight home or to a restaurant to be cooked. The accent is always on freshness.

There are many cooking techniques which the Chinese use to ensure that the flesh of the fish or shellfish retains its natural juices and flavor. Steaming is a favorite method. Many Chinese chefs consider this to be the ideal way of cooking fish. It allows the fragrance and natural flavors of the fish to develop, while at the same time preserving the delicate texture, moistness and shape of the fish. Quick-braising is another popular method, and deep-frying and shallow-frying are also often used.

The Chinese prefer to cook fish whole, although fish fillets and steaks can be satisfactorily used instead. We believe that the flesh remains moist and the flavor is best when the whole fish is used, head and tail included. To serve a fish whole is also a symbol of prosperity. The head of the fish should always point in the direction of the guest of honor, a courtesy that assures him or her good fortune.

Shellfish is especially important in Chinese cuisine. Shrimp, oysters, scallops, crab, lobster, squid and abalone are just some of the most popular varieties. Because shellfish is so delicate it requires a minimum amount of handling and the simplest preparation. The most common techniques used are stir-frying, steaming, deep-frying and braising. Recipes for shellfish are usually interchangeable; what works for prawns will work just as well for crab, lobster or scallops.

When fresh seafood is not available, Chinese cooks make imaginative use of dried seafood as the main ingredient or as a flavoring in soups, stir-fried dishes, braised dishes and stuffings. Drying concentrates the flavors of the seafood as well as preserving it.

The Chinese try to complement the delicate flavor, texture and color of fish and shellfish with contrasting flavorings and textures. For example, in the dish Sweet and Sour Shrimp, the subtle taste and crisp texture of the shrimp contrast nicely with the tasty spiciness of the sauce. Most Chinese recipes call for fresh, uncooked shrimp. If you can't find fresh shrimp, look for good-quality frozen (uncooked) shrimp. Crabs can sometimes still be bought live, or at least freshly cooked. Instructions for dealing with live crab and crab cooked in the shell are given on page 136.

There is a wide variety of fish to choose from. Cod and halibut are available everywhere and are perfect for deep-frying, stir-frying or braising. Other good choices are red snapper, sea bass, and rockfish. Dover sole, lemon sole and flounder are ideal for steaming. Oily fish such as red mullet, carp and eel are best braised, and trout should be shallow-fried. Get to know your fish dealer and be assertive in asking for the freshest fish and shellfish. Fresh fish should be firm, have clear eyes, bright gills and a shiny sheen to the skin. Shellfish should be firm and not smell fishy. Learn to be as finicky about selecting fish and shellfish as the Chinese are. It will open up a whole new world of flavor for you.

Ken selects only the freshest fish at Monterey Fish, Berkeley.

Fried Fish with Ginger

Ginger goes very well with fish. It is used rather as lemon is in Western fish cookery. In this easy dish it imparts a subtle fragrance to the fish. This goes well with Braised Spicy Eggplant (page 143) and Garlic Chicken with Cucumber (page 97).

Sprinkle the fish filets evenly on both sides with the salt. Cut the fish into strips 1 inch wide and let these sit for 20 minutes. Then dust them with the cornstarch.

Heat the oil in a wok or large skillet. When it is hot, add the ginger and, a few seconds later, the fish. Shallow-fry the fish strips until they are crisp and brown. Remove them with a slotted spoon and drain on paper towels.

Pour off all the oil and discard it. Wipe the wok clean and then add to it the rest of the ingredients. Bring them to a boil and then return the fish slices to the pan and coat them with the sauce. Turn the fish gently in the sauce for 1 minute, taking care not to break up the slices. Remove to a platter and serve at once.

Region: eastern
Method: shallow-frying

Serves 4
½ pound fish filets, such as cod, rockfish, or red snapper
¼ teaspoon salt
1½ tablespoons cornstarch
⅓ cup oil, preferably peanut
1½ tablespoons finely shredded ginger root
1 tablespoon Chicken Stock (page 60) or water
½ teaspoon salt
1 tablespoon rice wine or dry sherry
1 teaspoon sugar

(pictured on page 65)

Fish in Hot Sauce

I like to make this quick and easy dish when I am in the mood for fish. A firm, white fish such as cod or haddock is most suitable for shallow-frying because it is meaty and holds its shape during the cooking process. (Carp would be used in China for this recipe.) Serve with plain rice and any stir-fried vegetable.

Cut the fish filets into evenly sized slices about 2 inches wide. Sprinkle them with the salt and then with the cornstarch. Cut the scallions into 2-inch diagonal slices.

Heat a wok or large skillet until it is hot. Add the oil and heat it until it is almost smoking. Fry the filets on both sides until they are brown. (This should take about 5 minutes.) Then remove and drain the fish on paper towels. Pour off most of the oil, leaving about 1 tablespoon in the pan.

Reheat the wok and then add the scallions, garlic and ginger. Stir-fry them for 30 seconds. Then add the sauce ingredients and bring the mixture to a boil. Turn the heat down to a simmer and return the fish to the pan. Simmer for about 2 minutes, then turn the fish and sauce onto a platter and serve.

Region: western
Method: shallow-frying

Serves 4
¾ pound fresh fish filets, such as cod, rockfish, or sea bass
½ teaspoon salt
1 to 1½ tablespoons cornstarch
2 scallions
⅓ cup oil, preferably peanut
2 teaspoons finely chopped garlic
1 teaspoon finely chopped ginger root

Sauce
⅓ cup Chicken Stock (page 60)
2 teaspoons bean sauce
½ teaspoon chili bean sauce or chili powder
1 tablespoon rice wine or dry sherry
2 teaspoons light soy sauce
1 teaspoon sesame oil

Fish in Hot and Sour Sauce

Region: western
Method: shallow-frying

Serves 4
¾ pound fish filets, preferably
    flounder
⅓ cup oil, preferably peanut

Hot & Sour Sauce
⅓ cup Chicken Stock (page 60)
1 tablespoon rice wine or dry sherry
1 tablespoon dark soy sauce
2 teaspoons tomato paste
½ teaspoon chili bean sauce or chili
    powder
½ teaspoon ground white pepper
1 tablespoon Chinese black rice
    vinegar or cider vinegar
1 teaspoon sugar

Garnish
1 tablespoon finely chopped
    scallions

The combination of hot and sour is a popular one in western China. This is a quick and simple dish which is perfect for a light family meal. Stir-fried Spinach with Garlic (page 151) is a suitable accompaniment.

Have your fish dealer remove the dark skin of the flounder or else remove it yourself using a small, sharp knife. Cut the fish filets, across the width and at a slight diagonal, into 1-inch-wide strips.

Heat a wok or large skillet until it is quite hot. Add the oil and heat it until it is almost smoking. Fry the fish strips for 2 to 3 minutes, until they are golden brown. You may have to do this in several batches. Drain the cooked fish strips on paper towels.

Pour off all the oil, wipe the wok clean and reheat it. Add all the hot and sour sauce ingredients. Bring the sauce to a boil, then lower the heat to a simmer. Add the fried fish strips and simmer them in the sauce for 2 minutes. Serve garnished with the scallions.

Fish in Hot and Sour Sauce.

Stir-fried Fish with Peas

This dish is often made in southern China with grouper, a firm, white, fleshy fish. It works equally well with cod filets. It is important to use a firm-textured fish which will not fall apart during the stir-frying process. Serve it with Deep-fried Green Beans (page 143) and Ham and Zucchini Soup (page 64).

Cut the fish filets into strips 1 inch wide and sprinkle the salt evenly over them. Let them sit for 20 minutes. Cook the peas for 5 minutes in a saucepan of boiling water and then drain them in a colander.

Heat a wok or large skillet and, when it is hot, add the oil. Let the oil heat up and then add the fish strips. Stir-fry these gently, taking care not to break them up. Cook the strips for about 2 minutes, and then add the ham, peas and all the sauce ingredients except the cornstarch mixture. Bring the sauce to a boil, add the cornstarch mixture and stir this in well. Cook for another minute and then serve at once.

Region: southern
Method: stir-frying and braising

Serves 4
- ¾ pound fresh fish filets, cod or other firm white fish
- 1 teaspoon salt
- 2 ounces fresh or frozen peas (¼ cup)
- 1 tablespoon oil
- 1 ounce Smithfield ham or prosciutto, shredded (about 3 tablespoons)

Sauce
- ⅓ cup Chicken Stock (page 60) or water
- 2 teaspoons rice wine or dry sherry
- 2 teaspoons light soy sauce
- ½ teaspoon salt
- 1 teaspoon sugar
- 1 teaspoon cornstarch, blended with 1 teaspoon water

Fried Fish with Garlic and Scallions

This eastern fish dish is simple to make and works especially well with flounder. In coastal areas of China saltwater fish similar to a type of red snapper would be used for this recipe. In this dish the wine, egg and spicy sauce nicely complement the taste and texture of the fish, but do be careful not to overcook it. Serve this with rice and a simple stir-fried vegetable such as Chinese Cabbage in Soy Sauce (page 148).

Have your fish dealer remove the dark skin of the flounder or else remove it yourself with a small, sharp knife. Cut the fish filets into 1-inch strips. Sprinkle the strips with salt and let them sit for 15 minutes. Beat the egg in a small bowl. Dip the pieces of fish into the cornstarch and then into the beaten egg.

Heat the oil in a wok or large skillet until it is hot. Shallow-fry the fish pieces on each side, in several batches, until they are golden brown. Drain them on paper towels. Pour off the oil and discard it. Wipe the wok clean and add the rest of the ingredients. Simmer for 2 minutes. Put the fried fish filets on a warm serving platter and pour the hot sauce over. Serve at once.

Region: eastern
Method: shallow-frying

Serves 4
- ¾ pound flounder filets
- ½ teaspoon salt
- 1 egg
- ¼ cup cornstarch
- ⅓ cup oil, preferably peanut
- 1 tablespoon finely chopped garlic
- 1½ tablespoons finely chopped scallions
- 1 tablespoon rice wine or dry sherry
- ½ teaspoon salt
- 1 teaspoon sesame oil

Fish Balls with Broccoli

Region: eastern
Method: poaching and stir-frying

Serves 4 to 6
 1 pound fish filets, preferably cod
 1 egg white
 1 teaspoon salt
 2 teaspoons cornstarch
 2 teaspoons sesame oil
 1 pound broccoli
 1½ tablespoons oil, preferably
   peanut
 2 tablespoons finely shredded
   ginger root
 2 ounces Smithfield ham or
   prosciutto, finely shredded
   (about ¼ cup)
 1 tablespoon light soy sauce
 2 tablespoons rice wine or dry
   sherry
 1⅓ cups Chicken Stock (page 60)
 2 teaspoons cornstarch, blended
   with 2 teaspoons water

We often made this dish in our family restaurant, but usually just for the Chinese customers. My uncle thought his non-Chinese diners would not enjoy it. I remember how laborious it was, mincing the fish until it was smooth and like a paste. Now, thanks to modern kitchen equipment, this dish can be easily prepared at home in minutes. And I eventually discovered how much my European friends love it! Serve this with plain steamed rice and Hot and Sour Soup (page 68).

Remove the skin from the fish filets and then cut them into small pieces about 1 inch square. Combine the fish, egg white, salt, cornstarch and sesame oil in a blender or food processor, and blend the mixture until you have a smooth paste.

Bring a large pot of water to the simmering point. Take spoonfuls of the fish paste and form the mixture into balls about 1 inch in diameter. Poach the fish balls in the boiling water until they float to the top. (This should take about 3 to 4 minutes.) Remove them with a slotted spoon and drain them on paper towels.

Divide the broccoli heads into small florets. Peel the skin off the stems (it is often fibrous and stringy), and then cut them into thin slices at a slight diagonal. This will ensure that the stems cook evenly with the florets. Bring a pot of water to a boil, add the broccoli florets and stems and cook for about 5 minutes. Then drain them, plunge into cold water, and drain again.

Heat a wok or large skillet. When it is hot, add the oil and heat it. Then add the broccoli, ginger, ham and soy sauce and stir-fry for 1 minute. Then add the rice wine or sherry, stock and the cornstarch mixture. Bring to a boil and then add the poached fish balls. Stir over high heat for 1 minute to mix, and then turn the mixture onto a serving platter. Serve at once.

Fish Balls with Broccoli (facing page).

Steamed Fish with Garlic

Steaming fish is a great southern Chinese tradition and it is my favorite method of cooking fish. Steaming brings out the purest flavors of the fish. Because it is such a gentle cooking technique, nothing masks the fresh taste of the fish, which also remains moist and tender. Ask your fish dealer for the freshest possible fish.

If you are using a whole fish, remove the gills. Pat the fish or fish filets dry with paper towels. Rub with the salt on both sides, and then set aside for 30 minutes. (This helps the flesh to firm up and draws out moisture.)

Set up a steamer or put a rack into a wok or deep pan. Fill it with about 2 inches of water. Bring the water to a boil, then reduce the heat to a low simmer. Put the fish on a plate and scatter the ginger evenly over the top. Put the plate of fish into the steamer or onto the rack. Cover the pan tightly and gently steam the fish until it is just cooked. Flat fish will take about 5 minutes to cook. Thicker fish or filets such as sea bass will take 15 minutes.

Remove the plate of cooked fish and sprinkle with the scallions and light soy sauce. Heat the two oils together in a small saucepan. When they are hot, add the garlic slices and brown them. Pour the garlic-oil mixture over the fish. Serve at once.

Region: southern
Method: steaming

Serves 4
  ¾ to 1 pound firm white fish filets, such as cod or sole, or a whole fish such as sole
  1 teaspoon kosher salt
  1 tablespoon finely chopped ginger root

Garnish
  2 tablespoons finely chopped scallions
  1 tablespoon light soy sauce
  1 tablespoon oil, preferably peanut
  1 teaspoon sesame oil
  2 garlic cloves, peeled and thinly sliced

(pictured on page 69)

Braised Fish

Region: eastern
Method: shallow-frying and braising

Serves 4 to 6

1 pound fish filets, preferably cod
  or halibut
1 teaspoon salt
⅔ cup oil, preferably peanut
10 ounces small shallots or pearl
  onions, peeled and left whole
1 tablespoon finely chopped ginger
  root
1 tablespoon light soy sauce
1 tablespoon dark soy sauce
2 teaspoons granulated sugar
2 tablespoons rice wine or dry
  sherry
⅔ cup Chicken Stock (page 60)

Onions in all forms are popular in Chinese cookery, but shallots are especially prized for their distinctive flavor. I think they complement fish beautifully. If you can't get shallots for this recipe you can use pearl onions instead. A firm, white fish such as cod, halibut or bass will work better than delicate ones such as flounder or sole. Plain steamed rice and a fresh green vegetable would go well with this dish.

Pat the fish filets dry with paper towels. Rub both sides with salt and then cut them into 1½-inch-wide diagonal strips. Set the fish aside for 20 minutes, then again pat dry with paper towels. The salt will have extracted some of the excess moisture from the fish.

Heat the oil in a wok or large skillet. Then brown the fish in two batches, draining each cooked batch on paper towels. Drain all but 1 tablespoon of oil from the pan and discard the rest.

Reheat the pan and add the shallots and ginger. Stir-fry them for 1 minute, and then add the rest of the ingredients. Bring this mixture to a boil, then turn the heat down to a simmer. Return the fish to the pan, cover it and braise the fish in the sauce for 2 to 3 minutes. Using a slotted spoon, gently remove the fish and shallots and arrange them on a warm platter. Then pour the sauce over the top and serve at once.

Sweet and Sour Fish (facing page).

A sweet and sour sauce is a perfect foil for fish. The sugar and vinegar in the sauce contrast well with the rich flavor of the fish. This Chinese dish is at its most impressive when a whole fish is used, but it can be just as successfully made with filets. The best fish to use are cod, haddock or sea bass. The sauce can be made in advance and reheated.

If you are using fish filets, select ones which are at least 1 inch or more thick, and remove the skin. If you are using a whole fish it should be cleaned and gutted, and the gills removed. Either leave the head on as the Chinese do or remove it if you prefer. Using a sharp knife or cleaver, make crisscross slashes across the top of the fish or each filet. Do not cut right through, but keep the fish or filets intact.

Next prepare the vegetables. Peel and shred the carrots. Blanch the carrots, peas and snow peas or pepper in a pot of boiling water for about 4 minutes each. Then plunge them into cold water and then drain them. Put all the blanched vegetables into a pot with all the sauce ingredients. Bring the mixture to a simmer and remove the pot from the heat.

Heat the oil in a deep-fat fryer or large wok until it is almost smoking. Coat the fish filets or whole fish well with cornstarch, shaking off any excess. Then deep-fry one of the filets (or whole fish) until it is crisp and brown. Do the same with the other filets. Drain on paper towels. Bring the sauce to a simmer. Arrange the fish filets or whole fish on a warm serving platter and pour the reheated sauce over the top. Serve at once.

Region: eastern
Method: deep-frying

Serves 4 to 6
   1 pound whole fish or fish filets, preferably cod, halibut or sea bass
   2 to 3 carrots
   4 ounces peas, fresh or frozen (½ cup)
   4 ounces snow peas, or 1 green bell pepper, diced
   5 cups oil, preferably peanut (see Deep-fat fryers, page 35)
   ¼ cup cornstarch

Sauce
   2 tablespoons finely chopped scallions
   1 tablespoon finely chopped ginger root
   1⅓ cups Chicken Stock (page 60)
   1 tablespoon light soy sauce
   2 tablespoons rice wine or dry sherry
   1½ tablespoons tomato paste
   2 tablespoons Chinese white rice vinegar or cider vinegar
   2 tablespoons sugar
   2 teaspoons cornstarch blended with 2 teaspoons water

Sichuan-style Scallops

Scallops are a favorite with the Chinese. We love them in two forms, fresh and dried. Stir-frying works especially well with scallops because if they are overcooked they become tough. Just five minutes' stir-frying, as in this recipe, is quite sufficient to cook them thoroughly without robbing them of their sweet flavor. They are particularly tasty prepared with this spicy Sichuan sauce. This dish goes well with plain rice and Ham and Bean Sprout Soup (page 63).

Heat a wok or large skillet until it is hot. Add the oil and let it get hot. Add the ginger and scallions and stir-fry quickly. Next add the scallops and stir-fry them for 30 seconds. Then add all the sauce ingredients except the sesame oil. Continue to stir-fry for 4 minutes, until the scallops are firm and thoroughly coated with the sauce. Now add the sesame oil and stir-fry for another minute. Serve at once.

Region: western
Method: stir-frying

Serves 4
   1 tablespoon oil, preferably peanut
   1 teaspoon finely chopped ginger root
   2 teaspoons finely chopped scallions
   ½ pound scallops including the corals

Sauce
   2 teaspoons rice wine or dry sherry
   2 teaspoons light soy sauce
   1 to 2 teaspoons chili bean sauce
   2 teaspoons tomato paste
   1 teaspoon sugar
   1 teaspoon sesame oil

Deep-fried Oysters

Region: southern
Method: deep-frying

Serves 4
 1 pint shucked oysters
 1 small egg
 1 tablespoon cornstarch
 2 teaspoons water
 1 teaspoon baking powder
 ½ teaspoon salt
 ½ teaspoon oil, preferably peanut
 ¼ cup toasted breadcrumbs
 2 cups oil, preferably peanut (see
  Deep-fat fryers, page 35)

Garnish
 lemon wedges or Roasted Salt and
  Pepper (page 31)

Oysters are a favorite of the Hong Kong Chinese. The variety found in the South China Sea is quite large and they are usually cut up, dipped in batter and deep-fried. The Chinese never eat oysters raw, believing them to be unhealthy when uncooked. This dish is based on a recipe given to me by a friend who is a chef in the fishing village of Lau Fau Shan in the New Territories in Hong Kong. I have added a Western touch to it by using breadcrumbs on top of the batter. This dish makes an excellent cocktail snack.

Drain the oysters in a colander and then pat them dry with paper towels. Prepare a batter by mixing the egg, cornstarch, water, baking powder, salt and ½ teaspoon of oil together in a small bowl. Let the mixture sit for about 20 minutes. Then dip some of the oysters into the batter and then in the breadcrumbs. Set them on a plate. Prepare all the oysters in this way.

Heat the oil in a deep-fat fryer or large wok. When it is almost smoking, deep-fry the coated oysters until they are golden brown. (This should take just a few minutes.) Drain them on paper towels and serve with Roasted Salt and Pepper or lemon wedges.

Stir-fried Scallops with Pork Kidneys

Region: western
Method: stir-frying

Serves 4
 ½ pound pork kidneys
 ½ teaspoon baking soda
 1 teaspoon Chinese white rice
  vinegar or cider vinegar
 ½ teaspoon salt
 ¼ pound scallops, including the
  corals
 2 tablespoons oil, preferably peanut
 1 teaspoon finely chopped ginger
  root
 2 teaspoons finely chopped scallions
 2 teaspoons rice wine or dry sherry
 1 tablespoon light soy sauce
 ½ teaspoon sugar
 ¼ teaspoon salt
 ½ teaspoon cornstarch, blended
  with 2 teaspoons of stock or water

(pictured on page 185)

This regional dish was a favorite in our family. My mother varied the traditional recipe a little by adding oyster sauce. Be assured that scallops and kidneys go very well together, even though they may seem an unlikely combination. If the kidneys are properly prepared their texture is quite similar to that of scallops, and their two quite different flavors blend deliciously together. The richness of this dish means that it is best for special occasions. It goes very well with plain steamed rice and Braised Cauliflower with Oyster Sauce (page 155).

Using a sharp knife, remove the thin outer kidney membrane. Then, with a sharp cleaver or knife, split the kidney in half lengthwise by cutting horizontally as described on page 39. Now cut away the small knobs of fat and any tough membrane surrounding them. Score the top surface of the kidneys in a crisscross pattern (see page 41), then cut the halved kidneys into thin slices. Toss the kidney slices in the baking soda and let them sit for about 20 minutes. Then rinse them thoroughly with cold water and toss them in the vinegar and salt. Put them into a colander and let them drain for at least 30 minutes, preferably longer.

Cut the scallops into slices and put them in a small bowl. Blot the kidney slices dry with paper towels. Heat a wok or large skillet over high heat until it is hot. Add half of the oil and then the scallops. Stir-fry them for about 30 seconds and then add the ginger and scallions. Stir-fry for another 30 seconds and then remove them with a slotted spoon.

Immediately reheat the wok and then add the rest of the oil. Stir-fry the kidneys for 1 minute and then add all the other ingredients except the cornstarch mixture. Stir-fry for 1 minute and then return the scallops to the pan. Add the cornstarch mixture and stir for a minute or so. Turn onto a warm serving platter and serve at once.

Deep-fried Oysters (facing page).

Shrimp

Fresh shrimps are more and more available throughout the country. I even see them sometimes in supermarkets. The larger ones are often labeled "prawns," but both terms are used, depending on what part of the country you come from. If the shrimps are very fresh and come with the heads on, I tend to leave them on. I think that not only does it look attractive, but the heads also have a great deal of flavor. Look for shrimps with hard shells and smell them before buying. They should not have a "fishy" smell. If you can't get fresh shrimps, look for large frozen ones; be sure to thaw them thoroughly before using. Avoid any precooked shrimps.

To peel shrimp

First twist off the head (if not already removed) and pull off the tail. It should then be quite easy to peel off the shell, and with it the tiny legs. If you are using large shrimp make a shallow cut down the back of each shrimp and remove the fine digestive cord which runs the length of the shrimp. Wash the shrimp before you use them.

Stir-fried Squid with Vegetables

Region: southern
Method: blanching and stir-frying

Serves 4
  ¾ pound squid, fresh or frozen
  ½ red or green bell pepper
  1 tablespoon oil, preferably peanut
  4 ounces snow peas, trimmed
  ⅓ cup Chicken Stock (page 60)
  2 teaspoons rice wine or dry sherry
  1½ tablespoons oyster sauce
  1 teaspoon cornstarch, blended
    with 1 teaspoon water

Squid cooked the Chinese way is both tender and tasty. The secret is to use very hot water for blanching it and then a minimum amount of cooking time—just enough for the squid to firm up slightly. Too long will make it tough. Unlike most seafood, frozen squid can be quite good, and when properly cooked it is sometimes impossible to tell it from fresh. This simple recipe can also be prepared with shrimp if you find squid difficult to obtain. Serve this dish with Hot and Sour Soup (page 68) and plain rice.

The edible parts of the squid are the tentacles and the body. If it has not been cleaned by your fish dealer, you can do it yourself by pulling the head and tentacles away from the body. Then pull off and discard the skin. Using a small sharp knife, split the body in half. Remove the transparent bony section. Wash the halves thoroughly under cold running water and then pull off and discard the skin. Cut the tentacles from the head, cutting just above the eye. (You may also have to remove the polyp or beak from the base of the ring of tentacles.) If you are using frozen squid, make sure it is properly thawed before cooking it.

Cut the squid meat into 1½ inch strips. Blanch the strips and the tentacles in a large pot of boiling water for 30 seconds. The squid will firm up slightly and turn an opaque white color. Remove and drain in a colander.

Cut the pepper into 1½-inch strips. Heat a wok or large skillet until it is hot. Then add the oil and let it get hot. Add the pepper strips and snow peas and stir-fry for 1 minute. Then add the rest of the ingredients, except the squid, and bring the mixture to a boil. Give it a quick stir, then add the squid and mix it in well. Cook for 30 seconds more. Serve at once.

Braised Shrimp

This is one of the simplest shrimp recipes in Chinese cookery. It takes only minutes to prepare.

Peel the shrimp and, if you are using large ones, cut them to remove the fine digestive cord (see page 130). Wash the shrimp and pat them dry with paper towels.

Combine the sauce ingredients in a wok or large skillet. Bring it to a simmer and then add the shrimp. Braise the shrimp slowly over a low heat for 3 to 4 minutes. Serve at once.

Region: northern
Method: braising

Serves 4
½ pound shrimp, unpeeled

Sauce
⅓ cup Chicken Stock (page 60)
2 teaspoons rice wine or dry sherry
¼ teaspoon salt
2 teaspoons sugar
1 teaspoon Chinese black rice vinegar or cider vinegar
2 tablespoons finely chopped scallions
2 teaspoons finely chopped ginger root
½ teaspoon cornstarch, blended with ½ teaspoon water

Shrimp in Scallion and Ginger Sauce

This method of quick braising is very simple. Street vendors and sidewalk cafés throughout southern China sell this dish because it is uncomplicated and takes only minutes to prepare. It is also excellent cold and makes a very nice dish for an exotic picnic. Serve as part of a meal with Country-style Chicken (page 100) and rice.

Peel the shrimp and, if you are using large ones, cut them to remove the fine digestive cord (see page 130). Wash the shrimp and pat them dry with paper towels.

Combine the braising sauce ingredients in a wok or large saucepan and bring the mixture to a boil. Turn the heat down to low and simmer for 2 minutes. Then add the shrimp and stir, mixing them in well. Cover the pan and braise for 2 minutes. Serve at once or allow to cool and serve cold.

Region: southern
Method: braising

Serves 4
½ pound shrimp

Braising sauce
1½ tablespoons finely chopped scallions
2 teaspoons finely chopped ginger root
1 tablespoon rice wine or dry sherry
1 tablespoon light soy sauce
⅓ cup Chicken Stock (page 60)

Peking Shrimp

Region: northern
Method: shallow-frying

Serves 4
½ pound large unshelled shrimp
3 tablespoons all-purpose flour
3 tablespoons toasted breadcrumbs
1 egg
½ teaspoon sesame oil
¼ teaspoon salt
⅔ cup oil, preferably peanut

Dipping sauce
1½ tablespoons hoisin sauce
¼ teaspoon sesame oil

This is my adaptation of a favorite northern Chinese shrimp dish. The use of breadcrumbs, is, of course, a Western touch but one that works perfectly for this recipe. It is so simple to make that it presents no problem even if you are serving it at a dinner party. The shallow-frying, however, must be done at the last minute.

Peel the shrimp but leave the tail shell on. Using a sharp knife, split each shrimp lengthwise but leave it still attached at the back. Open the shrimp out so that it splays out flat in a butterfly shape. Remove the fine digestive cord. Pat the shrimp dry with paper towels.

Spread out the flour and breadcrumbs on separate plates. Beat the egg in another small bowl, then add the sesame oil and salt and mix well.

Heat the oil in a wok or deep skillet. Dip the shrimp into the flour, then into the egg mixture, and finally into the breadcrumbs, shaking off any excess. When the oil is hot, shallow-fry the shrimp in two batches, and then drain them on paper towels.

Mix the hoisin sauce with the sesame oil in a small dish. Serve this with the hot shrimp.

Sweet and Sour Shrimp

Region: eastern
Method: stir-frying and
simmering

Serves 4
½ pound raw shrimp
4 ounces water chestnuts, canned
  or fresh
1 or 2 red or green bell peppers
2 scallions
2 teaspoons oil, preferably peanut
2 teaspoons finely chopped garlic

Sauce
⅓ cup Chicken Stock (page 60)
1 tablespoon rice wine or dry sherry
2 teaspoons light soy sauce
1 tablespoon tomato paste
1 tablespoon Chinese white rice
  vinegar or cider vinegar
1 tablespoon sugar
2 teaspoons cornstarch blended
  with 2 teaspoons water

This is a very popular Chinese dish. The sweet and pungent flavors of the sauce combine well with the firm and succulent shrimp. It is simple to make, and can be served as part of a Chinese meal or on its own as a first course.

Peel the shrimp and, if you are using large ones, cut them to remove the fine digestive cord (see page 130). Wash them and pat dry with paper towels. Slice the water chestnuts, dice the pepper, and slice the scallions diagonally into 1½-inch pieces.

Heat a wok or large skillet. When it is hot add the oil and stir-fry the shrimp for 1 minute. Remove them with a slotted spoon and drain on paper towels. Add the garlic and scallions to the pan and stir-fry them for a few seconds. Then add the pepper and the fresh water chestnuts if you are using them. Stir-fry for 30 seconds, and then add the sauce ingredients. Bring the mixture to a boil and simmer for 4 minutes. If you are using canned water chestnuts, add these now. Return the shrimp to the sauce and boil over high heat for another 30 seconds. Serve immediately with steamed rice.

Sichuan Shrimp in Chili Sauce

Sichuan cooking is becoming increasingly popular. This is one of the best-known dishes from that area, but beware of versions which err on the side of excessive sweetness. This dish is quick and easy and makes a wholesome and delicious meal served with a stir-fried vegetable and steamed rice.

Peel the shrimp and cut them to remove the fine digestive cord (see page 130). Wash them and pat them dry with paper towels. Heat a wok or large skillet until it is hot. Add the oil and then the ginger and scallions. Stir-fry quickly and then add the shrimp. Stir-fry the shrimp for about 30 seconds. Add the sauce ingredients and continue to stir-fry for another 5 minutes over a high heat. Serve at once.

Region: western
Method: stir-frying

Serves 4
  ½ pound large shrimp, unpeeled
  2 teaspoons oil, preferably peanut
  2 teaspoons finely chopped ginger root
  1 tablespoon finely chopped scallions

Sauce
  2 teaspoons tomato paste
  1 teaspoon chili bean sauce, or ½ teaspoon chili powder
  ¼ teaspoon salt
  ½ teaspoon sugar
  ¼ teaspoon sesame oil

(pictured, in the shell, on page 13)

Stir-fried Shrimp with Eggs

This dish is commonly known in the West as Egg Foo Young. It is very popular because it tastes delicious, is easy to make and uses familiar ingredients. You can substitute crab, fish or even ground pork or beef for the shrimp. However, I think it is at its best made with good quality shrimp. This distinctive dish goes well with Hot and Sour Soup (page 68) and Stir-fried Beef with Ginger (page 81).

Peel the shrimp and, if you are using large ones, cut them to remove the fine digestive cord (see page 130). Wash the shrimp and pat them dry with paper towels. Put the shrimp into a bowl, and mix in the egg white and cornstarch. Let the mixture sit in the refrigerator for 20 minutes. Combine the eggs, sesame oil and the rest of the ingredients except the cooking oil in a bowl.

    Heat a wok or large skillet and then add half the oil. When it is hot and almost smoking add the shrimp and stir-fry them for 2 minutes. Remove them with a slotted spoon. Rinse the wok clean, then put the rest of the oil into the pan. Quickly add the egg mixture. Stir-fry for 1 minute or until the egg begins to set. Return the shrimp to the egg mixture and continue to stir-fry for 1 minute more. Garnish with scallions and serve.

Region: southern
Method: stir-frying

Serves 4
  ½ pound shrimp
  1 small egg white
  1 teaspoon cornstarch
  2 large eggs, beaten
  1 teaspoon sesame oil
  3 tablespoons Chicken Stock (page 60) or water
  2 teaspoons rice wine or dry sherry
  ½ teaspoon salt
  2 teaspoons light soy sauce
  ½ teaspoon sugar
  2 tablespoons oil, preferably peanut

Garnish
  1 tablespoon finely chopped scallions

Sizzling-Rice Shrimp

Region: western
Method: stir-frying and deep-frying

Serves 6 to 8
1 pound shrimp
2 tablespoons oil, preferably peanut
2 teaspoons finely chopped ginger root
1 tablespoon finely chopped garlic
1½ tablespoons finely chopped scallions
5 cups oil, preferably peanut (see Deep-fat fryers, page 35)
1 Rice Cake (page 162), broken into pieces

Sauce
1 large green or red bell pepper, diced
1 tablespoon Chinese black rice vinegar or cider vinegar
1 tablespoon dark soy sauce
1 tablespoon chili bean sauce or 2 dried red chilies
1½ tablespoons tomato paste
1 teaspoon light soy sauce
1½ tablespoons rice wine or dry sherry
1 teaspoon sugar
1⅓ cups Chicken Stock (page 60)
1 tablespoon cornstarch, blended with 1 tablespoon water

This is a dramatic dish which is sure to earn you compliments. It is moderately easy to make but requires organization and some experience in Chinese cooking. Attempt this dish after you have cooked some of the other, simpler recipes in this book. I'm sure that once you have tried it, it will become a regular feature of your repertoire. The key to success is that the shrimp sauce mixture and rice cake should both be fairly hot. You will then be sure to achieve a dramatic sizzle when the two are combined. Serve Sizzling-Rice Shrimp with Cold Marinated Bean Sprouts (page 145) and Stir-fried Bok Choi (page 148).

Peel the shrimp and discard the shells. Using a small sharp knife, split the shrimp in half but leave them still attached at the back so that they splay out like butterflies. If you are using large shrimp, remove the fine digestive cord. Rinse the shrimp well in cold water and blot them dry with paper towels.

Heat a wok or large skillet until it is quite hot. Add the 2 tablespoons of oil. Let it heat for a few seconds until it is almost smoking. Add the ginger and stir it quickly for a few seconds, then add the garlic and scallions. A few seconds later add the shrimp and stir-fry them quickly until they become firm. (This takes about 30 seconds.) Then add all the sauce ingredients except the cornstarch mixture. Bring the mixture to a boil, remove it from the heat and add the cornstarch mixture. Bring back to a boil and then reduce the heat to a very slow simmer. The shrimp sauce may be cooked ahead up to this point and reheated when required.

Now you are ready to fry the rice cake. Heat the 5 cups of oil in a deep-fat fryer or large wok until it is nearly smoking. Drop in a small piece of rice cake to test the heat. It should bubble all over and immediately come up to the surface. Now deep-fry the pieces of rice cake for about 1 to 2 minutes until they puff up and brown slightly. Remove them immediately with a slotted spoon and set them to drain on a plate lined with paper towels. Then quickly transfer the pieces to a platter and pour the hot shrimp and sauce mixture over them. It should sizzle dramatically. Once you are skilled at preparing this dish, you can attempt to perform this trick at the dinner table. (The oil used for deep-frying the rice cake can be saved and reused once it has cooled. Filter it through coffee filter papers before storing it.)

Sizzling-Rice Shrimp (facing page).

One of the things I most dislike about deep-fried foods in many Chinese restaurants outside China is the use of a dense batter coating. Such a thick coating soaks up the oil and makes the food very greasy. I prefer a light, almost transparent coating of batter. This way shrimp will be tender and sweet and the flavor will not be obstructed.

Peel the shrimp and, if you are using large ones, cut them to remove the fine digestive cord (see page 130). Wash them and pat them dry with paper towels. Combine the batter ingredients in a small bowl and beat them well until they are thoroughly blended.

   Put the oil into a deep-fat fryer or large wok and heat it until it almost smokes. Put the shrimp into the batter. Then, using a slotted spoon, remove them from the batter, leaving them with just a light coating. Now deep-fry them for about 2 minutes, and then drain on paper towels. Serve the cooked shrimp with Roasted Salt and Pepper or with lemon wedges.

Region: eastern
Method: deep-frying

Serves 4
   ½ pound shrimp
   2 cups oil, preferably peanut (see Deep-fat fryers, page 35)

Batter
   1 small egg
   1 tablespoon cornstarch
   2 teaspoons cold water
   1 teaspoon sesame oil
   1 teaspoon salt
   2 tablespoons finely chopped scallions

Garnish
   lemon wedges or Roasted Salt and Pepper (page 31)

Crabs

Choosing a crab

Where possible the Chinese prefer to buy crabs live and cook them when they are needed. In this country crabs are sold both cooked and live. If you are buying cooked crabs, take care to buy ones that are fresh and do not have a fishy smell. The heavier the crab the better.

Cooking live crabs

Bring a large pot of water to a boil, add 2 teaspoons of salt and then put in the crab. Cover the pot and cook the crab for about 5 to 7 minutes, until it turns bright red. Remove with a slotted spoon and drain in a colander. Leave to cool. (You can also steam it.)

Removing cooked crabmeat

Extracting the crabmeat is not difficult but it takes a little time and patience. Follow these steps:

1. Place the crab upside down with the shell on the worktop. Using your fingers, twist the claws from the body. Do the same with the rest of the legs. They should come off quite easily.

2. Now twist the bony tail flap on the underside of the crab and discard it. With your fingers, pry the body from the main shell.

3. Remove and discard the small bag-like stomach sac and its appendages, which are located just behind the crab's mouth.

4. With a teaspoon, scoop out the brown crabmeat.

5. Pull the soft feathery gills, which look a little like fingers, away from the body and discard them.

6. Using a cleaver or heavy knife, split the crab body in half, and, using a knife, fork or skewer, scrape out all the white crabmeat from the body and from the claws and legs.
   Combine the brown and white crabmeat.

Canned or frozen crabmeat

If you are using frozen crabmeat, thaw it thoroughly before you use it. Canned crabmeat has a fishy odor. If you are forced to use it, rinse it carefully first in cold water.

Crab with Black Bean Sauce

This recipe can only be made with fresh crabs in the shell since the shell has to protect the delicate crabmeat during the stir-frying process. If you can't get crab in the shell, use shrimp instead. I have added some ground pork to stretch the crab, which can be expensive. (Of course you can always use just crab if you are feeling extravagant.) I love to eat this dish with plain steamed rice and Braised Spicy Eggplant (page 143).

Remove the tail flap, stomach sac and feathery gills from the crab as described on page 136. Using a heavy knife or cleaver, cut the crab, shell included, into large pieces.

Heat the oil in a wok or large skillet. When it is hot, add the black beans, garlic, ginger and scallions and stir-fry quickly. Then add the pork and stir-fry for one minute. Add the crab pieces and the rest of the ingredients except the eggs and the sesame oil. Stir-fry the mixture over high heat for about 10 minutes. Combine the eggs with the sesame oil and then mix this into the crab mixture, stirring slowly. There should be light strands of egg trailing over the crab mixture. Turn it onto a large warm serving platter and serve. It is perfectly good manners to eat the crab with your fingers, but I suggest you have a large bowl of water decorated with lemon slices on the table so that your guests can rinse their fingers.

Region: southern
Method: stir-frying

Serves 4 to 6
> 3 pounds freshly cooked crab in the shell
> 2 tablespoons oil, preferably peanut
> 2 tablespoons coarsely chopped black beans
> 2 teaspoons finely chopped garlic
> 2 teaspoons finely chopped ginger root
> 2 tablespoons finely chopped scallions
> ½ pound ground pork
> 1 tablespoon rice wine or dry sherry
> 2 cups Chicken Stock (page 60) or water
> 2 eggs, beaten
> 1 teaspoon sesame oil

Crab in Egg Custard

There are many delicious and meaty varieties of crab which are harvested off the coast of northern China. A favorite way to prepare them is to steam them whole and then crack them at the table and dip them in vinegar and sugar. In this northern dish, cooked crab is mixed with a light egg custard and then steamed. The result is a sort of velvet- or satin-textured custard. Although canned or frozen crabmeat can be used, I recommend using fresh cooked crabmeat for this dish. It makes a satisfying main course with rice and Curried Corn Soup with Chicken (page 64).

Mix the custard ingredients in a bowl and then add the cooked crabmeat. Mix well to blend all the ingredients together. Put the mixture into a deep dish.

Set up a steamer or put a rack into a wok or deep pan. Pour about 1½ to 2 inches of water into the pan, and bring the water to a boil. Now place the dish of custard into the steamer or onto the rack. Cover the pan tightly and lower the heat. Gently steam for 25 minutes, or until the custard has set. Remove the custard and pour the soy sauce over the top. Serve at once.

Region: northern
Method: steaming

Serves 4
> ½ pound cooked white crabmeat

Custard
> 4 eggs
> 1⅓ cups Chicken Stock (page 60)
> 1 teaspoon finely chopped ginger root
> 3 tablespoons finely chopped scallions
> 1 tablespoon rice wine or dry sherry
> ½ teaspoon freshly ground black pepper
> 1 teaspoon salt

Garnish
> 2 teaspoons dark soy sauce (optional)

Fresh vegetables from Monterey Produce in Berkeley, California

VEGETABLES

蔬菜

Even as a child I loved vegetables. In this regard I am certainly very much Chinese. My Western friends often refuse to eat vegetables, and not without reason. Many people overcook them, draining them of their natural flavors and colors and rendering them limp and lifeless. In China vegetables are never overcooked. The techniques of stir-frying, blanching, deep-frying and even braising all preserve the flavors of vegetables while retaining their crispness and texture. The trick is to know when to stop cooking. Simplicity is another factor. The Chinese rarely cover their vegetables with heavy sauces, preferring the natural tastes and textures. But vegetables are rarely eaten raw unless they are pickled; even lettuce is cooked, and cold Chinese salads always consist of cooked or pickled vegetables too. All Chinese meals include one or two vegetable dishes, since apart from being highly nutritious they add color and texture to a well-balanced meal.

Westerners generally agree that vegetables cooked in the Chinese fashion are delectable. This excellence in the preparation of vegetables is, of course, based on thousands of years of culinary experience. China is also fortunate in having a vast array of native edible plants, supplemented in recent centuries by foreign imports such as tomatoes, carrots, sweet potatoes and various types of squash.

The Buddhist-Taoist tradition is one source of the Chinese people's expertise with vegetables. Buddhists avoid meat because they abhor killing any living animal, since this contradicts their doctrine of reincarnation. Taoists are vegetarian because they believe that to kill animals is to shatter the essential unity of the universe. For the past 1500 years, therefore, these minority groups have promoted vegetarianism, and their chefs have made imaginative and creative use of vegetables. They have concocted imitations of meat, fish and shellfish dishes which are so realistic and delicious that people are hard put to distinguish the replica from the real thing. Because vegetables are not good sources of protein, the soybean, that miracle protein food which is found everywhere in China, was pressed into service. Bean curd, soybean milk and other bean curd products became staples in the vegetarian diet. Instead of poultry or meat broths, the liquid left from soaking dried Chinese black mushrooms provided the base for sauce and soups. All of these innovations slowly spread beyond the Buddhist and Taoist groups to the much larger society of non-vegetarian Chinese.

Technique is especially important in vegetable cookery. We cook with a minimum of water or oil to obtain the best results. The use of high heat and rapid cooking seals in the flavors and nutrients but retains texture and crispness. Blanching vegetables in hot water and then plunging them

139

into cold water after brief cooking ensures that the natural flavor and color are retained. This process is particularly important when stir-frying harder vegetables such as carrots or broccoli, which need to be partly cooked before being stir-fried.

Deep-frying is another favorite method of cooking vegetables, since hot oil seals in the flavors and gives vegetables a crunchy texture. Whatever technique you use, I hope you will discover the same pleasure that the Chinese have been deriving from vegetables for centuries. Most of the vegetables used in the following recipes are well known in this country. I have, however, included some which may be less familiar.

BEAN SPROUTS

Bean sprouts are now widely available in greengroceries, supermarkets and Chinese groceries. They are the sprouts of the green mung bean, although some Chinese grocers also stock yellow soybean sprouts, which are much larger. Bean sprouts should always be very fresh and crunchy. They will keep for several days wrapped in a plastic bag and stored in the vegetable compartment of a refrigerator. Never use canned bean sprouts as these have been precooked and are soggy and tasteless.

To grow bean sprouts
It is very easy to grow your own bean sprouts. Dried mung beans are available in supermarkets, Asian groceries and health-food shops. You will need a perforated flat surface. An aluminum foil pan punched with holes or a bamboo steamer is ideal. You will also need two pieces of cheesecloth and about ¼ cup dried green mung beans.

Wash the beans several times in water. Then leave them to soak in lukewarm water for 8 hours or overnight. Once soaking is complete, rinse the beans again under warm running water until the water runs clear. Dampen the cheesecloth and spread one piece over the aluminum pan or steamer. Spread the beans over the cloth and sprinkle them with more lukewarm water. Cover the beans with the second piece of cheesecloth and then put them in a warm, dark place. Keep them moist by sprinkling them with water over the next few days. In 3 days you should have white crisp sprouts ready for use.

BOK CHOI

This is an attractive vegetable *(Brassica chinensis)* with a long, smooth, milky-white stem and large, crinkly, dark green leaves. It looks like Swiss chard and has been grown in China for centuries. Commonly known as *bok choi* in the U.S., it may also be called Chinese white cabbage, Chinese greens, or Chinese chard. It has a light fresh taste and requires little cooking. Both the leaves and the stems are used, but peel the stems first. It is usually available from Chinese groceries. Swiss chard or spinach can be substituted if you cannot obtain *bok choi*.

CHINESE BROCCOLI

Chinese broccoli, or *gai lan (Brassica oleracea capitata),* does not taste like Western broccoli (calabrese). It is very crunchy and slightly bitter and is more like Swiss chard in flavor. It has deep olive green leaves and sometimes has white flowers. It is usually only available at Chinese groceries. If you can find it, look for firm stems and leaves that look fresh and green. It is prepared in exactly the same way as calabrese and should be stored in a plastic bag in the vegetable compartment of the refrigerator, where it will keep for several days. If you cannot find Chinese broccoli use calabrese instead.

Chinese Flowering Cabbage

Chinese flowering cabbage *(Brassica rapa)* is usually known by its more familiar Cantonese name, *choi sam.* It has yellowish green leaves and may have small yellow flowers, which are eaten along with the leaves and stems. It is obtainable from Chinese groceries and is delicious stir-fried. *Choi sam* can be used in place of *bok choi.*

Chinese Cabbage

Chinese cabbage *(Brassica pekinensis)* looks rather like a large, tightly packed Romaine lettuce with firm, pale green, crinkled leaves. It is sometimes known as celery cabbage, Napa or Peking cabbage, or Chinese leaves, and is widely available in greengrocers, supermarkets and Chinese groceries. This is a delicious crunchy vegetable with a distinctive but mild taste. If you cannot find it, use regular white cabbage instead.

Chinese White Radish *(mooli)*

Chinese white radish is a winter radish from Asia which can withstand long cooking without disintegrating, so it absorbs the flavor of a sauce yet retains its distinctive radish taste and texture. It is long and white and rather like a carrot in shape but usually very much larger. It must be peeled before it is used. Chinese white radish can be bought in many supermarkets and greengrocers, and in Asian and Chinese groceries. Look for ones that are firm, heavy and unblemished. They should be slightly translucent inside and not tough and fibrous. Store in a plastic bag in the vegetable compartment of your refrigerator, where they will keep for over a week. If you cannot find white radish use turnips instead.

Eggplant

These pleasing purple-skinned vegetables range in size from the huge fat ones which are easy to find in all greengrocers, to the small thin variety which the Chinese prefer because they have a more delicate flavor.

Do not peel eggplants since the skin preserves their texture, shape and taste. Large eggplants should be cut according to the recipe, sprinkled with a little salt and left to sit for 20 minutes. They should then be rinsed and any liquid blotted dry with paper towels. This process extracts excess moisture from the vegetable before it is cooked.

SHALLOTS

Shallots are mild-flavored members of the onion family. They are small—about the size of pearl onions—with copper-red skins. They have a distinctive onion taste without being as strong or overpowering as ordinary onions, and I think they are an excellent substitute for Chinese onions, which are unobtainable here. They are expensive but few go a long way. Buy them at good greengrocers, supermarkets and delicatessens. Keep them in a cool, dry place (not the refrigerator) and peel them as you would an onion. If you cannot find shallots use pearl onions or scallions.

SPINACH

Western varieties of spinach are quite different from those used in China, although they make satisfactory substitutes for the real thing. Spinach is most commonly stir-fried, so frozen spinach is obviously unsuitable. Chinese water spinach (*Ipomoea aquatica*) is available in some greengrocers and in Chinese groceries. It has hollow stems and delicate, green, pointed leaves, lighter in color than common spinach and with a milder taste. It should be cooked when it is very fresh, preferably on the day on which it is bought.

Ken in his kitchen, Berkeley.

Braised Spicy Eggplant

Eggplant is one of my favorite vegetables. I like its color, taste and texture. The subtle flavor is receptive to a good zesty sauce, such as this one from western China. It's worth trying to get the small, long, thin Chinese eggplants for their sweet taste. However, this recipe also works perfectly well with the large Western variety. The Chinese prefer to leave the skin on because it holds the eggplant together throughout the cooking and because the skin is tender, tasty and nutritious.

Two techniques are employed here: a quick stir-frying to blend the seasonings, and braising, which cooks the eggplant and makes a sauce in which it is served. The result is a tender and distinctively flavored vegetable dish.

Roll-cut the Chinese eggplants (see page 40), or if you are using the regular large variety, trim and cut them into 1-inch cubes. Sprinkle the cubes with salt and leave them in a sieve to drain for 20 minutes. Then rinse them under cold running water and pat them dry with paper towels.

Heat a wok or large skillet to a moderate heat. Add the oil and let it heat up for a few seconds. Then add the eggplant, garlic, ginger and scallions and stir-fry them for 1 minute until they are thoroughly mixed together. Then add the rest of the ingredients. Turn the heat down and cook uncovered for 10 to 15 minutes, until the eggplant is tender, stirring occasionally.

Return the heat to high and continue to stir until the liquid has been reduced and has thickened slightly. Turn the mixture onto a serving dish and garnish with the chopped scallion tops.

Region: western
Method: stir-frying and braising

Serves 4
- 1 pound eggplants
- 2 teaspoons salt
- 1 tablespoon oil
- 1 tablespoon finely chopped garlic
- 1 tablespoon finely chopped ginger root
- 2 tablespoons finely chopped scallions
- 2 tablespoons dark soy sauce
- 1 to 2 teaspoons chili bean sauce, or 1 dried red chili
- 1 tablespoon bean sauce
- 1 tablespoon granulated sugar
- 1⅓ cups water

Optional garnish
- 2 tablespoons chopped scallions

(pictured on page 52)

Deep-fried Green Beans

This tasty dish originated in western China, as its seasonings indicate. The traditional recipe calls for Chinese asparagus or long beans but I have found string beans equally suitable. The beans are deep-fried to transform their texture, but they should remain green and not be overcooked. (Deep-frying merely gives them a chewy instead of a crunchy texture.) After deep-frying, the beans are then stir-fried in an array of spices to create a delectable dish. They should be slightly oily, but if they are too oily for your taste you can blot them with paper towels before stir-frying them. For best results serve them as soon as they are cooked.

Heat the oil in a deep-fat fryer or large wok until it is fairly hot. When a single bean is dropped into the oil, it should bubble all over. Deep-fry half the beans until they are slightly wrinkled, which should take about 3 to 4 minutes. Remove the beans and drain them. Deep-fry the second batch in the same way.

Transfer about 1 tablespoon of the oil in which you have cooked the beans to a clean wok or skillet. (The rest can be retained for future use in cooking vegetables.) Add the garlic, ginger and scallions and stir-fry quickly. Add the chilies and stir-fry them for about 30 seconds, until they turn black. Remove the chilies, and then add all the other ingredients. Stir-fry the mixture for a few seconds, and then add the cooked, drained beans. Mix well until all the beans are thoroughly coated with the spicy mixture. Serve as soon as the beans have heated through.

Region: western
Method: deep-frying and stir-frying

Serves 2 to 4
- 2 cups oil (see Deep-fat fryers, page 35)
- 1 pound string beans, trimmed and cut into 5-inch pieces
- 1 tablespoon finely chopped garlic
- 1 tablespoon finely chopped ginger root
- 2 tablespoons finely chopped scallions
- 4 dried red chilies
- 1 tablespoon bean sauce
- 1 tablespoon rice wine or dry sherry
- 1 tablespoon dark soy sauce
- 1 teaspoon sugar
- 1 tablespoon water

Bean Curd with Vegetables

Region: southern
**Method: shallow-frying and
     stir-frying**

Serves 4
  8 ounces fresh bean curd (1 cake)
  3 fresh water chestnuts, or ¼
    8-ounce can
  2 ounces canned bamboo shoots
  2 ounces snow peas, trimmed
  ⅔ cup oil, preferably peanut

Sauce
  1 tablespoon rice wine or dry sherry
  2 tablespoons oyster sauce
  1 teaspoon sugar
  ¼ cup Chicken Stock (page 60)
  1 teaspoon cornstarch, blended
    with 1 teaspoon water
  2 teaspoons sesame oil

Bean curd changes its texture when it is shallow-fried, from slippery soft to light and spongy. Cooked in this way, the bean curd does not absorb the oil in which it is fried but forms a sort of skin which helps to hold it together during the stir-frying stage. This is a simple, tasty dish which reheats well.

Drain and rinse the bean curd in cold water. Blot it dry with paper towels and cut into ½-inch cubes. If you are using fresh water chestnuts, peel and slice them. If you are using canned water chestnuts, rinse them in cold water and then slice them. Slice the bamboo shoots on the diagonal into 1-inch pieces and trim the snow peas.

Heat a wok or large skillet and then add the oil. Heat the oil until it is moderately hot. Add the bean curd cubes and shallow-fry until they are lightly brown on all sides. Remove with a slotted spoon and drain on paper towels.

Pour off most of the oil, leaving about 1 tablespoon in the pan. Reheat the oil, add the vegetables and stir-fry for about 2 minutes. Then add all the sauce ingredients except for the cornstarch mixture and the sesame oil. Bring the mixture to a boil, remove from the heat, and then add the cornstarch mixture. Return the pan to the heat and bring it back to a boil. Return the bean curd to the pan and add the sesame oil. Give the mixture a few stirs and turn onto a warm serving platter. Serve at once.

Braised Bean Curd with Mushrooms

Region: western
Method: deep-frying and braising

Serves 2 to 4
  8 ounces fresh bean curd (1 cake)
  2 to 3 scallions
  2 cups oil (see Deep-fat fryers, page
   35)
  1 tablespoon oil
  1 tablespoon finely chopped garlic
  ¼ pound small whole button
    mushrooms, washed
  ½ teaspoon finely chopped ginger
    root
  1 teaspoon chili bean sauce, or 1
    dried red chili
  1 tablespoon rice wine or dry sherry
  1 tablespoon dark soy sauce
  2 tablespoons Chicken Stock (page
    60) or water

Bean curd, which is also known as tofu *(see page 18), is a versatile and nutritious food. It is derived from the soybean, which is exceedingly rich in protein. Bean curd is rather bland, but this is easily remedied by recipes such as this one, in which it is deep-fried, which alters its texture, and then braised, which makes it tasty. The result is a delicious and unusual vegetable dish. An additional bonus is that it reheats well.*

Cut the bean curd into 1-inch cubes. Trim the scallions and cut them into 1-inch segments.

Heat the 2 cups of oil in a deep-fat fryer or large wok until it almost smokes, and then deep-fry the bean curd cubes in 2 batches. When each batch of bean-curd cubes is lightly browned, remove and drain well on paper towels. Let the cooking oil cool and then discard it.

Heat a clean skillet or wok. When it is hot, add 1 tablespoon of oil, and then add the garlic, scallions and ginger. Stir-fry for a few seconds and then add the mushrooms. Stir-fry for 30 seconds, and add all the other ingredients. Reduce the heat to very low and then add the bean-curd cubes. Cover the pan and slowly simmer the mixture for 8 minutes. It is then ready to serve.

Cold Marinated Bean Sprouts

This is a nutritious salad, easy to make and perfect either as an appetizer or as a salad course with grilled meat or fish. Always use fresh bean sprouts—never canned ones, which are soggy and tasteless. Fresh ones are widely available and are also very easy to grow (see page 140). I prefer to trim the sprouts at both ends. Although this is a bit laborious, it is well worth the effort as it makes the finished dish look more elegant. This dish may be prepared up to 4 hours in advance, and may be served cold or at room temperature. It is perfect for warm summer days.

Trim and discard both ends of the bean sprouts and put the trimmed sprouts in a glass bowl. If you are using a fresh chili, split it in half and carefully remove and discard the seeds. Shred the chili as finely as possible. Remember to wash your hands immediately after handling the chili. Add the chili, together with all the other ingredients, to the trimmed bean sprouts. Mix well. Let the mixture marinate for at least 2 to 3 hours, turning the bean sprouts in the marinade from time to time. When you are ready to serve the salad, drain the bean sprouts and discard the marinade.

Region: northern
Method: marinating

Serves 4
  1 pound fresh bean sprouts
  1 fresh red or green chili, or ¼
    teaspoon chili powder
  3 tablespoons Chinese white rice
    vinegar or cider vinegar
  2 tablespoons light soy sauce
  1 tablespoon finely chopped fresh
    coriander
  ½ teaspoon finely chopped garlic

(pictured on page 147)

Cold Sesame Broccoli

This dish makes a good garnish for meats or a wonderful vegetable dish for summer picnics. The cold crunchiness of the broccoli goes well with the texture of the sesame seeds. For a tangy alternative, you could substitute finely chopped fresh ginger for the sesame seeds (using roughly the same amounts). Think of this dish as a cold vegetable salad with a Chinese touch, which goes well with almost any menu. It can be prepared a day in advance and actually tastes even better if you do this.

Cut off the broccoli heads and break them into small florets. Peel and slice the broccoli stems. Blanch the broccoli heads and stems in a large pot of boiling salted water for 4 to 5 minutes. Then plunge them into cold water. Next, drain the broccoli dry in a colander or a salad spinner, and put it into a clean bowl.

  Roast the sesame seeds in a preheated oven at 375°F or under the broiler, until they are brown. In a small glass bowl combine the roasted sesame seeds with the rest of the ingredients and mix them together well. Then pour the mixture into the bowl of broccoli and toss well. If you are serving this dish the next day, tightly cover the bowl with plastic wrap and keep it in the refrigerator until it is needed.

Region: northern
Method: blanching

Serves 4 to 6
  1 to 1½ pounds broccoli
  1 tablespoon white sesame seeds
  1 tablespoon oil
  2 teaspoons sesame oil
  1 teaspoon finely chopped garlic
  1½ tablespoons light soy sauce
  2 tablespoons finely chopped
    scallions

(pictured on page 76)

Stir-fried Ginger Broccoli

Region: southern
Method: stir-frying

Serves 2 to 4
  1 pound fresh broccoli
  1 tablespoon oil
  1 small slice ginger root, finely
    shredded
  ½ teaspoon salt
  ½ teaspoon sesame oil

(pictured opposite)

Broccoli as it is known in the West is different from the Chinese variety. The Western variety is often considered to combine the best features of cauliflower and asparagus, and its distinctive flavor is milder than the Chinese type. It goes well with many seasonings but ginger is one of its most congenial companions. After stir-frying this dish, I let it cool and serve it at room temperature, so it is particularly suitable for summertime.

Separate the broccoli heads into small florets, and peel and slice the stems. Blanch the broccoli pieces in a large pot of boiling salted water for several minutes, and then immerse them in cold water. Drain thoroughly.

Heat the oil in a large wok or skillet. When it is moderately hot, add the ginger shreds and salt. Stir-fry for a few seconds, and then add the blanched broccoli. If it seems dry, add a few tablespoons of water. Stir-fry at a moderate to high heat for 4 minutes, until the broccoli is thoroughly heated through. Add the sesame oil and continue to stir-fry for 30 seconds, and the broccoli is ready to serve.

Stir-fried Broccoli with Hoisin Sauce

Region: northern
Method: stir-frying

Serves 2 to 4
  1 pound fresh broccoli
  1 tablespoon oil, preferably peanut
  2 teaspoons finely chopped garlic
  2 tablespoons hoisin sauce
  3 tablespoons water

I find the sweet flavor of broccoli blends perfectly with the rich taste of hoisin sauce. This sauce gives a good color and pleasant fragrance to the broccoli, but remember that a little goes a long way. This dish is quick and easy to make. Served hot, it makes a perfect vegetable accompaniment to any meal. (Carrots or zucchini can be used instead of broccoli.)

Separate the broccoli heads into florets, and peel and slice the stems. Blanch all the broccoli pieces in a large pot of boiling salted water for several minutes. Then drain them and immerse them in cold water. Drain again thoroughly in a colander.

Heat the oil in a wok or large skillet. When it is moderately hot, add the garlic and broccoli pieces. Stir-fry them for about 1 minute, and then add the hoisin sauce and water. Continue to stir-fry at moderately high heat for about 5 minutes, or until the broccoli pieces are thoroughly cooked. Serve at once.

Clockwise from lower left: Stir-fried Ground Pork (page 74), Kidney and Bean-Curd Soup (page 67), Stir-fried Ginger Broccoli (page 146), Cold Marinated Bean Sprouts (page 145).

Stir-fried Bok Choi

Region: southern
Method: stir-frying

Serves 2 to 4
 1 tablespoon oil
 1½ pounds bok choi
 1 tablespoon light soy sauce
 1 teaspoon salt
 2 tablespoons Chicken Stock
  (page 60) or water

Bok choi was a staple food in my childhood as it was inexpensive, nutritious and readily available. Even today I look forward to this simple stir-fried dish. Sometimes the leaves are merely blanched, but I think they are delicious stir-fried with oil and garlic or with a little soy sauce and stock. It makes a delicious dish to serve with meat and fish and is excellent in vegetarian menus. You can get bok choi at Chinese groceries, but Swiss chard or snow peas work equally well in this recipe.

Heat a wok or large skillet over moderate heat. Add the oil and then the *bok choi*. Stir-fry for 3 to 4 minutes, until the leaves have wilted a little. Then add the soy sauce, salt and chicken stock or water. Continue to stir-fry for a few more minutes, until the *bok choi* is done but still slightly crisp.

Spiced Chinese Cabbage

Region: western
Method: braising

Serves 2 to 4
 1½ pounds Chinese cabbage
 1 tablespoon oil
 2 teaspoons finely chopped ginger
  root
 2 teaspoons finely chopped garlic
 1 dried red chili, or 1 teaspoon chili
  powder
 1 tablespoon rice wine or dry sherry
 2 tablespoons dark soy sauce
 2 teaspoons sugar
 ¼ cup water
 2 teaspoons sesame oil

Unlike the more familiar green and red cabbage, Chinese cabbage (page 141) has a bland, sweet, delicate flavor rather like lettuce. Cooking is needed to make it palatable, and because it is so light, it calls for a robust sauce. I like to serve it with this spicy sauce. For a variation you could substitute curry powder for the chili.

Separate the cabbage leaves and wash them well. Cut them into 1-inch strips.

Heat a large wok or skillet. When it is hot, add the oil. A few seconds later add the ginger and stir-fry it quickly. Then add the garlic and dried chili if you are using it. Toss them well for a few seconds and then add the rice wine or sherry, soy sauce, sugar, water and the chili powder if you are using it. Bring the mixture to a simmer and then add the Chinese cabbage. Boil over high heat for 5 minutes until it is thoroughly cooked, stirring occasionally. Just before you serve it, add the sesame oil and stir it in well.

Chinese Cabbage in Soy Sauce

Region: southern
Method: blanching

Serves 2 to 3
 1 pound Chinese cabbage
 1 tablespoon light soy sauce
 1 tablespoon oil, preferably peanut

This simple dish is one of my favorite ways of preparing Chinese cabbage. The blanching preserves its sweetness while the hot oil imparts a rich nutty flavor to the vegetable. It is quick and easy to make. You can also use white cabbage or any other leafy green vegetable for this dish.

Cut the cabbage leaves into 1½-inch strips and blanch them in a pot of boiling salted water for about 1 minute. Drain thoroughly, and put the blanched leaves onto a platter. Dribble the soy sauce over them.

Heat the oil in a wok or skillet until it is almost smoking and then pour the hot oil over the leaves. Serve at once. For a spicy taste, try using Chili Oil (page 29) instead of peanut oil.

Stir-fried Cucumbers with Hot Spices

It always mystified me when I was a child to see Americans eating cucumbers raw. We Chinese never eat them like this. If they are not pickled, then they must be cooked. We prefer them when they are in season, young, tender and bursting with juice. This is a simple stir-fried cucumber dish from western China. Once the ingredients are assembled, it is very quick to cook. The chili and garlic contrast well with the cool, crisp cucumber.

Peel the cucumbers, slice them in half lengthwise and, using a teaspoon, remove the seeds. Then cut the cucumber halves into 1-inch pieces. Sprinkle them with the salt and mix well. Put the mixture into a colander and let it sit for 20 minutes to drain. (This rids the cucumber of any excess liquid.) When the cucumber pieces have drained, rinse them in water and then blot them dry with paper towels.

Heat a wok or large skillet until it is hot. Add the oil, and when it is almost smoking add the chili bean sauce or chili powder, garlic and black beans and stir for about 30 seconds. Then add the cucumbers and stir for a few seconds until they are coated with the spices and flavorings. Add the water and continue to stir-fry over high heat for 3 to 4 minutes, until most of the water has evaporated and the cucumbers are cooked. At this point, add the sesame oil and serve immediately.

Region: western
Method: stir-frying

Serves 4 to 6
  2 medium cucumbers (about 1½ pounds)
  2 teaspoons salt
  1 tablespoon oil
  ½ teaspoon chili bean sauce or chili powder
  1½ tablespoons finely chopped garlic
  1½ tablespoons coarsely chopped black beans
  ½ cup water
  1 teaspoon sesame oil

(pictured on page 55)

Cold Sweet and Sour Chinese Cabbage

In northern China, with its short growing season and long cold winters, fresh vegetables are available for only a few months of the year. In the absence of modern refrigeration, other means of preserving foods are necessary. Some of the most common methods are pickling in brine, in salt and wine, in a mixture of sugar and salt, or by inducing fermentation.

In this recipe from the north, Chinese cabbage undergoes what is essentially a sweet and sour pickling process. It can be eaten at once or stored for later use. Dishes like this are served at room temperature at the beginning of a meal, and their sweet and sour flavors are designed to stimulate the palate and whet the appetite.

Blanch the Chinese cabbage strips in hot water for a few seconds until they wilt. Drain them and put them to one side in a glass bowl. Heat the two oils in a pan or wok until they are hot. Add the chilies and whole roasted peppercorns. When the chilies and peppercorns turn dark, turn the heat off. Pour the flavored oil through a strainer and then over the leaves. Wrap the chilies and peppercorns in cheesecloth and tie it into a bag like a bouquet garni, so that it can be removed later. Place it among the vegetable strips.

Now add the sugar and vinegar to the leaves and mix well. Add the salt, ginger and garlic and make sure that all the ingredients are mixed in well. Let the mixture sit at room temperature for several hours. It is now ready to be refrigerated overnight and then served. This dish will keep for up to 1 week in the refrigerator. Before you serve it, drain off all the marinade and remove the chili-peppercorn bouquet garni.

Region: northern
Method: blanching and pickling

Serves 4 to 6
  1½ pounds Chinese cabbage, cut into 2-inch strips
  ⅓ cup peanut oil
  1 tablespoon sesame oil
  5 dried red chilies
  2 tablespoons whole roasted Sichuan peppercorns (page 26)
  4 ounces Chinese rock sugar, or ¼ cup granulated
  ⅔ cup Chinese white rice vinegar or cider vinegar
  1½ tablespoons salt
  1 tablespoon finely chopped ginger root
  2 tablespoons finely chopped garlic

(pictured on page 185)

Spicy Stir-fried Mushrooms

Region: western
Method: stir-frying

Serves 4

1 tablespoon oil, preferably peanut
1 teaspoon finely chopped ginger
  root
2 teaspoons finely chopped scallions
1 teaspoon finely chopped garlic
½ pound small fresh mushrooms,
  whole
1 teaspoon chili bean sauce
2 teaspoons rice wine or dry sherry
2 teaspoons dark soy sauce
1 tablespoon Chicken Stock
  (page 60) or water
½ teaspoon sugar
¼ teaspoon salt
1 teaspoon sesame oil

The cultivated mushrooms common in Europe and America were virtually unknown in China until quite recently. They are now increasingly popular there. Their mild, subtle flavor makes them perfect for stir-frying with Chinese spices. This dish is simple to make and reheats well. Serve it with Braised Duck (page 114) and plain steamed rice. It also goes perfectly with grilled meats.

Heat a wok or large skillet over high heat until it is hot. Add the oil and then the ginger, scallions and garlic. Stir-fry for about 20 seconds. Then add the mushrooms and stir-fry them for about 30 seconds. Quickly add the rest of the ingredients except the sesame oil. Continue to stir-fry for about 5 minutes or until the mushrooms are cooked through and have absorbed all the spices and seasonings. Just before serving, add the sesame oil and give the mixture a couple of quick stirs. Turn it onto a warm serving dish and serve at once.

Three Mushrooms Braised

Region: southern
Method: stir-frying and braising

Serves 4 to 6

1 ounce Chinese dried mushrooms
  (about 10 large)
8 ounces canned Chinese straw
  mushrooms
3 ounces button mushrooms
1 tablespoon oil
1 tablespoon light soy sauce
2 tablespoons rice wine or
  dry sherry
3 tablespoons oyster sauce
2 teaspoons granulated sugar
2 teaspoons finely chopped garlic
⅓ cup Chicken Stock (page 60)
2 tablespoons finely chopped
  scallions

Mushrooms are very popular in China, especially in the south where the warm, moist climate is ideal for fungi. The varieties of mushrooms are endless. The three used in this recipe have very different characteristics: straw mushrooms have a musky scent and meaty texture; Chinese dried mushrooms are smoky-flavored and densely textured; button mushrooms are mild and soft. Combining all three in a substantial and rich sauce transforms the mushroom from a supporting ingredient to a vegetable dish in its own right. Straw and dried mushrooms can be bought at Chinese groceries but if you can't get them, this recipe is nearly as delicious made entirely with button ones (use 12 ounces button mushrooms).

Soak the Chinese dried mushrooms in warm water for 20 minutes, and then drain them. Rinse them well and squeeze out any excess liquid. Discard the tough stems, then shred the caps and put them aside. Drain and rinse the canned straw mushrooms, but leave them whole. Wash and slice the button mushrooms.

Heat a wok or large skillet, then add the oil. Now add all the mushrooms and stir-fry them, mixing them well, for a few seconds. Then quickly add the soy sauce, rice wine or sherry, oyster sauce, sugar, garlic and chicken stock. Turn the heat down and cook for about 7 minutes, stirring continuously until the fresh mushrooms are thoroughly cooked. Then mix in the scallions, stir for a few seconds, and serve at once.

Stir-fried Spinach with Garlic

Spinach has often been regarded with disdain in the West, probably because it is usually overcooked. This is a time-honored, delicious southern Chinese recipe. The spinach is quickly stir-fried and then seasoned. It is very simple to prepare and may be served hot or cold.

Wash the spinach thoroughly. Remove all the stems, leaving just the leaves. Heat a large wok or skillet over moderate heat. Add the oil, and then add the salt and spinach. Stir-fry for about 2 minutes to coat the spinach leaves thoroughly with the oil and salt. When the spinach has wilted to about one-third of its original size, add the sugar and garlic and continue to stir-fry for another 4 minutes. Transfer the spinach to a plate and pour off any excess liquid. Serve hot or cold.

Region: southern
Method: stir-frying

Serves 4
  1½ pounds fresh spinach
  1 tablespoon oil
  ½ teaspoon salt
  1 teaspoon granulated sugar
  2 teaspoons finely chopped garlic

(pictured on page 109)

Pickled Vegetables

Pickled vegetables were much more common in Western households before the advent of the domestic refrigerator. Now they are usually only available sold in jars and full of preservatives. This I regard as one of the losses we have incurred with progress. Even today pickled vegetables, fruits and ginger are still very popular with the Chinese, and deservedly so. I remember watching my mother pickling vegetables for use the following week. She often used to pickle carrots and turnips, but my favorite was pickled young fresh ginger. Pickled vegetables make delicious snacks and appetizers and can also be used to garnish cold platters. They are easy to make and may be prepared well ahead. They should rest in the brine mixture for at least 3 to 4 days; thereafter, they will keep in the refrigerator for up to 2 weeks.

First prepare all the vegetables. Cut the peeled carrots, white radish or turnips and the washed Chinese leaves or cabbage into chunks 1 inch × ½ inch. Thinly slice the fresh chilies, retaining the seeds.

   Now mix all the pickling brine ingredients together in a glass bowl and stir them to make sure the salt and sugar have dissolved. Put the vegetables into the brine and let them sit in the refrigerator, covered, for 3 or 4 days. Drain the vegetables and rinse them well in cold water before storing them in a covered glass bowl in the refrigerator. They will keep for 2 weeks. Before you serve the vegetables, discard any brine that has collected in the bowl. And remember that the longer you leave them in the brine, the stronger and saltier they will be.

Region: northern and western
Method: pickling

Makes 2 pounds
  ½ pound carrots, peeled
  1 pound white radish or turnips, peeled
  ½ pound Chinese cabbage
  2 fresh red or green chilies

Pickling brine
  ¼ cup salt
  9 cups water
  ⅓ cup rice wine or dry sherry
  ½ cup granulated sugar
  2 tablespoons finely chopped ginger root
  2 tablespoons finely chopped garlic

Fried Stuffed Cucumbers

Region: eastern
Method: shallow-frying

Serves 4 to 6
  2 medium cucumbers (about 1½
    pounds)
  2 tablespoons cornstarch
  1 tablespoon oil, more if needed

Stuffing
  ½ pound fatty pork, finely ground
  1 tablespoon finely chopped
    scallions
  2 teaspoons finely chopped ginger
    root
  2 teaspoons rice wine or dry sherry
  2 teaspoons light soy sauce
  2 teaspoons sugar
  ½ teaspoon salt
  1 small egg

Sauce
  1⅓ cups Chicken Stock (page 60)
  2 tablespoons rice wine or dry
    sherry
  2 tablespoons light soy sauce
  2 teaspoons sugar

Garnish
  1 teaspoon sesame oil
  1 tablespoon finely chopped fresh
    coriander

There are countless Chinese recipes for all kinds of stuffed vegetables. Even bean curd can be filled. Cucumbers, in particular, lend themselves to stuffing because their tender, succulent flesh is complemented by a savory filling. The stuffing in this recipe uses seasoned ground pork, but you can use ground beef instead if you prefer. Thick cucumber slices are stuffed and then shallow-fried; this seals in the flavors of the stuffing. Then the cucumbers are simmered to create the sauce. I think you will agree that cucumbers have never tasted so good!

Cut the cucumbers into 1-inch slices without peeling them. Remove the seeds and pulp from the center of each cucumber slice using a small sharp knife. Lightly dust the hollow interior of the cucumber slices with a little cornstarch. Mix all the stuffing ingredients together in a large bowl. Then stuff each cucumber ring with this mixture.

Heat a wok or large skillet and add the oil. When it is moderately hot, add the stuffed cucumber rings and cook them slowly until they are lightly browned. Turn them over and brown the other side, adding more oil if necessary. You may have to do this in several batches. When the cucumber rings are brown, remove them from the oil and put them on a plate. When you have fried all the cucumber rings, wipe the wok or pan clean.

Mix the sauce ingredients and put them into the reheated wok or pan. Bring the liquid to a simmer, and then add the stuffed cucumber rings. Cover with a lid and simmer slowly for 7 minutes, or until the cucumbers are completely cooked. Transfer them to a serving platter, lifting them out of the sauce with a slotted spoon.

Reduce the sauce by a third over high heat. Then add the sesame oil and fresh coriander. Pour the sauce over the stuffed cucumbers and serve at once.

Lettuce with Oyster Sauce

Region: southern
Method: blanching

Serves 2 to 4
  1 head Romaine or iceberg lettuce
    (about 1½ pounds)
  3 tablespoons oyster sauce
  1 tablespoon oil

(pictured on page 69)

Here is lettuce prepared in a very familiar Chinese way—blanched and served with oyster sauce. Lettuce prepared like this retains a crispy texture and its delicate flavor is unimpaired by cooking. The combination makes a simple, quickly prepared, tasty vegetable dish.

Separate the lettuce leaves and blanch them in a pot of boiling salted water for about 30 seconds, or until they have wilted slightly. Remove them and drain well. Mix the oyster sauce with the oil. Arrange the lettuce leaves on a serving dish, pour the oyster sauce mixture over it, and serve immediately.

Fried Stuffed Cucumbers (facing page).

Snow Peas with Water Chestnuts

Fresh water chestnuts are cultivated between rows of rice plants. You can some-times buy them fresh, but canned ones are easier to find. Fresh water chestnuts are often dipped into a sugar syrup and eaten as a snack. Cooked, they have a sweet taste and a crunchy texture. This is a straightforward recipe which should be made with the freshest snow peas you can find. Asparagus, when in season, makes a delightful alternative.

If you are using fresh water chestnuts, peel them. If you are using canned water chestnuts, drain them well and rinse in cold water. Thinly slice the water chestnuts.

Heat a wok or large skillet over medium heat. Add the oil, and when it is hot, add the scallions. A few seconds later, add the snow peas and fresh water chestnuts if you are using them, and stir-fry for 1 minute. Make sure you coat them thoroughly with the oil. Then add the rest of the ingredients and continue to stir-fry for another 3 minutes. If you are using canned water chestnuts, add these now and cook for a further 2 minutes or until the vegetables are cooked. Serve at once.

Region: eastern and southern
Method: stir-frying

Serves 2 to 4
12 fresh water chestnuts, or 1
   8-ounce can, drained
1 tablespoon oil, preferably peanut
3 tablespoons finely chopped
   scallions
½ pound snow peas, trimmed
1 tablespoon light soy sauce
2 tablespoons water
½ teaspoon salt
½ teaspoon granulated sugar
1 teaspoon sesame oil

(pictured on pages 65 and 112)

Buddhist Casserole (facing page).

Buddhist Casserole

This is my adaptation of a famous Buddhist dish. The original recipe calls for many obscure dried Chinese vegetables but my version uses vegetables that are readily available. I like to add a little coriander, which Buddhists do not eat. A deeply satisfying dish, this casserole is suitable for both summer and winter. I prefer to cook it in a Chinese clay pot (see page 37) but you can also use a good, small cast-iron pot. Take care not to overcook the vegetables. The casserole may be made in advance and reheated very slowly. It is delicious with rice, noodles or even with fresh bread.

Cut the bean curd into 1-inch cubes. Next prepare all the vegetables. Separate the broccoli heads and break them into small florets. Peel and slice the broccoli stems. Cut the Chinese cabbage into 1-inch chunks. Slice the zucchini into rounds ¼ inch thick, or roll cut them (see page 40). Thinly slice the pepper. Leave the snow peas whole, but trim the ends.

Heat the oil in a deep-fat fryer or large wok. When the oil is almost smoking, deep-fry the bean curd cubes in two batches. Drain each cooked batch on paper towels.

Put the chicken stock, soy sauce, hoisin sauce and bean sauce into a large cast-iron enamel pot or Chinese clay pot and bring it to a boil. Next add the broccoli and stir in the Chinese leaves or cabbage. Boil for 2 minutes. Then add the zucchini and pepper and cook for another 2 minutes. Finally add the snow peas and bean curd cubes. Cook for 1 minute more, then stir in the fresh coriander and the dish is ready to serve. (The dish should be quite liquid.) To reheat, bring to a simmer over very low heat until all the vegetables are hot.

Region: eastern
Method: deep-frying and braising

Serves 4 to 6
   8 ounces fresh bean curd (1 cake)
   ¼ pound broccoli
   ¼ pound Chinese cabbage
   1 to 2 small zucchini
   1 red bell pepper, sliced
   ¼ pound snow peas, washed and
      trimmed
   2 cups oil (see Deep-fat fryers,
      page 35)
   3½ cups Chicken Stock (page 60)
   2 tablespoons light soy sauce
   3 tablespoons hoisin sauce
   2 tablespoons bean sauce
   1 tablespoon finely chopped fresh
      coriander

Braised Cauliflower with Oyster Sauce

I find cauliflower a versatile vegetable, both delicious and easy to prepare. It has a distinct but rather mild taste which goes very well with oyster sauce. It takes a little while to cook, so stir-frying is not the most appropriate method. I prefer to braise it in oyster sauce.

Cut the cauliflower into small florets about 1 to 1½ inches wide.

Heat a wok or large skillet over a moderate heat. Add the oil and then add the garlic and ginger. Stir-fry for about 20 seconds to flavor the oil. Then remove the garlic and ginger and discard them. Add the cauliflower florets and stir-fry them for a few seconds. Next add the salt, oyster sauce and the stock or water. Bring the mixture to a simmer and cook for 5 to 10 minutes, or until the cauliflower is tender. Turn onto a warm serving platter and sprinkle with the scallions. Serve at once.

Region: southern
Method: braising

Serves 4
   1½ pounds cauliflower
   1 tablespoon oil, preferably peanut
   2 garlic cloves, crushed
   2 slices ginger root
   ½ teaspoon salt
   3 tablespoons oyster sauce
   2 cups Chicken Stock (page 60) or
      water

Garnish
   2 tablespoons finely chopped
      scallions

(pictured on page 13)

Assorted Chinese noodles: Dried egg noodles, dried rice noodles, bean thread noodles and fresh egg noodles.

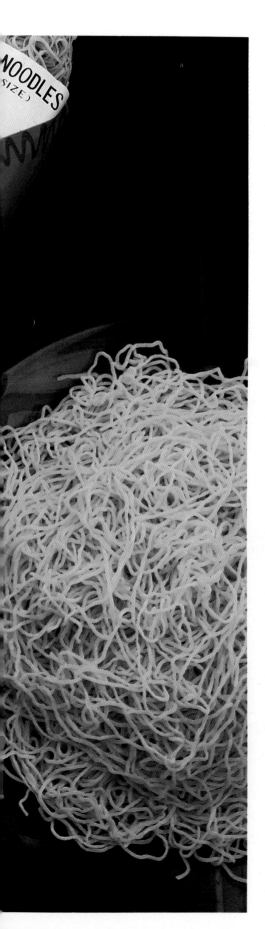

RICE, NOODLES AND DOUGHS

麵飯

All Chinese meals must be composed of two parts: the *cai*, or meat, fish, poultry and vegetable dishes, and the *fan*, or staple. Both parts are important. As one Chinese sage put it, "Without the *cai* the meal is less tasteful, but without the *fan* one's hunger cannot be satisfied." Most Westerners think that rice is the only Chinese staple food, but in the northern parts of China where it is too cold to grow it, wheat takes precedence and so noodles, dumplings and pancakes are eaten more often than rice. This chapter is divided into three sections: rice; noodles; and doughs, which include dumplings, buns and pancakes. I have given detailed information on different types of rice, noodles and flour in the appropriate sections.

Rice

There are many types of rice, including long-grain, short-grain and glutinous varieties, and all are made into flour, noodles, wines and vinegars as well as being used in cooking. Brown rice, which is popular in the West, is not used by the Chinese, who dislike its texture. Plain boiled or steamed white rice is eaten with meals. Fried rice, now popular in Chinese restaurants all over the world, is served in China as a snack or as the last course at a banquet, and never with other *cai* dishes.

LONG-GRAIN RICE

This is the most popular rice for cooking in southern China and it is my favorite too. It needs to be washed before it is cooked. Do not confuse it with the "easy-cook" and precooked varieties which are now widely available, as these are unsuitable for Chinese cooking. They lack the starchy flavor, texture and clean white color which is so essential to Chinese cuisine.

SHORT-GRAIN RICE

Short-grain rice is usually used in Chinese cooking for making congee and is more popular outside southern China. Varieties known as "American Rose" or "Japanese Rose" are very suitable and can be found in many Chinese groceries. If you cannot find the short-grain rice, use long-grain instead.

GLUTINOUS RICE

Glutinous rice is also known as sweet rice or sticky rice. It is short, round and pearl-like, and is not to be confused with regular short-grain rice or pudding rice. It has more gluten than ordinary rice, and when cooked is stickier and sweeter. It is used mainly for stuffings and desserts and for making Chinese rice wine and vinegar. Most Chinese grocers stock it. Glutinous rice must be washed and soaked for at least 2 hours before cooking. You may cook it in the same way as long-grain rice (see page 157) or by steaming. If you want to steam it, soak the rice for at least 8 hours or overnight. Then line a bamboo steamer with cheesecloth and spread the rice over it. Steam it for about 40 minutes or until the rice is cooked.

TO WASH RICE

Put the required amount of rice in a large bowl. Fill the bowl with cold water and swish the rice around with a spoon or with your hands. Carefully pour off the cloudy water, keeping the rice in the bowl. Repeat this process several times until the water is clear.

Ken at the Monterey Market, Berkeley.

Steaming rice the Chinese way is quite easy. I prefer to use long-grain white rice, which is drier and fluffier when cooked. Don't use precooked or "easy-cook" rice for Chinese cookery as both have insufficient flavor and lack the texture and starchy taste which is fundamental to Chinese rice.

The secret of preparing rice without it being sticky is to cook it first at a high heat until most of the water has evaporated. Then the heat should be turned very low, the pot covered and the rice cooked slowly in the remaining steam. As a child I was always instructed never to peek into the rice pot during this stage or else precious steam would escape and the rice would not be cooked properly, bringing bad luck.

Here is a good trick to remember: if you make sure that you cover the rice with about 1 inch of water, it should always cook properly without sticking. Many package recipes for rice use too much water and result in a gluey mess. Follow my method and you will have perfect steamed rice, the easy Chinese way.

Most Chinese eat quite large quantities of rice (as much as 2 cups of cooked rice in one meal, which is more than many Westerners are able to manage). This recipe and the one for Fried Rice allow 2 cups uncooked rice for 4 people. If you want more than that, just increase the quantity of rice, but remember to add enough water so that the level of water is about 1 inch above the top of the rice.

Put the rice into a large bowl and wash it in several changes of water until the water runs clear. Drain the rice and put it into a heavy pot with the water and bring it to a boil. Continue boiling until most of the surface liquid has evaporated. This should take about 15 to 20 minutes. The surface of the rice should have small indentations like a pitted crater. At this point, cover the pot with a very tight-fitting lid, turn the heat as low as possible and let the rice cook undisturbed for 15 to 20 minutes. There is no need to "fluff" the rice before serving it.

Region: all
Method: steaming

Serves 4
2 cups uncooked long-grain rice
3½ cups water

Fried Rice

Region: eastern
Method: stir-frying

Serves 4
   2 ounces Smithfield ham or
      prosciutto
   ¼ pound fresh or frozen peas
      (¼ cup)
   2 tablespoons oil, preferably peanut
   2 cups long-grain rice, steamed
      (page 159) and chilled
   1 teaspoon salt
   2 eggs, beaten
   4 ounces fresh bean sprouts
      (about 1 cup)

Garnish
   2 tablespoons finely chopped
      scallions

In China fried rice is eaten as a "filler" at the end of a dinner party. It is not eaten with other dishes in place of steamed rice, though many Westerners do so. Although fried rice is common in Chinese restaurants, it is frequently incorrectly cooked. Often the rice is sticky and colored with soy sauce. Here are a few important points to remember when making authentic fried rice.

● The cooked rice should be thoroughly cool, preferably cold. Once cooled, much of the moisture in the rice evaporates, allowing the oil to coat the dry grains and keep them from sticking. (For hygienic reasons, always store cooked rice in the refrigerator, never at room temperature, and only remove it when you are ready to cook it.)

● Never put any soy sauce into fried rice. This not only colors the rice unnaturally but also makes it too salty.

● Some recipes for fried rice involve cooking the eggs ahead of time and then adding them to the fried rice. Never do this, as the eggs will get tough and dry.

● Always be sure the oil is hot enough to avoid saturating the rice. Saturated rice is greasy and heavy.

If you follow these simple guidelines, you will be rewarded with fried rice as it should be. Fried rice goes with almost any dish, but in China it is usually served at the end of a dinner to clean the palate.

Cut the ham into fine dice. Blanch the peas in a saucepan of boiling water for about 5 minutes if they are fresh or 2 minutes if they are frozen. Drain them in a colander.

   Heat a wok or large skillet until it is hot. Then add the oil and wait until it is almost smoking. Add the cooked rice and stir-fry it for 1 minute, and then add the ham or bacon, peas and salt. Continue to stir-fry the mixture for 5 minutes over high heat. Next add the beaten egg and bean sprouts and continue to stir-fry for 2 minutes or until the eggs have set. Turn the mixture onto a plate and garnish it with the scallions. Serve at once, or let it cool and serve as a cold rice salad.

This is a popular rice dish in the south. At first glance the recipe may seem similar to that for Fried Rice (page 160), but it is really quite different since the rice and the other ingredients all have to be cooked separately and then combined. It is a substantial dish, beautifully colored and ideal for a special dinner.

Prepare the rice as instructed in the recipe on page 159. While it is steaming, soak the dried mushrooms in warm water for about 20 minutes, until they are soft. Meanwhile cut the red pepper, carrot and sausages or ham into small dice. Squeeze the excess liquid from the mushrooms and remove and discard their stems. Cut the caps into small dice. If you are using frozen peas make sure they are thoroughly thawed.

Heat a wok or large skillet. Add the oil and scallions and stir-fry for about 30 seconds. Then add all the vegetables and the sausages or ham. Stir-fry the mixture for about 2 minutes and then add the soy sauce. Give the mixture a few stirs and then add the sesame oil. Remove the pan from the heat and let the mixture cool.

When the rice is almost ready, pour the cooked mixture over it to cover the rice. Let the rice and the stir-fried mixture cook for a further 5 minutes. Then stir to mix well. Turn onto a serving platter and serve at once.

Region: southern
Method: stir-frying

Serves 4 to 6
2 cups long-grain rice
2 ounces Chinese dried mushrooms (about 20)
½ red bell pepper
1 to 2 carrots
4 ounces Chinese sausages or Smithfield ham
3 tablespoons green peas, fresh or frozen
2 tablespoons oil, preferably peanut
3 tablespoons finely chopped scallions
1 tablespoon light soy sauce
2 teaspoons sesame oil

Rainbow Rice.

Rice Cake

Region: all
Method: steaming

Makes a 9-inch rice cake
1 cup long-grain rice
2⅓ cups water
2 teaspoons oil, preferably peanut

Rice cakes were probably invented by a thrifty cook centuries ago in order to make use of that thin layer of rice which sometimes gets stuck at the bottom of the pot. This crispy leftover has evolved into an accompaniment to many dishes. After trying rice cakes you will never discard your leftover rice crust again.

Do not use "converted" rice for this dish because it does not have enough starch to form a crust; use long-grain white rice. Basically the method is the same as for steamed rice, but the cooking time is longer.

Wash the rice and put it, with the water, in a 9- or 9½-inch-wide heavy pot. Bring the water to a boil over high heat. Then turn the heat down as low as possible, cover and let the rice cook for about 45 minutes. The rice should form a heavy crust on the bottom. Remove all the loose surface rice, leaving the heavy crust. This loose rice can be used for making Fried Rice (page 160).

Dribble the oil evenly over the top of the crust and let it cook over a very low heat for 5 minutes. The crust should lift off easily at this point. If it is still sticky, add another teaspoon of oil and continue to cook until the whole thing comes loose. Put the crust onto a plate until it is ready for use. Once it has been cooked, it can be left out at room temperature for several days. Do not cover it, as moisture will form and make the cake soggy. Let the rice cake dry out, and it is then ready to be deep-fried and added to hot chicken stock for a sizzling rice soup or shrimp (page 134).

Chicken, Sausage and Rice Casserole.

Rice congee is what many Chinese eat for breakfast; it is simply a boiled rice porridge. In various areas of China, fried dough bread, fermented bean curd, pickles, preserved salt or spicy mustard greens may be added to the congee. In the south, meat, chicken, roast duck, peanuts or fermented eggs are added. Interestingly enough, the word congee is a Hindi word and this perhaps indicates the origin of the dish.

The technique used in making congee is to boil the rice and then simmer it slowly. The starch is released gradually, thickening the porridge without the rice grains disintegrating. I find short-grain rice best for making congee, but you can use long-grain. In this recipe the rice needs no washing as all the starch is needed to thicken the porridge.

Cut the Chinese sausage, or whatever flavoring you are using, into fine dice and set aside. You should have ⅓ to ½ cup.

Bring the water to a boil in a large pot and add the rice and salt. Let the mixture come back to a boil and give it several good stirs. Then turn the heat down to low and cover the pot. Let the mixture simmer for about 35 minutes, stirring occasionally. Then add the Chinese sausages or other flavoring and simmer for a further 5 minutes with the pot uncovered. Just before serving, add the scallions and fresh coriander. Serve it at once. If you like, congee can be made in advance. In this case reheat it slowly and add some more water if the porridge is too thick.

Region: southern
Method: simmering

Serves 4
¼ pound Chinese sausages (or any other flavoring of your choice, such as Sichuan preserved vegetable, or diced cooked chicken or duck)
3 cups water
2 cups short-grain rice
½ teaspoon salt
2 tablespoons finely chopped scallions
1 tablespoon finely chopped fresh coriander

I have many pleasant memories of this dish. Even though I grew up in America, I often took a typically Chinese lunch to school. Very early in the morning, my mother would steam chicken and sausage with rice and put it in a thermos to keep it warm. I would often exchange bits of my hot lunch for portions of my classmates' sandwiches! This dish is easy to make and is a simple but fully satisfying meal in itself.

It is well worth the effort to try to get authentic Chinese sausages from a Chinese food shop. Pork sausages could be substituted, but they should be browned first to rid them of their excess fat, and, of course, the taste will be quite different.

Cut the chicken into 2-inch pieces. Put these into a bowl and combine them with the rice wine or dry sherry, soy sauce, sugar and sesame oil. Let the mixture sit for at least 20 minutes. If you are using the dried mushrooms, soak them in warm water for 20 minutes. Then drain them, squeeze out any excess liquid, cut off and discard the stems and coarsely chop the mushroom caps. Slice the Chinese sausages thinly into 2-inch pieces at a slight diagonal. If you are using pork sausages, grill them for 3 minutes to partially cook them, and then slice them into 2-inch rounds.

Combine the rice and stock in a large pot and bring to a boil. Continue to boil until most of the surface liquid above the rice has evaporated. Then mix in the chicken, mushrooms, ginger, scallions and sausages. Turn the heat down low, cover, and cook for about 25 minutes until the rice, chicken and pork are cooked. Serve at once. You might serve this with Braised Spicy Eggplant (page 143) or Spiced Chinese Cabbage (page 148).

Region: southern
Method: steaming

Serves 4 to 6
2 pounds boneless chicken pieces, skinned
1 tablespoon rice wine or dry sherry
1 tablespoon light soy sauce
2 teaspoons sugar
1 teaspoon sesame oil
1 ounce Chinese dried mushrooms (about 10) (optional)
6 ounces Chinese sausages or pork sausages
2 cups long-grain rice, washed
3½ cups Chicken Stock (page 60) or water
1½ tablespoons finely chopped ginger root
2 tablespoons finely chopped scallions

Noodles

There has always been an argument about whether the Chinese invented noodles before the Italians discovered spaghetti. Chinese noodles are more varied than Italian ones. They come in all shapes and sizes and are made from a variety of flours. They are most commonly made from wheat or rice flour and water, and in the south from wheat flour, water and eggs. There is also a type which is made from mung beans, although this is strictly speaking not a noodle but a vegetable.

To see an expert noodle maker at work is a real treat. Handmade noodles are formed by an elaborate but rapid process of kneading, pulling, tossing and twisting of the dough into a cascade of fine long noodles. This spectacular skill takes four to five years to acquire and is a delight to watch.

Noodles play an important part in Chinese tradition since they are a symbol of longevity. For this reason they are often served at Chinese New Year and at birthday dinners, and it is considered bad luck to cut them since this might shorten one's life! Noodles can be boiled and eaten plain instead of rice, with sauces, cold as salads, or in soups. Alternatively, fried with meat and vegetables they make a delicious and sustaining light meal. Here are some of the most common types of noodles.

WHEAT NOODLES AND EGG NOODLES

These are made from hard or soft wheat flour and water. If egg has been added the noodles are usually labeled as egg noodles. They can be bought dried or fresh from Chinese grocers, and many supermarkets and delicatessens also stock the dried variety. Flat noodles are usually used in soups and rounded noodles are best for stir-frying. If you can't get Chinese noodles you can use Italian egg noddles (dried or fresh) instead.

RICE NOODLES

Rice noodles are popular in southern China, especially with seafood. They are usually dried and can be found in Chinese groceries. They are white and come in a variety of shapes. One of the most common is rice stick noodles, which are flat and about the length of a chopstick. Rice noodles are very easy to use. Simply soak them in warm water for 15 minutes until they are soft. Drain them in a colander or a sieve and they are then ready to be used in soups or to be stir-fried.

BEAN THREAD (CELLOPHANE) NOODLES

These noodles, also called transparent noodles, are made from ground mung beans and not from a grain. They are available dried, and are very fine and white. Easy to recognize, packed in their neat, plastic-wrapped bundles, they are stocked by most Chinese grocers and some supermarkets. I like to buy the small (1.7 ounce) size package. Bean thread noodles are never served on their own but are added to soups or braised dishes or are deep-fried as a garnish. They must be soaked in warm water for about 5 minutes before use. As they are rather long you might find it easier to cut them into shorter lengths after soaking.

Stir-fried Rice Noodles with Vegetables (page 169).

Boiled Wheat or Egg Noodles

Serves 2 to 4
½ pound fresh or dried noodles

Noodles are very good boiled and served with main dishes instead of plain rice. I think dried wheat or fresh egg noodles are best for this.

If you are using fresh noodles, immerse them in a pot of boiling water and cook them for 3 to 5 minutes, until they are soft. If you are using dried noodles, either cook them according to the instructions on the package, or cook them in boiling water for 4 to 5 minutes. Then drain and serve.

If you are cooking noodles ahead of time, before using them in another dish or before stir-frying them, toss the cooked drained noodles in 2 teaspoons of sesame oil and put them in a bowl. Cover this with plastic wrap and put it in the refrigerator. The cooked noodles will keep like this for about 2 hours.

Bean Sauce Noodles

Region: northern
**Method: stir-frying and
          simmering**

Serves 4
1 pound dried or fresh egg noodles
1½ tablespoons sesame oil

Sauce
1 tablespoon oil, preferably peanut
1½ tablespoons finely chopped
    garlic
2 tablespoons finely chopped
    scallions
1 pound ground pork
3 tablespoons bean sauce
1 to 2 teaspoons chili bean sauce
    (optional)
1 tablespoon rice wine or dry sherry
2 tablespoons dark soy sauce
2 teaspoons salt
1 teaspoon Chili Oil (page 29), or 2
    teaspoons chili powder
2 teaspoons granulated sugar
1⅓ cups Chicken Stock (page 60)
    or water

Garnish
2 tablespoons coarsely chopped
    scallions

Noodles are so popular in northern China that they are even eaten for breakfast, usually in soup. They are also a common snack. This recipe is an adaptation of a common noodle dish on which there are hundreds of variations. Once you have mastered this recipe you can add your own touches, just as the Chinese do. Serve with snacks such as Spring Rolls (page 177) and Fried Wonton (page 179).

If you are using fresh noodles, blanch them first by boiling them for 3 to 5 minutes in a pot of boiling water. If you are using dried noodles, cook them in boiling water for 4 or 5 minutes. Drain the noodles, toss them in the sesame oil and put them aside until you are ready to use them. They can be kept in this state, if tightly covered with plastic wrap, for up to 2 hours in the refrigerator.

Heat a wok or large skillet until it is hot. Then add the oil and when it is hot add the garlic and scallions. A few seconds later add the pork. Stir well to break up all the pieces and continue to stir-fry for about 1 minute or more until it loses its pink color. Then add the rest of the sauce ingredients, stirring all the time. Bring the mixture to a boil, turn the heat down to low and simmer for 5 minutes. Plunge the noodles into boiling water for 20 seconds and then drain them well in a colander or sieve. Then quickly tip the noodles into a large bowl and pour the hot sauce over the top. Sprinkle on the scallions, mix everything together well and serve at once.

Chow mein literally means "stir-fried noodles," and this dish is as popular outside China as it is in southern China. It is a quick and delicious way to prepare egg noodles. Almost any ingredients you like, such as fish, meat, poultry or vegetables, can be added to it. It is a popular lunch dish, either served at the end of the meal or eaten by itself. It also makes a tasty noodle salad when served cold.

If you are using dried noodles, cook them according to the instructions on the package or else boil them for 4 to 5 minutes. Then cool them in cold water until you are ready to use them. If you are using fresh Chinese noodles, boil them for 3 to 5 minutes and then immerse them in cold water.

Using a cleaver or sharp knife, slice the chicken breasts into fine shreds 2 inches long. Combine the chicken shreds with the 2 teaspoons of light soy sauce and rice wine or sherry in a small bowl. Mix well together and let the chicken marinate for about 10 minutes.

Heat a wok or large skillet, then add the 2 teaspoons of oil and then the chicken shreds. Stir-fry the mixture for about 2 minutes and then transfer to a plate. Clean the wok or pan.

Drain the noodles, shaking off as much water as possible. Reheat the pan and add the 1 tablespoon of oil and then the garlic. Stir-fry for 10 seconds and then add the snow peas and ham. Stir-fry for about 1 minute, and then add the noodles, 1 teaspoon of soy sauce, sugar and scallions. Continue to stir-fry for about 2 minutes and then return the chicken to the noodle mixture. Continue to stir-fry for about 3 to 4 minutes, or until the chicken is cooked. Next add the sesame oil and give the mixture a few final stirs. Turn it onto a warm platter and serve at once.

Region: southern
Method: stir-frying

Serves 4
½ pound dried or fresh egg noodles
¼ pound boneless chicken breasts, skinned
2 teaspoons light soy sauce
2 teaspoons rice wine or dry sherry
2 teaspoons oil, preferably peanut
1 tablespoon oil, preferably peanut
1 teaspoon finely chopped garlic
2 ounces snow peas, trimmed
1 ounce Smithfield ham or prosciutto, finely shredded (about 3 tablespoons)
1 teaspoon light soy sauce
½ teaspoon granulated sugar
1 tablespoon finely chopped scallions
1 teaspoon sesame oil

Noodles with Bean Sprouts and Ham

Like many Chinese noodle dishes this one is very easy to make. It is suitable for a simple lunch or for a picnic. Serve the noodles with snacks such as Stuffed Peppers (page 180) or Steamed Buns (page 172).

Cook the fresh or dried noodles for 3 to 5 minutes in a pot of boiling water. Then immerse them in cold water until you are ready to use them. (They can be left in the cold water for up to 1 hour.)

Now prepare the bean sprouts. I prefer to remove both ends of the sprouts as I think this gives them a cleaner look and taste. Shred the ham or bacon into 2-inch lengths.

Heat a wok or large skillet. Add all the sauce ingredients, except the sesame oil, and bring the liquid to a simmer. Add the cooked noodles and stir-fry them to mix them in well with the sauce. Then turn the heat back to high and add the bean sprouts, sesame oil and ham. Continue to stir-fry for about 3 minutes, until the noodles are thoroughly heated. Turn them onto a warm serving platter and serve at once.

Region: eastern
Method: stir-frying

Serves 4 to 6
1 pound dried or fresh egg noodles
¾ pound fresh bean sprouts (about 3 cups)
2 ounces Smithfield ham or prosciutto, shredded (about ¼ cup)

Sauce
1⅓ cups Chicken Stock (page 60)
2 tablespoons dark soy sauce
1 tablespoon light soy sauce
2 tablespoons rice wine or dry sherry
1 tablespoon finely chopped garlic
3 tablespoons finely chopped scallions
2 teaspoons sesame oil

Cold Spicy Noodles

Region: western
Method: blanching

Serves 4
1 pound dried or fresh egg noodles
1 tablespoon sesame oil

Sauce
3 tablespoons sesame paste or
    peanut butter
2 teaspoons chili powder
1½ tablespoons finely chopped
    garlic
2 teaspoons Chili Oil (page 29)
2 tablespoons light soy sauce
1 tablespoon dark soy sauce
1 tablespoon sesame oil
1 tablespoon chili bean sauce
2 teaspoons chopped ginger
1 teaspoon salt
2 teaspoons sugar

Garnish
3 tablespoons finely chopped
    scallions

(pictured on pages 65 and 185)

These savory noodles are perfect for summertime, and I enjoy making them because much of the work can be done ahead of time. Most people enjoy the fragrance of the sesame paste in this recipe, but if you can't get it you can use peanut butter instead. Cold Spicy Noodles makes a good picnic dish.

Cook the noodles by boiling them for 3 to 5 minutes in a pot of boiling water, and then put them into cold water until you are ready to use them.

Mix the sauce ingredients together in a bowl or in a blender. This can be done in advance and kept refrigerated, as the sauce is meant to be cold.

Drain the cooked noodles, and toss them with the sesame oil to make sure none of the noodles stick together. Arrange the noodles on a platter or in a large bowl. Pour the sauce over the top and sprinkle on the scallions. Toss the noodles well with the sauce before serving.

Beef Noodle Soup

Region: northern
Method: blanching and braising

Serves 4 to 6
2 pounds boneless beef
1 Chinese cinnamon bark or whole
    cinnamon stick
2 star anise (optional)
2 tablespoons light soy sauce
6 dried red chilies
2 dried citrus peels, soaked and
    finely chopped (page 19)
    (optional)
1 teaspoon salt
4⅔ cups Chicken Stock (page 60)
¾ pound egg noodles, fresh or dried

(pictured on page 55)

This is a warming, satisfying dish, rich in beefy flavor—one of my favorite northern Chinese dishes. It reheats wonderfully and is especially delicious on cold winter nights. Don't use an expensive cut of meat for this recipe. Even sirloin steak is too extravagant as it has insufficient flavor and will be too dry. Use a coarse, gristly cut of beef, such as chuck, brisket or shank.

Cut the meat into 2-inch cubes. Blanch the meat by plunging it into boiling water for 5 minutes. Then remove the meat and discard the water.

Combine the meat cubes with all the other ingredients except the noodles in a large pot. Bring the mixture to a boil and then lower the heat to a simmer. Skim any scum or fat off the surface for the first 15 minutes. Then cover the pot and simmer gently for 2 to 2½ hours or until the meat is tender.

Cook the noodles for 3 to 5 minutes in a pot of boiling water. Then put them in cold water until you are ready to use them. When the meat is tender, drain the noodles, put them into the pot and let them warm through. Ladle some meat, broth and noodles into individual serving bowls. (This dish reheats well.)

Hot Bean Thread Noodles

Bean thread, or cellophane, noodles are delightfully light. They are very fine, white and almost transparent and can be easily obtained from Chinese grocers and some supermarkets. They are quite easy to prepare and go well with almost any kind of sauce. Unlike other types of noodle, they can be very successfully reheated. The spicy sauce in this recipe gives the noodles body and character, and I think it makes an excellent dish for lunch or a light supper.

Soak the noodles in a large bowl of warm water for 15 minutes. When they are soft, drain them and discard the water. Cut them into 3-inch lengths using scissors or a knife.

   Put 1 tablespoon of oil into a hot wok or pot. Then add the scallions and garlic and stir-fry quickly for a few seconds. Add the meat and stir-fry until it is cooked. (This should take between 5 and 10 minutes.) Then add all the sauce ingredients except the sesame oil and cook the mixture over a gentle heat for about 5 minutes. Now add the drained noodles and sesame oil and cook the mixture for a further 5 minutes. Ladle some noodles and sauce into individual bowls or into one large serving bowl, and serve at once.

Region: western
Method: stir-frying

Serves 4
   ¼ pound bean thread (transparent)
      noodles (about 2½ packages)
   1 tablespoon oil
   3 tablespoons finely chopped
      scallions
   2 tablespoons finely chopped garlic
   1 pound ground beef

Sauce
   2 cups Chicken Stock (page 60)
   1½ tablespoons chili bean sauce
   1 tablespoon bean sauce
   1 dried red chili, or 1 teaspoon
      chili powder
   2 tablespoons light soy sauce
   1 teaspoon sesame oil

Stir-fried Rice Noodles with Vegetables

My mother often used to cook rice noodles as an alternative to egg noodles. I like the drier texture of the rice noodles and the way they absorb the flavor of a sauce. I think my mother liked them because they needed little cooking! Instead of blanching the noodles before stir-frying, all she had to do was to soak them. She often cooked them with small dried shrimps, but they are equally good with vegetables as in this recipe. Rice noodles can be found in Chinese groceries, but if you can't get them, this recipe can be made with egg noodles. As with most noodles, this dish is best served with snacks such as Steamed Spareribs with Black Beans (page 180) or Sesame Shrimp Toast (page 179).

Soak the rice noodles in a bowl of warm water for 25 minutes. Then drain them in a colander or sieve. If you are using dried egg noodles, cook them for 3 to 5 minutes in boiling water, drain and immerse in cold water until you are ready to use them.

   If you prefer (and have the time), trim the bean sprouts at both ends. Finely shred the pepper. If you are using fresh water chestnuts, peel them, then slice and finely shred them. If you are using canned water chestnuts, drain them and rinse them well in cold water before shredding them finely.

   Heat a wok or large pot over a high heat. Add the oil and when it is almost smoking add the scallions. After a few seconds add the bean sprouts, shredded pepper and shredded water chestnuts and stir-fry for about 1 minute. Then put in the rest of the ingredients and the drained noodles. Stir-fry the mixture for about 3 minutes, until it is well mixed and heated through. Serve at once.

Region: eastern and southern
Method: stir-frying

Serves 3 to 4
   ½ pound rice noodles, rice
      vermicelli or rice sticks
   ½ pound fresh bean sprouts (about
      2 cups)
   1 red or green bell pepper
   12 fresh water chestnuts, or
      1 8-ounce can, drained
   2 tablespoons oil, preferably peanut
   6 scallions, shredded
   1 teaspoon salt
   2 tablespoons light soy sauce
   2 tablespoons rice wine or
      dry sherry
   2½ tablespoons tomato paste
   5 tablespoons Chicken Stock
      (page 60) or water

Dumplings, Buns and Pancakes

Many types of flour are used in China to make dough for pancakes, buns and dumplings. Rice flour, especially that made from glutinous rice, is particularly favored for desserts and pastries. I have used two types of flour in the recipes in this book. Neither of them are Chinese flours but both work very satisfactorily and they are easy to find and to handle.

ALL-PURPOSE WHITE FLOUR

Plain white wheat flour is a soft flour which is ideal for making Chinese pancakes. It contains relatively little gluten and can be quickly mixed and rolled out. Whole-wheat flour is not suitable for Chinese cookery.

SELF-RISING FLOUR

This is not at all Chinese but I find it works well for buns and dumplings, and it is easier and quicker to use since it avoids the need for yeast. (Of course your buns will be slightly heavier than the authentic Chinese ones.)

Potsticker Dumplings

Region: northern
Method: shallow-frying

Makes about 18
1 cup all-purpose flour
½ cup very hot water
2 tablespoons oil, preferably peanut
⅔ cup water

Stuffing
3 ounces ground pork
1 ounce Chinese cabbage or spinach, finely chopped (¼ cup)
1 teaspoon finely chopped ginger root
1 tablespoon rice wine or dry sherry
1 tablespoon dark soy sauce
½ teaspoon salt
1 tablespoon finely chopped scallions
1 teaspoon sesame oil
½ teaspoon sugar
1 tablespoon Chicken Stock (page 60) or water

This is a popular and rather substantial snack from northern China where, during the harsh cold winter, the dumplings are often frozen outside until they are needed. At Chinese New Year whole families gather round and stuff the dumplings together. The dumplings can be shallow-fried, boiled or steamed, but I find shallow-frying to be the tastiest way of cooking them. Shallow-fried dumplings are called potstickers because once they have been fried they are covered with liquid and cooked until they literally stick to the pan. They should be crispy on the bottom, soft on the top, and juicy inside. A dipping sauce made from Chili Oil (page 29), vinegar and soy sauce is generally served with the potstickers. Potsticker dumplings can be made in advance and then frozen, uncooked. If you do this you don't need to thaw them before cooking them, but you will need to cook them for a little longer.

First make the dough. Put the flour into a large bowl and stir the hot water gradually into it, mixing it all the while with a fork or with chopsticks until the water is incorporated. Add more water if the mixture seems dry. Then remove the mixture from the bowl and knead it with your hands until it is smooth. This should take about 8 minutes. Put the dough back into the bowl, cover it with a clean, damp towel and let it rest for about 20 minutes. While the dough is resting, combine the stuffing ingredients in a large bowl and mix them together thoroughly.

After the resting period, take the dough out of the bowl and knead it again for about 5 minutes, dusting with a little flour if it is sticky. Once the dough is smooth, form it into a roll about 9 inches long and 1 inch in diameter. Take a knife and cut the roll into equal segments. There should be about 18.

Roll each of the dough segments into a small ball. Then roll each ball into a small, round, flat pancake about 2½ inches in diameter. Arrange the rounds on a lightly floured tray and cover them with a damp kitchen towel to keep them from drying out until you are ready to use them.

Put about 1 teaspoon of filling in the center of each pancake and then fold in half. Moisten the edges with water and pinch together with your fingers. Pleat around the edge, pinching to seal well. (The dumpling should look like a small turnover with a flat base and a rounded top.) Transfer the finished dumpling to the floured tray and keep it covered until you have stuffed all the dumplings in this way.

Heat a skillet (preferably a non-stick pan) over high heat until it is hot. Add 1 tablespoon of oil and place the dumplings flat-side down in the pan. Turn down the heat and cook for about 2 minutes until they are lightly browned. (You may need to cook the dumplings in two batches.) Add the ⅔ cup of water, cover the pan tightly and cook for about 12 minutes or until most of the liquid is absorbed. Uncover the pan and continue to cook for another 2 minutes. Remove the dumplings and serve.

Provide each person with three small bowls, one with some Chinese white rice vinegar, one with Chili Oil (page 29), and one with light soy sauce. The idea is to concoct your own dipping sauce by mixing these three things exactly to your taste.

Potsticker Dumplings.

Steamed Buns

Region: all
Method: steaming

Serves 6 to 8
1 package dry yeast
1 cup warm water or milk
3 cups all-purpose flour
½ cup sugar
3½ tablespoons lard
cooking parchment or waxed paper

Steamed buns are popular throughout all of China. Being steamed, they have no crust. Their texture is soft and light, fluffy yet firm. They make a pleasing foil for savory dishes. In the south they are often stuffed with savory meats or sweet bean paste and served as dim sum *snacks. In the north and west they are served with such dishes as Crispy Sichuan Duck (page 110). Steamed buns reheat well and can also be frozen and, once thawed, resteamed. They make a delightful alternative to rice.*

Combine the yeast and warm water or milk in a small bowl. Place in a warm spot, or in a warm oven which has been turned off, for about 5 minutes, or until double in size. Then combine the yeast mixture with the flour, sugar, and lard. Knead well. Cover the dough with a damp dish towel and let it rest for about 1 hour in a warm place. After this period the dough should have risen a little. Meanwhile, cut the sheets of paper into 16 pieces, each 2½ inches square.

Take the risen dough out of the bowl and knead it again for about 5 minutes on a floured board. If it is still sticky, dust lightly with a few tablespoons of flour. Then form it into a roll about 18 inches long and 2 inches wide. Take a sharp knife and cut the roll into equal segments. There should be about 18 pieces. Take a segment of dough and work it in the palm of your hand until it forms a smooth ball. Put the ball onto a paper square. Do the same with all the rest of the pieces, and put them, together with their paper bases, onto a heatproof plate.

Set up a steamer or put a rack into a wok or deep pan and fill it with 2 inches of water. Bring the water to a boil and then put the plate of dough balls into the steamer or onto the stand. Cover the pan tightly and turn the heat to low. Steam the buns for about 25 minutes. (You may have to do this in two batches.)

The steamed buns are now ready to be served with Crispy Sichuan Duck (page 110) or Peking Duck (page 113). Or you can let them cool and then pack them into a plastic bag and freeze them. Be sure to thaw them completely before reheating. The best way to reheat them is by steaming, as above, for 10 to 15 minutes, until they are thoroughly hot.

These pancakes are the classic accompaniment to Peking Duck (page 113) and reflect the northern Chinese use of wheat instead of rice. The pancakes are easy to make once you get the knack, which comes with practice. The unusual method of rolling double pancakes is designed to ensure thinner, moister pancakes with less risk of overcooking them. Since they can be frozen it is possible to make them weeks ahead. They can also be used with other dishes, such as Stir-fried Ground Pork (page 74) or instead of the lettuce leaves in Rainbow Beef in Lettuce Leaves (page 85).

Region: northern

Serves 6 to 8
2 cups all-purpose flour
¾ to 1 cup very hot water
2 tablespoons sesame oil

(pictured on page 112)

Put the flour into a large bowl. Stir the hot water gradually into the flour, mixing all the while with chopsticks or a fork until the water is fully incorporated. Add more water if the mixture seems dry. Then remove the mixture from the bowl and knead it with your hands until it is smooth. This should take about 8 minutes. Put the dough back into the bowl, cover it with a clean, damp towel and let it rest for about 30 seconds.

After the resting period take the dough out of the bowl and knead it again for about 5 minutes, dusting with a little flour if it is sticky. Once the dough is smooth, form it into a roll about 18 inches long and 1 inch in diameter. Take a knife and cut the roll into equal segments. There should be about 18. Roll each segment into a ball.

Take two of the dough balls. Dip one side of one ball into the sesame oil and place the oiled side on top of the other ball. Take a rolling pin, and roll the two together into a circle about 6 inches in diameter. It is important to roll double pancakes in this way because the resulting dough will remain moist inside and you will be able to roll them thinner but avoid the risk of overcooking them later.

Heat a skillet or wok over a very low heat. Put the double pancake into the wok or pan and cook it until it has dried on one side. Flip it over and cook the other side. Remove from the pan, peel the 2 pancakes apart and set them aside. Repeat this process until all the dough balls have been cooked.

Steam the pancakes to reheat them, or you can wrap them tightly in a double sheet of foil and put them into a pan containing 1 inch of boiling water. Cover the pan, turn the heat down very low and simmer until they are reheated. Don't be tempted to reheat them in the oven, as this will dry them out too much. If you want to freeze the cooked pancakes, wrap them tightly in plastic wrap first. When using pancakes that have been frozen, let them thaw in the refrigerator first before reheating them.

Potstickers and exotic fresh fruits

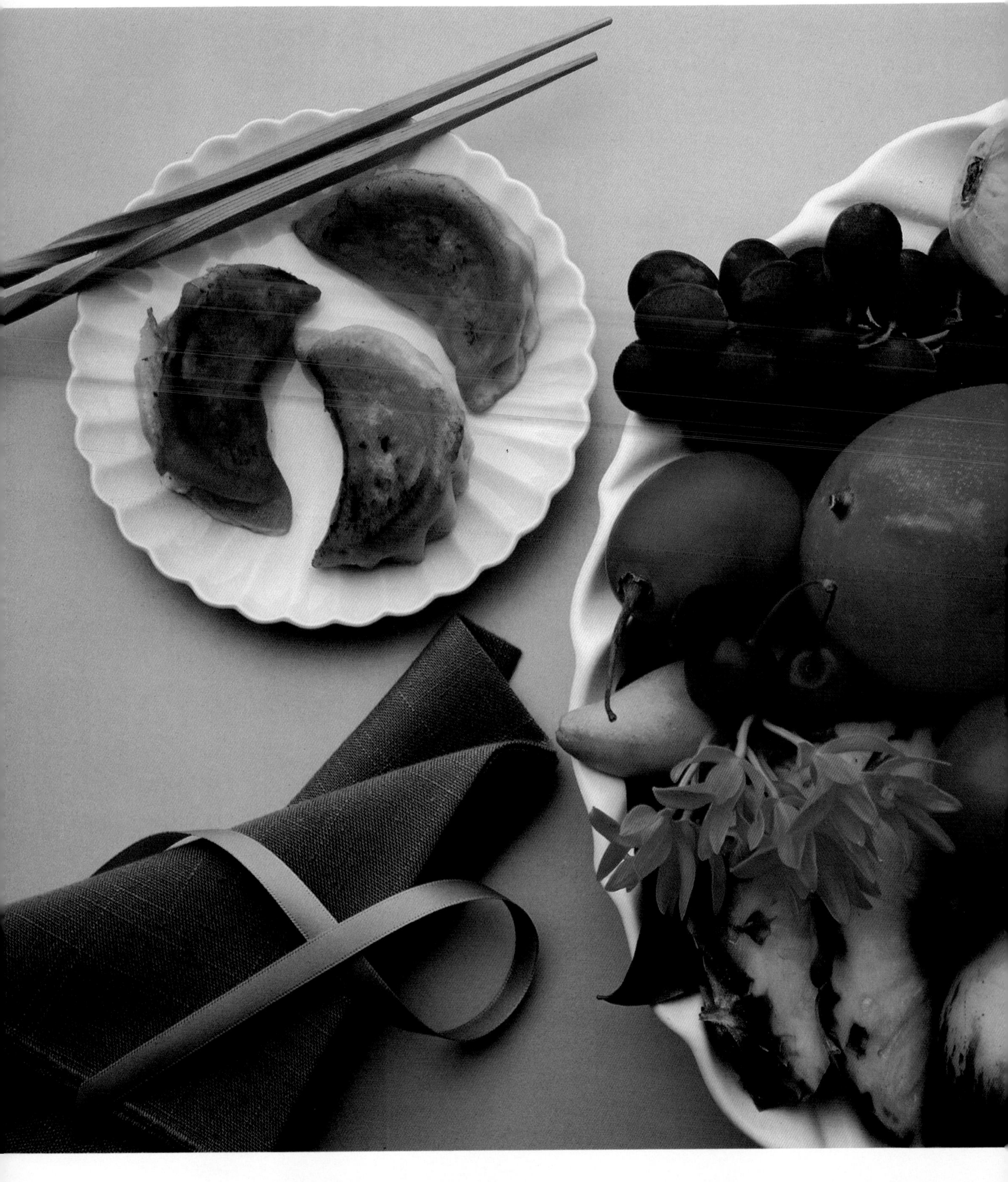

SNACKS AND SWEETS

點心

There is an enormous variety of Chinese savory and sweet snacks which are eaten between meals and during banquets. Originally they were enjoyed only by members of the Imperial household, whose chefs concocted savory delicacies such as minced pheasant dumplings and sweet ones made from steamed milk and sweet bean sauce. Over the centuries these and many less expensive versions have found their way into the diet of the ordinary Chinese. By 1900, Cantonese restaurants were the acknowledged masters of this specialty. Appropriately, the Cantonese term for such snacks is *dim sum,* which means "eating snacks for pleasure" or "order what you fancy." Today, Hong Kong's Cantonese restaurants are some of the best places to enjoy *dim sum* because there the range of snacks is both wide and adventurous.

Dim sum are eaten between midmorning and late afternoon, usually as a light, inexpensive lunch. Many *dim sum* restaurants in Hong Kong are enormous, consisting of a number of cavernous rooms which are jam-packed at lunchtime as family and friends meet to gossip or discuss business. The noise is deafening.

In many restaurants no menu is presented. Diners are provided with a pot of tea, cups, small plates and chopsticks. Waiters and waitresses circulate around the huge rooms pushing carts containing various *dim sum.* Diners stop the carts and select whatever appeals to them, sometimes accumulating as many as 3 dozen different small dishes. Tea is drunk throughout the meal, which is why *dim sum* is sometimes referred to as *yam cha*—the Cantonese words for drinking tea. At the end of the meal the bill is calculated by counting up the number of small plates or steamers on the table. It is all great fun.

Dim sum come in all flavors and can be hot, sour, sweet or spicy. They are prepared in many different ways, although some of the most popular are cooked in attractive little round bamboo steamers which are then transported in stacks on *dim sum* carts. Some of the most popular *dim sum* snacks are:

- Spring roll *(chun guen)*: the familiar deep-fried pastry filled with vegetables and meat.
- Barbecued pork bun *(cha siu bau)*: steamed or baked buns filled with delicious pieces of roasted pork.
- Pork dumplings *(siu mai)*: dumplings filled with ground pork and steamed.
- Steamed spareribs *(pai gwat)*: spareribs cut into short pieces and steamed with black bean sauce.
- Shrimp dumplings *(har gau)*: delicate light dumplings filled with shrimp and pork, and steamed.
- Fried taro dumplings *(woo kok)*: mashed taro root filled with pork and deep-fried.

There are dozens of other simple and exotic varieties. In this chapter I have included recipes for some of the simpler *dim sum* which can be successfully made at home. If you have never tried *dim sum*, do seek out a Chinese restaurant that serves them. (You will find not every Chinese restaurant offers them, as they require the expertise of special *dim sum* chefs.)

As for desserts, I knew nothing of them as a child. In authentic Chinese tradition my mother served fresh fruit at the end of a family meal, usually fresh oranges cut into wedges. Ice cream and candy were unknown to me until I ventured out into the non-Chinese world. Of course Chinese desserts do exist, although they are not a feature of the cuisine as they are in the West. They sometimes come in the form of sweet *dim sum*, but I find most of them overpoweringly sweet. I have therefore included recipes for some of the simpler and lighter Chinese desserts. Of course, one may serve Western-style desserts at the end of a Chinese meal, but my experience is that the subtle and complex tastes and flavors of Chinese dishes are best appreciated when followed by a simple dessert of fresh fruit.

I have always had a fondness for crispy snacks, especially shrimp crackers. They are made from a combination of shrimp meat, starch, salt and sugar which is pounded into a paste and then dried into hard, round crisps. They are sold in many supermarkets and Chinese groceries and need only to be deep-fried. They are terrific for serving with drinks.

Heat the oil in a deep-fat fryer or large wok until it is hot. Test the oil to see if it is hot enough by dropping in one shrimp cracker. If it puffs up and floats immediately to the top then the oil is ready. If not, wait a few minutes more and test again.

Deep-fry a handful of the shrimp crackers. Once they have puffed up, scoop them out immediately with a slotted spoon and drain them on paper towels. Then deep-fry the rest, a handful at a time.

Region: southern
Method: deep-frying

Serves 4 to 6
2 cups oil, preferably peanut (see Deep-fat fryers, page 35)
3½ ounces shrimp crackers

Spring rolls are among the best-known Chinese snacks. They are not difficult to make and are a perfect starter for any meal. Spring rolls should be crisp, light and delicate. Avoid all greasy, bulky imitations which are sometimes called egg rolls. The skins for spring rolls can be obtained fresh or frozen from Chinese grocers. Be sure to let them thaw thoroughly if they are frozen.

Finely shred the ham and pepper into very thin slices using a sharp knife or cleaver. If you are using fresh water chestnuts, peel them and then thinly slice them. If you are using canned water chestnuts, rinse them well in cold water, drain and then slice them finely.

Heat a wok or large skillet, add the oil and, when it is hot, stir-fry the ham and all the vegetables for 1 minute. Add the salt, sugar, soy sauces, sesame oil and rice wine or sherry. Stir-fry this mixture for 3 minutes and then turn it into a colander to drain and cool.

Mix the flour paste seal in a small bowl. Put about 3 tablespoons of the cooled filling on each spring roll skin. Fold in each side and then roll it up tightly. Use the flour paste to seal the open end by brushing a small amount on the edge. Then press the edge onto the roll. You should have a roll about 4 inches long, a little like an oversized cigar.

Heat the 4 cups oil in a deep-fat fryer or large wok until it is hot and almost smoking. Deep-fry the spring rolls in several batches until they are golden brown. Drain them on paper towels. Serve at once with your choice of dipping sauces (pages 28 to 30).

Region: all
Method: deep-frying

Makes 12 to 15
1 package spring roll skins
6 ounces Smithfield ham or prosciutto
¼ pound snow peas, trimmed
1 large red or green bell pepper
6 fresh water chestnuts, or ½ 8-ounce can, drained
1 tablespoon oil, preferably peanut
¼ pound fresh bean sprouts (about 1 cup)
4 finely shredded scallions
1 teaspoon salt
1 teaspoon granulated sugar
1 teaspoon light soy sauce
1 teaspoon dark soy sauce
1 teaspoon sesame oil
1½ tablespoons rice wine or dry sherry
4 cups oil, preferably peanut, for deep-frying (see Deep-fat fryers, page 35)

Flour paste seal
3 tablespoons all-purpose flour blended with 2 tablespoons water

Steamed Open Dumplings

Region: southern
Method: steaming

Serves 4 to 6
  1 package wonton skins (about 30
    to 35 skins)

Filling
  ¾ pound ground pork
  2 tablespoons finely chopped
    Smithfield ham or prosciutto
  1 tablespoon light soy sauce
  2 teaspoons rice wine or dry sherry
  1½ tablespoons finely chopped
    scallions
  1 teaspoon finely chopped ginger
    root
  1 teaspoon sesame oil
  1 egg, beaten
  1 teaspoon granulated sugar

This is a favorite snack in many dim sum *teahouses throughout southern China. It is merely a wonton or egg dough dumpling which is filled and steamed instead of being poached and deep-fried. The steamed dumpling has a character wholly different from pan-fried or boiled dumplings. The texture and taste of the steamed dumpling filling is more pronounced, yet delicate and subtle at the same time. The steamed skin retains a slightly chewy texture. Wonton skins can be obtained fresh or frozen from Chinese grocers. This dish can be made ahead of time and reheated by resteaming when you are ready to serve it.*

Combine the filling ingredients and mix them together well. Spoon a generous portion of filling onto each wonton skin. Bring up the sides and press them around the filling mixture. Tap the dumpling on the bottom to make a flat base. The top should be wide open, exposing the meat filling.

Set up a steamer or put a rack inside a wok or large deep pot. Pour in about 2 inches of water and bring it to a boil. Put the dumplings on a plate and place this into the steamer or onto the rack.

Cover the pot tightly, turn the heat to low, and steam gently for about 20 minutes. (You may have to do this in several batches.) Serve the dumplings hot with your choice of dipping sauce (see pages 28 to 30). Keep the first batch warm by covering them with foil and placing them in a warm but switched-off oven until all the dumplings are ready to serve.

Steamed Open Dumplings.

Although I have rarely seen fried wonton in China, they are common in Chinese restaurants in the West. This is perhaps because they are easily prepared and their crisp, dry texture goes well with drinks. Wonton skins can be bought fresh or frozen from Chinese grocers. (Be sure to thaw them thoroughly if they are frozen.) Filled uncooked wonton can be frozen successfully.

Combine the filling ingredients in a large bowl and mix well. Then, using a teaspoon, put a small amount of filling in the center of a wonton skin. Fold the bottom corner up over the filling, moisten the edges with a little water, and pinch the edges closed to form a triangle. Then fold the two bottom corners up over the filled section so they overlap, moisten them, and pinch them together to form a little ring. The filling should be well sealed in—somewhat like a large tortellini.

Heat the oil in a deep-fat fryer or a large wok until it is very hot. Deep-fry the filled wontons in several batches until golden, about 5 minutes.

Drain them on paper towels and serve at once with your choice of dipping sauces (see pages 28 to 30).

Region: southern
Method: deep-frying

Serves 6
1 package wonton skins (about 30 to 35 skins)
2 cups oil, preferably peanut (see Deep-fat fryers, page 35)

Filling
¾ pound ground pork
2 tablespoons finely chopped Smithfield ham or prosciutto
1 tablespoon dark soy sauce
1 tablespoon rice wine or dry sherry
1½ tablespoons finely chopped scallions
2 teaspoons finely chopped ginger root
1 teaspoon sesame oil
1 egg, beaten
½ teaspoon cornstarch
1 teaspoon sugar

(pictured on page 55)

Sesame Shrimp Toast

Sesame Shrimp Toast is a savory snack which is often served in dim sum restaurants outside China. Its origins are rather obscure, but I suspect it is a variation on the shrimp paste used widely in southern China for stuffings or for deep-frying into crispy balls. Whatever its origin, it is delicious and easy to make.

Using a cleaver or sharp knife, chop the shrimp coarsely and then mince them finely into a paste. Put the paste into a bowl and mix in the rest of the ingredients. (You could do this in a food processor.) This step can be done hours in advance, but you should then wrap the paste well in plastic wrap and put it into the refrigerator until you need it.

If the bread is fresh, place it in a warm oven to dry out. (Dried bread will absorb less oil.) Remove the crusts and cut the bread into rectangles about 3 inches × 1 inch. (You should have about 3 pieces per slice.) Spread the shrimp paste thickly on each piece of bread. The paste should form a mound about ⅛ inch deep, although you can spread it more thinly if you prefer. Sprinkle the toasts with the sesame seeds.

Heat the oil in a deep-fat fryer or wok to a moderate heat. Deep-fry several shrimp toasts at a time, paste-side down, for 2 to 3 minutes. Then turn them over and deep-fry for about 2 minutes, or until they are golden brown. Repeat the process until they are all done. Remove with a slotted spoon, drain on paper towels and serve.

Region: southern
Method: deep-frying

Makes about 30 pieces
10 very thin slices white bread
3 tablespoons white sesame seeds, untoasted
2 cups oil, preferably peanut (see Deep-fat fryers, page 35)

Shrimp paste
1 pound peeled shrimp
1 teaspoon salt
1 egg
2 tablespoons finely chopped scallions
2 teaspoons finely chopped ginger root
1 tablespoon light soy sauce
1 teaspoon sesame oil

(pictured on page 109)

Stuffed Peppers

Region: southern
Method: steaming and shallow-
frying

Serves 4 to 6
2 medium-size red or green bell
  peppers
3 tablespoons cornstarch
1½ tablespoons oil, preferably
  peanut

Filling
6 fresh water chestnuts, or
  ½ 8-ounce can, drained
½ pound raw shrimp or white fish
  filets, skinned
½ pound ground pork
1 egg white
1 teaspoon cornstarch
1 teaspoon salt
1½ tablespoons light soy sauce
2 teaspoons sesame oil
1 tablespoon rice wine or dry sherry
1 teaspoon granulated sugar
2 tablespoons finely chopped
  scallions

Red or green bell peppers are delicious when they are stuffed. These snacks are featured on many dim sum menus in southern China. Easy to make, they also reheat well. The quick pan-frying before serving gives the snacks a crusty brownish top. They make an attractive dish for a light luncheon.

Halve the peppers and remove the seeds and pulp. Next prepare the stuffing. If you are using fresh water chestnuts, peel and chop them finely. If you are using canned water chestnuts, first rinse them well in cold water. Drain in a colander and then chop them finely. Shell the shrimp and, if you are using large ones, remove the fine digestive cord. Coarsely chop the shrimp or fish. Put the water chestnuts and shrimp or fish into a bowl with the rest of the filling ingredients and mix them together very well. Dust the pepper halves lightly with cornstarch and stuff them with the filling mixture. Now cut each stuffed pepper half into 2 or 4 chunks and arrange them on a plate.

Set up a steamer or put a rack into a wok or deep pan and pour in 2 inches of water. Bring the water to a boil and then carefully put the plate of stuffed peppers into the steamer or onto the rack. Cover the wok or pan tightly and steam gently for 20 minutes. (You may have to do this in two batches.) The snacks may be prepared in advance up to this point.

When you are ready to serve the peppers, heat the oil in a wok or large frying-pan until it is moderately hot. Fry the peppers, stuffing-side down, until they are lightly brown and heated through. Serve immediately.

Steamed Spareribs with Black Beans

Region: southern
Method: steaming

Serves 2 to 4
1½ pounds pork spareribs
1 teaspoon salt
½ cup Chicken Stock (page 60)
1 tablespoon light soy sauce
1 teaspoon sesame oil
1 teaspoon finely chopped
  ginger root
1½ tablespoons coarsely chopped
  black beans
2 teaspoons finely chopped garlic
½ teaspoon salt
1 teaspoon granulated sugar
1 tablespoon rice wine or dry sherry

This is a popular dim sum snack. The spareribs are steamed until they are so tender they melt in your mouth. The steaming process ensures that the meat is permeated by the pungent flavor and smell of the black beans.

If possible, ask your butcher to cut the spareribs into individual ribs and then into 2-inch segments. Otherwise do this yourself with a cleaver or a sharp, heavy knife. Rub the spareribs with salt and let them sit in a bowl for about 20 to 25 minutes. Fill a large saucepan with water and bring it to a boil. Turn the heat to low, add the spareribs and simmer them for 10 minutes. Drain them and discard the water.

Mix the other ingredients together in a large bowl and stir in the spareribs, coating them well with the mixture. Transfer the mixture to a deep plate or dish.

Set up a steamer or put a rack into a wok or large deep pot. Pour in 2 inches of water. Bring the water to a boil, and then reduce the heat. Lower the plate of spareribs carefully into the steamer or onto the rack. Cover it with a lid and steam gently for 1 hour or until the spareribs are very tender. Remember to keep a careful watch on the water level, and replenish it with hot water when necessary. Skim off any surface fat, and serve.

You can make this dish ahead of time and reheat the ribs by steaming for 20 minutes or until they are hot.

Stuffed Peppers (facing page).

Marbled Tea Eggs

Region: southern
Method: simmering

Serves 4 to 6
  6 eggs
  7 cups water

Tea mixture
  3 tablespoons black tea, preferably
    Chinese
  2 tablespoons dark soy sauce
  1 teaspoon salt
  1 piece Chinese cinnamon bark or
    cinnamon stick
  1 star anise (optional)

This unique method of cooking eggs in spiced tea derives its name from the marbled texture and web of cracks which appear on the surface of the eggs when they are shelled. Traditionally tea eggs are served cold and they make a wonderful and easy garnish for cold platters. Not only are they delicious but they are also beautiful to look at. Once the eggs have cooled they can be kept in the tea liquid and stored in the refrigerator for up to 2 days.

If you keep your eggs in the refrigerator, take them out and let them warm to room temperature. (This will help prevent premature cracking of the egg shells when they are boiled.)

Fill a large pot with the water and bring to a boil. Using a spoon, lower the eggs into the pot and turn the heat down to a simmer. Cook the eggs for 10 minutes, then remove them and place in a bowl of cold water. (Do not discard the water in which you have cooked them.) In about 10 minutes, when the eggs have cooled, *gently* crack each shell with the back of a spoon until the entire shell is a network of cracks.

Add all the tea mixture ingredients to the pot of water in which you have cooked the eggs. Bring the mixture to a boil and return the cracked eggs to the pot. Reduce the heat to a simmer and cook them for about 25 minutes. Remove the pot from the heat and allow the eggs to cool in the liquid.

Remove the eggs from the cooled liquid and gently peel off the cracked shells. You should have a beautiful marble-like web on each egg. Serve them cut in half or quarters as a snack with other cold dishes or use them as garnish. They are also a glamorous dish for a picnic.

Cold Marinated Peanuts

Region: northern
Method: marinating

Serves 6 to 8
  1 pound raw peanuts
  3 tablespoons light soy sauce
  3 tablespoons dark soy sauce
  1 tablespoon finely chopped garlic
  2/3 cup Chinese white rice vinegar
    or cider vinegar
  1/3 cup rice wine or dry sherry

Peanuts were not introduced into China until the sixteenth century, but they quickly won an important place in Chinese agriculture. The peanut plant replenishes the soil as it grows, and the nuts themselves are a nutritious supplement to the diet both in their natural form and as peanut oil. This dish may be made a day or two in advance and can be served cold or at room temperature.

First blanch the peanuts by immersing them in a pot of boiling water for about 2 minutes. Drain them and let them cool and the skins should come off easily.

Put the blanched peanuts in a bowl. Mix in all the other ingredients. Let the peanuts marinate in this mixture for 2 or 3 hours, stirring from time to time to ensure an even distribution of the marinade. Most of it will be absorbed by the peanuts. Serve with Pickled Vegetables (page 151) as snacks or appetizers. We Chinese eat them one by one using chopsticks!

Egg Custard

One of the delights I have enjoyed since childhood, whether at a formal dinner or at a casual dim sum *lunch, is egg custard. I love it served on its own in a cup or as a filling for little pastry tartlets. The secret of this light, velvety and satin-textured custard lies both in the addition of sugar-water to lighten the eggs and in the steaming technique. I have added my own touch of crystallized ginger, or you could use fresh orange zest. It can be served hot or cold.*

Region: southern
Method: steaming

Serves 4 to 6
    2 cups water
    ½ cup sugar
    eggs, beaten
    6 eggs, beaten
    ¼ teaspoon almond or vanilla extract
    2 tablespoons finely chopped
        crystallized ginger or fresh
        orange zest

Combine the water and sugar in a large pot and bring it to a boil. Continue to boil the mixture until the sugar has entirely dissolved. Let the mixture cool completely.

In a large bowl combine the eggs, almond or vanilla extract and ginger or orange. Mix them thoroughly and add the cooled sugar-water mixture. Pour the mixture into a heatproof shallow bowl. Cut a round piece of waxed paper or parchment paper to cover the top of the bowl. (This will prevent the top of the custard from drying out.)

Set up a steamer or put a rack into a wok or pan. Add 2 inches of water and bring to a simmer. Put the bowl of custard into the steamer or onto the rack and cover the wok or pan tightly. Gently steam for about 20 minutes or until the custard has set. Remove the cooked custard and allow it to cool slightly before serving it. Or let it cool completely, then wrap it in plastic wrap and put it in the refrigerator until you are ready to serve it.

Caramel Walnuts

The first time I had this delicious snack was at a Beijing restaurant in Hong Kong and I was determined to learn how to make them. As it turned out they were surprisingly easy. The shelled walnuts must be blanched first to rid them of any bitterness. They are then rolled in sugar, left to dry for several hours, then deep-fried to caramelize the sugar coating. Finally they are rolled in sesame seeds. The result is a classic contrast of tastes and textures. They can be served cold or hot and they are perfect with drinks.

Region: northern
Method: deep-frying

Serves 4
    ½ pound shelled walnuts
    ½ cup granulated sugar
    2 cups oil, preferably peanut (see
        Deep-fat fryers, page 35)
    3 tablespoons white sesame seeds,
        toasted

(pictured on page 112)

Bring a pot of water to a boil. Add the walnuts and cook for about 10 minutes to blanch them. Drain the nuts in a colander or sieve, and then pat dry with paper towels and spread them on a baking pan. Sprinkle the sugar over the walnuts and roll them around in the sugar to cover them completely. Put the tray of sugared walnuts into an oven which has been heated to a low temperature and switched off. Let them dry for at least 2 hours.

Heat the oil in a deep-fat fryer or wok to a moderate heat. Fry a batch of the walnuts for about 2 minutes or until the sugar melts and the walnuts turn golden. (Watch the heat to prevent burning.) Remove the walnuts from the oil with a slotted spoon or strainer. Sprinkle them with some of the sesame seeds and lay them on a cake rack to cool. (Do not drain them on paper toweling as the sugar will stick to it when it dries.) Deep-fry and drain the rest of the walnuts in the same way. Once cooled, the caramel walnuts can be kept in a sealed glass jar for about 2 weeks. Serve them warm or cold.

Fresh Fruit

Region: all

Our family meals always ended with a plate of fresh oranges sliced into wedges. Occasionally during the summer we had special treats such as wedges of watermelon or honeydew melon instead. It has always struck me how appropriate simple fresh fruits are after a Chinese meal. They are invariably refreshing, cleansing the palate and adding a final sweet note to the end of a meal. I think it is probably one of the most pleasing and sensible desserts for a Chinese or any other meal, and it is easy!

Clockwise from lower left: Chicken Pieces in Black Bean Sauce (page 95), Cold Spicy Noodles (page 168), Strawberries, Stir-fried Scallops with Pork Kidneys (page 128), Cold Sweet and Sour Chinese Cabbage (page 149).

Fruit Compote

Region: southern

Serves 4 to 6
2 apples
2 oranges
1 small cantaloupe
14 ounces lychees, drained

(pictured on page 109)

Southern China is fortunate in having a bountiful supply of fruits, some of which are very exotic, such as lychees, loquats and kumquats. Lychees were so sought after by the Imperial Court that, once picked, they were rushed to the Court by special fast horse relays. Some of these special fruits are now available in cans. They are acceptable but should be served without their sickeningly sweet syrup. A mixed compote of fresh and canned fruits is a delicious and most appropriate dessert for any dinner party.

Using a sharp knife, peel, core and slice the apples into thin wedges. Peel and slice the oranges into segments. Cut the melon in half, scoop out and discard the pulp and seeds. Cut the melon flesh into 1-inch cubes, or use a melon baller. Combine all the fruits in a large bowl. Mix them gently together. Wrap the bowl tightly in plastic wrap until you are ready to serve the compote.

Peaches in Honey Syrup

Region: western
Method: simmering

Serves 4
2 large firm peaches
3 ounces Chinese rock sugar, or 4 tablespoons granulated
2/3 cup water

(pictured on page 55)

Any list of the classical fruits of China should begin with the peach, which figures prominently in folklore, traditional religion, literature and popular affection. New exotic varieties were introduced into China from central Asia during the Tang dynasty (618–907 A.D.). In this recipe, peaches are poached in a sugar syrup and then the liquid is reduced to a honey-like consistency. The dish can be served warm or cold and makes a simple, light, sweet dessert.

Bring a pot of water to a boil and quickly blanch the peaches in it for a few seconds. Remove them with a slotted spoon. With a sharp knife, peel the skin off the peaches and split each one in half, discarding the pit.

Combine the sugar and water in a small pot and boil the mixture together until the sugar dissolves. Then add the peach halves and turn the heat down to a low simmer. Simmer the peach mixture for about 15 minutes or until the peaches are tender. Gently remove them with a slotted spoon. Turn the heat to high and reduce the liquid to about half the amount—it should become a sweet syrup. If you are serving the dish hot, pour the liquid over the peaches and serve at once. If you are serving it cold, let the liquid cool, pour it over the peaches and refrigerate until you are ready to serve it.

Walnut Cookies

Region: southern
Method: baking

Makes about 12 cookies
12 walnut halves
3 tablespoons lard
¾ cup flour
2 teaspoons baking powder
½ cup sugar
2 eggs

Although baking is not a common Chinese method of cooking, cookies of all kinds are quite popular in the south. The most famous is the almond cookie, but walnut cookies are equally delicious. They can be served alone or with fresh fruit.

Immerse the walnut pieces in a pot of boiling water for about 5 minutes. Remove them with a slotted spoon, pat dry with paper towels and set aside.

Preheat the oven to 400°F. In a large bowl blend the lard into the flour and baking powder until it is well mixed. Next mix in the sugar and 1 egg to form a thick paste. Divide the mixture into 12 balls of dough and press them into flattish cookie shapes about 2 inches in diameter. Put them on a non-stick baking pan or use a plain baking sheet greased with 1 teaspoon of oil. Press a piece of walnut on the top of each cookie. Using a pastry brush, glaze the top of the cookies with 1 beaten egg. Put them in the oven and bake them for about 20 minutes. Remove the cookies and set them on a cake rack. Once cooled, the cookies can be stored in a tightly covered jar, where they will keep for about a week.

Steamed Pears

Region: northern
Method: steaming

Serves 4
4 firm pears
3 tablespoons sugar, preferably
    Chinese rock sugar
⅓ cup water
2 pieces Chinese cinnamon bark or
    cinnamon sticks

Pears are a northern Chinese fruit which are eaten fresh, cooked in soups, deep-fried, and are especially delicious when steamed. The steaming process cooks the pears without drying them out. The Chinese traditionally serve this dish hot, but I find it equally good cold.

Peel the pears and cut them in half. Remove the core and seeds. Combine the sugar and water in a small pot and boil it until the sugar has completely dissolved. Allow it to cool slightly.

Put the pears, sugar-water and cinnamon together into a shallow bowl. Set up a steamer or put a rack into a wok or pan. Add about 2 inches of water and bring to a boil. Put the bowl of pears into the steamer or onto the rack, turn the heat down to a simmer and cover the wok or pot tightly with a lid. Slowly steam the pears for about 15 to 25 minutes, until they are tender. (The cooking time will depend on the ripeness of the pears.)

When the pears are cooked, drain all the liquid and cinnamon stick or bark into a small saucepan and reduce the liquid to a syrup by boiling it fast. Remove and discard the cinnamon stick. Pour the syrup over the pears and serve at once. Or you can let the mixture cool, cover it with plastic wrap and refrigerate until you are ready to serve it.

Toffee Apples and Bananas

Although apples and bananas are most often associated with southern China, they are glazed with honey or sugar and eaten as snacks throughout the country. The dish requires some dexterity, which will come with experience. Make it for yourself a few times before you attempt it for guests.

Region: northern
Method: deep-frying

Serves 4
  2 large firm apples
  2 firm bananas
  ¼ cup all-purpose flour
  ¼ cup cornstarch
  1 large egg
  1 teaspoon sesame oil
  1⅓ cups oil, preferably peanut (see
    Deep-fat fryers, page 35)
  2 teaspoons sesame oil
  ¾ cup granulated sugar
  2 tablespoons white sesame seeds,
    toasted

Peel and core the apples and cut each into 8 large wedges. Peel the bananas and cut them into 1½-inch chunks. Combine the flour, cornstarch, egg and 1 teaspoon of sesame oil in a small bowl. Mix them well to form a smooth, very thick batter.

Combine the peanut oil and 2 teaspoons of sesame oil in a deep-fat fryer or wok and heat the mixture until it is moderately hot. Put the fruit into the batter mixture. Then lift out several pieces of fruit at a time, using a slotted spoon, and drain off any excess batter. Deep-fry for about 2 minutes, until they are golden. Remove with a slotted spoon and drain on paper towels. Repeat the process until you have deep-fried all the fruit.

Just before serving, prepare a bowl of ice water filled with ice cubes. Reheat the oil over moderate heat and deep-fry the fruit a second time for about 2 minutes. Drain again on paper towels. Put the sugar, sesame seeds and 2 tablespoons of oil from the deep-frying oil into a pot. Heat the mixture until the sugar melts and begins to caramelize. (Watch the heat to prevent it from burning.) When the caramel is light brown, add the fruit sections. Stir them gently in the caramel syrup to coat them. Then take them out and put them into the ice water to harden. Do a few at a time to prevent them from sticking together. Remove them from the water and place on a serving platter. Serve at once.

Almond Jelly with Fresh Oranges

This is my version of a classic Chinese dessert. In the original version, which involves a long and laborious process, agar-agar (a type of seaweed) is used instead of gelatin, ground almond juice is used instead of almond extract, and a sugar syrup is served with it instead of orange juice. I think this recipe, although it departs from the original, is nevertheless delicious and refreshing.

Region: southern
  1 tablespoon gelatin
  1⅓ cups water
  1⅓ cups milk
  3 tablespoons granulated sugar
  1 teaspoon almond extract
  1⅓ cups fresh orange juice
  2 oranges

Put the gelatin into a small bowl. Add half the water to dissolve the gelatin and bring the other half to a boil in a small pot. Pour the hot water into the gelatin and cold water and stir until the gelatin has completely dissolved. Combine this with the milk, sugar and almond extract in a large bowl. Pour the mixture into a baking pan about 8 inches square and 1½ inches deep. Put it in the refrigerator for about 2 hours or until it has completely set.

Peel the oranges and remove all the white pith. Separate them into segments. When the almond jelly is ready, cut it into 1-inch cubes. Put some orange segments into individual bowls. Add some almond jelly cubes, and then pour a little orange juice over each portion.

A Note from the Publisher

Ken Hom demonstrates many of the recipes and techniques described in this volume on his television show, *Ken Hom's Chinese Cookery*, an eight-part series produced by the BBC and seen on public television in the U.S.

In the first program, Ken Hom prepares Peking Duck (page 113) with all the trimmings and Potsticker Dumplings (page 170), a popular snack from northern China.

In Program 2, he introduces the classic technique of stir-frying and visits a Chinese family in Hong Kong. He offers demonstrations of three simple stir-fried dishes—Chicken in Black Bean Sauce (page 95), Stir-fried Shrimp with Eggs (page 133), and Stir-fried Ginger Broccoli (page 146).

Program 3 includes a visit to a Taoist Temple and its vegetarian restaurant. He demonstrates Braised Spicy Eggplant from western China (page 143), Buddhist Casserole (page 155), and Sweet and Sour Pork (page 75).

In Program 4, Ken Hom shows how to make delicious Stir-fried Noodles with Vegetables (page 169) and, in Hong Kong, a young chef demonstrates the spectacular art of noodle-making. Ken also makes a winter dish, Peking Braised Lamb (page 90), and a quick and easy vegetable dish, Lettuce with Oyster Sauce (page 152).

Program 5 focuses on some of the key techniques used to cook meat in China, with recipes for Steamed Beef Meatballs (page 86), spicy Chili Pork Spareribs (page 78) and Stir-fried Hot and Sour Kidneys (page 91). Included is a visit to a soy sauce factory.

In Program 6 Ken offers Steamed Rice (page 159) and Stir-fried Beef with Orange (page 82), as well as a Hot and Sour Soup (page 68). Also a fascinating look at the exciting food market in Hong Kong.

In Program 7 Ken Hom joins his family for a special dim sum lunch at a restaurant in Hong Kong and demonstrates Deep-fried Sesame Shrimp Toast (page 179), Stuffed Peppers with an unusual pork and fish filling (page 180), and Cold Peking Pork (page 76).

In the final program of the series (Program 8), Ken Hom offers advice on cooking seafood and fish. After a visit to a Chinese fishing village, he prepares a Corn Soup with Crabmeat (page 61) and Steamed Fish with Garlic, Scallions and Ginger (page 125), as well as a quick and delicious Shredded Chicken with Sesame Seeds (page 101).

Certain ingredients are called by different names in the U.K., and the following list is offered as an aid to viewers:

British	American
aubergine	eggplant
cornflour	cornstarch
cos lettuce	romaine
courgette	squash
fillet steak	tenderloin
groundnut oil	peanut oil
junket	custard
mange-tout	snow peas
pigeon	squab
plaice	flounder
plain flour	all-purpose flour
prawn	shrimp
raw English smoked bacon or Parma ham	Smithfield ham